# FROM THATCHED-ROOF HOUSES TO IMMIGRANT ENTREPRENEURSHIP

*First Generation Lemko-American Businessmen*

Bogdan Horbal

Carpathian Institute

Higganum, Connecticut

Copyright © 2024 Bogdan Horbal
All Rights Reserved

Library of Congress Control Number: 2022949631

ISBN: 978-1-938292-15-6

First Edition 2024

Layout by Jeffrey Paison

Cover by Michael Decerbo and Walter Maksimovich

Carpathian Institute
184 Old County Road
Higganum, CT 06441

Publisher's Cataloging-in-Publication
(Provided by Cassidy Cataloguing Services, Inc.).

| | |
|---|---|
| Names: | Horbal, Bogdan, 1965- author. |
| Title: | From thatched-roof houses to immigrant entrepreneurship : first generation Lemko-American businessmen / Bogdan Horbal. |
| Description: | Higganum, Connecticut : Carpathian Institute, [2024] | Includes bibliographical references and index. |
| Identifiers: | ISBN: 978-1-938292-15-6 (paperback) | 978-1-938292-16-3 (hardcover) | LCCN: 2022949631 |
| Subjects: | LCSH: Carpatho-Rusyn Americans--Biography. | Lemky--United States--Biography. | Businesspeople--United States--Biography. | Immigrant business enterprises--United States--History. | Entrepreneurship. | LCGFT: Biographies. | BISAC: BUSINESS & ECONOMICS / Small Business. | HISTORY / United States / 19th Century. | HISTORY / United States / 20th Century. | BIOGRAPHY & AUTOBIOGRAPHY / Business. |
| Classification: | LCC: E184.U5 H67 2024 | DDC: 973.0491791--dc23 |

*To my wife, Danuta*

*On the cover*

*Dimitry Karlak in his store in Beacon Falls, Connecticut, and a ten dollar bill issued by the Market Street National Bank of Shamokin, Pa., 1929.*

# TABLE OF CONTENTS

Introduction ........................................................................... 1

Biographies ......................................................................... 32

Illustration Credits ........................................................... 188

Index .................................................................................. 191

# INTRODUCTION

In 1892, the Polish author Bolesław Malinowski (1835–1935), better known as the "Nestor" of modern Polish socialism, published a general overview of Galicia in which he devoted one paragraph to Lemkos. He described them as "the weakest physically and the most intellectually restricted population in all of Galicia."[1] In his review of the book, Ukrainian author and ethnographer Ivan Franko (1856–1916), also known as a political radical and a founder of the Socialist movement in Western Ukraine, argued that Lemkos received too little attention. He also added that "their immigration and vigorous earnings in America proved their vitality and uncommon willpower, as well as the capacity for civilized life."[2]

The Lemko people[3] are a numerically small population of highlanders who, for centuries, inhabited the northern slopes of their Carpathian Mountains in what is today Polish borderland with Slovakia. Before their expulsion from the Carpathian homeland in the 1940s, the Lemkos made their living in forest- and farm-related professions, particularly sheep-herding. Their spiritual and cultural life, especially their adherence to Eastern Christianity and use of the Cyrillic alphabet, placed them squarely within the East Slavic sphere.

Lemko community life was traditional and has almost never evolved in a rapid manner. Village life was close and insular, providing the Lemkos with the cultural and conceptual space necessary to form a distinct collective consciousness. Lemkos have traditionally described themselves as Rus' people/*rusky liude*, or simply as Rusyns or Rusnaks. Under the influence of their own national and religious movements and those of their neighbors, the Lemkos have, at various points in their history, considered themselves or been considered by others to be Carpatho-Russian, Russian, Ukrainian, Polish, or Carpatho-Rusyn.

Because conditions in the Lemko Region were harsh, mostly due to the lack of quality arable land, an ever-increasing number of men left the region in search of work. Hundreds went south each summer to find seasonal work on the Hungarian Plain. Some began emigrating southward in the mid 18th century and again at the turn of the 19th and 20th centuries. They settled primarily in what is today Serbia, Croatia and Bosnia. A much larger emigration, however, sent Lemkos to North America.

## Immigration to America

The first Lemko to arrive in America is believed to be Iurko Kashytskii, who had lost his property in his native village of Nowa Wieś due to a natural disaster. He arrived in New York in 1872 and worked in a laundry for $1.75 a day. Mykhal Zoliak from Hańczowa supposedly followed him just a year later, then one year after that Il'ko Pyvovarchyk came from Uhryń. Other Lemkos came in the 1870s, but massive emigration started only in the 1880s.

---

[1] Bolesław Limanowski, *Galicya przedstawiona słowem i ołówkiem* (Warszawa: Wydawnictwo Przeglądu Tygodniowego, 1892): 28.

[2] The review appeared in 1892 under the title "Krajoznawstwo galicyjskie" in several installments in a newspaper *Kurier Lwowski*, no. 212, 218-219, and 221-226.

[3] For a general introduction to Lemkos, see my *Lemko Studies: A Handbook* (New York: Columbia University Press/East European Monographs, 2010).

1. M.J. Burs (artist), Immigrants' Waiting-room, Hamburg, 1902

Steamship lines sent ticket agents to many regions in Europe to recruit labor, and they often used any means necessary to make sure that ship companies operating cross-Atlantic routes had enough customers. These agents at times deliberately misrepresented conditions in America and various immigration crimes were committed, some of which were uncovered and led to trials.[4] It was noted that "two of the leading steamship lines before World War I had 5,000 or 6,000 ticket agents in Galicia alone, that there was 'a great hunt' for emigrants, and that the work was very successful there."[5]

It seems, however, that the most important impulse to emigrate came via letters from those who were already abroad. Also, in towns near the Lemko region, in the Austrian army, or at school, Lemkos often encountered people who had already been to America, including other Rusyns as well as Poles, Ukrainians, or Slovaks.

As much as a quarter of the total population of many Lemko villages left for the New World.[6] Besides Pennsylvania, large groups of Lemkos went to the industrial centers of

---

[4] Grzegorz Maria Kowalski, *Przestępstwa emigracyjne w Galicji, 1897-1918: z badań nad dziejami polskiego wychodźstwa* (Kraków: Wydawnictwo Uniwersytetu Jagiellońskiego, 2003).

[5] Jeremiah W. Jenks and W. Jett Lauck, *The Immigration Problem: A Study of American Immigration Conditions and Needs*, ed. 5 (New York-London: Funk & Wagnalls Co., 1922): 22.

[6] The best statistical data on the issue is in the *Shematyzms* of the Greek Catholic Eparchy of Przemyśl. The first one that noted statistical information on immigration is the one for 1894, but it was the one for 1909 which gave statistics on the number of immigrants currently staying in America for most of the villages.

New Jersey, New York, Connecticut, Ohio, Minnesota and other states. Because they often had only a fourth-grade education or were illiterate, these Lemkos initially had difficulty adapting to the New World. Just like Galician Poles or Ukrainians, Lemkos arrived in the United States with almost no resources and were forced to accept hard and dangerous labor that most of them kept for their entire working lives.

## Life and Work in America

Many Lemkos worked in the mines and steel mills of Pennsylvania and other states, while others did manual work in factories like Alexander Smith and Sons Carpet Company in Yonkers, N.Y. or American Brass Company in Ansonia, Conn. Unlike earlier generations of American immigrants, many among these newer immigrants sought only to exploit, temporarily, the economic opportunities of the New World and then return home to create a better life in the old country.

One of the early immigrants observed that "while our immigrant planned for his return home, life decreed otherwise. Gradually he became accustomed to America. If he had a wife in the old country, he brought her over here with any children that he may have had. If he was single, he began to look around for a wife. He still clung to the hope of returning back home, but constantly deferred his final decision in the matter. And when finally he got a job that looked permanent, became married, and especially when his children began to grow up here, then no matter how much he still talked about returning, he knew that he had to remain here. If ever he did return, it was only to visit his dear ones. By this time, he had begun to make real efforts to read and write in English; to organize his kind, and to set up his church, school, newspaper, clubs. These new activities and organizations gave more depth and meaning to his life, and made it so that he decided to make America his new permanent home."[7]

During those early years in America, Lemko immigrants focused on saving money. In the early twentieth century, Slavic immigrants were able to save fifteen to twenty dollars a month[8] or even as much as fifty dollars.[9] This allowed them to accumulate capital. Some then purchased land, engaging in the business of farming that they knew well. Nikolaj Zajacz, a Rusyn farmer in the Petersburg, Virginia area argued in a letter to *Amerikansky russky viestnik* (February 1919) that "It's the best security and freedom to have an American farmstead."[10]

## Boarding

Many more, however, purchased lots to build a house or bought houses in towns where they worked in factories or mines. Once the house was in place, keeping boarders was

---

[7] Dmytro Kapitula, "Early Immigrant Life," *Ukrainian Weekly* Jersey City, N.J., April 8, 1939, p. 3.

[8] Frank Julian Warne, *The Immigrant Invasion* (New York: Dodd, Mead and Company, 1913): 154. It is important to underline that around 1910 all of Ruthenians (and for that matter more than 95% of Slovaks and Poles) made less than $1,000 a year. *Reports of the Immigration Commission*, [v. 8:] *Immigrants in Industries (in twenty-five parts), pt. 2: Iron and Steel Manufacture*, v. 1, Senate doc. no. 633 (Washington: Government Printing Office, 1911): 60.

[9] Emily Greene Balch discussing bank deposits wrote: "Few of them, I was told, would deposit less than $20 a month, many as much as $50." See her *Our Slavic Fellow Citizens* (New York: Charities Publication Committee, 1910): 305.

[10] Two months later, he wrote to the ARV again boosting the "Ruthenian farmers' colony" in Claremont. Robert M. Zecker, *Race and America's Immigrant Press: How the Slovaks Were Taught to Think Like White People* (New York-London-New Delhi-Sydney: Bloomsbury, 2013); 19-20.

the earliest and most widespread form of business in which immigrants, including Lemkos, engaged. The strategy was to use the house to produce an income, offsetting expenses. Frank Julian Warne (1874–1948), an American journalist, economist, and statistician, noted that "not a few board with married members of their own nationality at an expense not to exceed twelve dollars a month. The Slav with family cannot save so much, but in not a few cases even with a wife and children his slightly higher cost of living is met by the wife taking in boarders."

The arrangement usually included a place to sleep with food, as well as cleaning and laundry. Boarding homes or houses were usually organized and run by women. In addition to their own, often large families, these women usually had three to five boarders to care for. By doing that, at the beginning of the 20th century, they were able to add $12 to $16 to their household's monthly income.[11] Among immigrant workers in the Central Competitive Field that comprised Indiana, Ohio, Illinois, and Western Pennsylvania, over one half of all Ruthenian, Croatian, Russian, Lithuanian, Hungarian, Polish and South Italian households took in boarders.[12] It was noted, however, that Slavs boarded so commonly that many believed it to be a phenomenon peculiar to them. It also elicited frequent condemnation.[13]

Many women also did sewing, weaving, or home manufacturing for outside clients. A good seamstress could make as much as her husband did at the mill. A skilled seamstress made about $100 a month in 1914,[14] but it seems that there were not that many of them among the Slavs.[15]

Although all these entrepreneurial women did more than their fair share to support their families, their names have never appeared in any annals of small business.

In 1910 some 95 percent of Slavic immigrants in Johnstown, Pa., and its vicinity were employed as laborers in the mills and coal mines.[16] This was the case for years to come in countless other places where Slavs,[17] including Lemkos, settled. Businessmen, however, were present in all communities where Slavs, including Rusyns,

---

[11] David M. Reimers, "Immigrants and Thrift," in: Joshua J. Yates and James Davison Hunter, eds., *Thrift and Thriving in America: Capitalism and Moral Order from The Puritans to the Present* (New York, N.Y.: Oxford University Press, 2011): 357.

[12] Thomas Mackaman, *New Immigrants and the Radicalization of American Labor, 1914-1924* (Jefferson, N.C.: McFarland & Company, Inc., Publishers, 2016): 47.

[13] Karel D. Bicha, "Hunkies: Stereotyping the Slavic Immigrants, 1890-1920," *Journal of American Ethnic History* 2:1 (Fall 1982): 24.

[14] Thaddeus C. Radzilowski, "Family, Women, and Gender: The Polish Experience," in John J. Bukowczyk, ed., *Polish Americans and Their History: Community, Culture, and Politics* (Pittsburgh, Pa.: University of Pittsburgh Press, 1996): 75.

[15] "Families whose heads were Serbian, Romanian, Ruthenian, and Croatian, in the order named, show between 65 and 80 per cent of their entire income from the husband and boarders or lodgers." *Reports of the Immigration Commission,* [v. 8:] *Immigrants in Industries (in twenty-five parts), pt. 2: Iron and Steel Manufacture*, v. 1, Senate doc. no. 633 (Washington: Government Printing Office, 1911): 82.

[16] Ewa Morawska, "A Replica of the "Old-Country" Relationship in the Ethnic Niche: East European Jews and Gentiles in Small-town Western Pennsylvania, 1880s–1930s.," *American Jewish History* 77:1 (Sept. 1987): 58.

[17] In 200 interviews used in the preparation of a study by John Bodnar, "Immigration and Modernization: The Case of Slavic Peasants in Industrial America," *Journal of Social History* 10:1 (1976): 44-71, only ten immigrants ever indicated an attempt to leave their industrial pursuits to enter business for themselves. One of them opened a small saloon in Pittsburgh which failed a year later. Of those who did enter private business, several did so only upon retirement from industrial work.

lived.[18] In 1904 Frank Julian Warne noted that "at first the Slav was found only in the 'patch'— the small group of buildings usually located near a colliery. But today he is filling up and overflowing the small town, and is appearing in the principal thoroughfares of the mining cities with his saloon and his butcher shop."[19] For first-generation Lemkos who entered business, groceries/butcher shops and saloons/hotels were indeed the most popular business choices.

## Grocery/Butcher Stores

A few hundred dollars were needed to open a small, rather unattractive store stocked with an assortment of simple goods. This store sometimes combined selling goods with the sale of steamship and railroad tickets and possibly served as an informal employment agency.[20] In the late 19th century most Americans grew some of their own food and often raised livestock. Mom-and-pop grocers sold food that did not require refrigeration. At the end of the 19th and the beginning of the 20th centuries a grocery store carried some 200 products. Food and supplies for the home were delivered by store-keepers who often worked long hours.[21] These stores, in fact, relied on self-employment and often unpaid family labor, including children.[22] In those instances in which immigrant businesses employed people from outside of their families, those were, with very few exceptions, people of the same ethnicity as the proprietors.[23] This kind of firm was typical in statistical terms because it represented the majority of first-generation immigrant businesses.

## Saloons/Hotels

Among many immigrant groups, including Carpatho-Rusyns,[24] the operation of a saloon in one of the rooms of the house or in a rented space was a common enterprise. The liquor sector was broad and also included hotels with bars and liquor dealerships. In Shenandoah, Pa., alone, the number of East European liquor dealers rose from 83 in 1890 (out of a total population of 15,944) to 166 in 1900 (when the total population was 20,321).[25]

---

[18]In 1899, a group of Greek-Catholic priests met in Philadelphia, PA to organize a fraternal society. The group requested that each parish sends in a statistical record of its members so that a directory/schematismus of Greek Catholic parishes in the United States and Canada for 1900 could be prepared. Among 18 questions, there were those about the occupation of the parishioners, whether parishoners own their own homes and what is the home value as well as about the number of businessmen belonging to each parish. John Slivka, *Historical Mirror, Sources of the Rusin and Hungarian Greek Rite Catholics in the United States of America, 1884-1963* (Brooklyn, N.Y., n.d.): 24.

[19]Frank Julian Warne, *The Slav Invasion and The Mine Workers: A Study in Immigration* (Philadelphia-London: J.B. Lippincott, 1904): 105.

[20]Emily Greene Balch, *Our Slavic Fellow Citizens* (New York: Charities Publication Committee, 1910): 307-308; Paul Robert Magocsi, *Our People: Carpatho-Rusyns and Their Descendants in North America*, 4th rev. ed. (Wauconda, Ill.: Bolehazy-Carducci Publishers, 2005): 23.

[21]Michael Ruhlman, *Grocery: The Buying and Selling of Food in America* (New York, N.Y.: Abrams Press, 2017): 30, 37.

[22]There was a widespread expectation that children should contribute to the material support of the family. In Pennsylvania mining districts Slavs not only exceeded all other ethnic groups in their use of child labor but routinely falsified their children's ages to obtain working permits. John Bodnar, "Immigration and Modernization: The Case of Slavic Peasants in Industrial America," *Journal of Social History* 10:1 (autumn 1976): 46.

[23]*Reports of the Immigration Commission, [v.8:] Immigrants in Industries (in twenty-five parts)*, pt. 2: *Iron and Steel Manufacture*, v. 1, Senate doc. no. 633 (Washington: Government Printing Office, 1911): 458.

[24]Paul Robert Magocsi, *Our People: Carpatho-Rusyns and Their Descendants in North America*, 4th rev. ed. (Wauconda, Ill.: Bolehazy-Carducci Publishers, 2005): 23.

[25]Ron Rothbart, "The Ethnic Saloon as a Form of Immigrant Enterprise," *The International Migration Review* 27:2 (summer, 1993): 338.

It was more profitable, and therefore more desired, to have a saloon/hotel rather than a store. At the same time, it took more capital. The cost estimate to set up a Polish saloon of the poorer sort in Chicago was $500 for furnishings and an equal amount for the license.[26] In smaller places where Lemkos lived, renting an unfurnished space for a saloon could cost $20 to $50 a month, while a furnished space could cost from $80 to $200 a month. The cost of the license apparently varied greatly from $200 to even $2,000 per year, depending on what the local regulations called for, and there was tax to be paid as well.[27]

The saloon-keeper was usually a man with a good deal of experience in the United States, strong attachments here, and some familiarity in operating within the new environment.[28] Saloons occupied an important role among immigrant workers and workers in general. They were vital when it came to the workingman's leisure-time activities. The saloon played three significant roles: it was a neighborhood center, an all-male establishment, and a transmitter of working-class and immigrant cultures.[29] Iuliian Bachyns'kyi (1870–1940), a Ukrainian politician and public figure who visited United States in 1905, went as far as stating that saloon owners

"(…) set the tone for the entire national and political life of the immigrants and create public opinion. These are the first 'patriots' and organizers of the entire national and most of all religious life among the immigrants. Immigrants own them, in most part, being organized in parishes. They [saloon owners] created parishes, built churches, and up to the most recent times, nominated priests to be pastors in their communities. This was done as it suited them best, nominating either a Greek Catholic, or an Orthodox or an 'independent' priest – whoever was the best for business. They [saloon owners] set up and support self-reliance organizations, brotherhoods, organize dances, trips, theatrical performances, and initiate all of this at least for the business. Nothing is surprising here. Everything has to evolve around their saloon. (…)"[30]

At the same time an integral part of the saloon's attraction was the alcohol.[31] It was also the place where men gambled on card games.[32] Thus arose "the saloon problem," as the resulting drunkeness and uncontrolled gambling came to be known. In order to resolve this, some advocated abolishing saloons altogether, while others wanted to regulate saloons and the liquor industry in general.[33] The backlash against saloon owners and wannabe owners was significant. In 1908, in Plymouth, Pa., a Slavic saloon-keeper lost his liquor license for selling alcohol to

---

[26] Emily Greene Balch, *Our Slavic Fellow Citizens* (New York: Charities Publication Committee, 1910): 308.

[27] Iuliian Bachyns'kyi, *Ukraïns'ka immigratsiia v Z'iedynenykh Derzhavakh Ameryky* (L'viv: Naukove tovarystvo imeni Shevchenka, 1914): 187-188.

[28] Ron Rothbart, "The Ethnic Saloon as a Form of Immigrant Enterprise," *The International Migration Review* 27:2 (summer, 1993): 340.

[29] Jon M. Kingsdale, "The 'Poor Man's Club': Social Functions of the Urban Working-Class Saloon," *American Quarterly* 25:4 (October 1973): 472.

[30] Iuliian Bachyns'kyi, *Ukraïns'ka immigratsiia v Z'iedynenykh Derzhavakh Ameryky* (L'viv: Naukove tovarystvo imeni Shevchenka, 1914): 189.

[31] Frequent and often daily visits by Rusyn and other immigrant workers to the local tavern after a long day at work cut deeply into the immigrants' savings. Paul Robert Magocsi, *Our People: Carpatho-Rusyns and Their Descendants in North America*, 4th rev. ed. (Wauconda, Ill.: Bolehazy-Carducci Publishers, 2005): 23.

[32] Karol K. Weaver, ""It's the Union Man That Holds the Winning Hand": Gambling in Pennsylvania's Anthracite Region," *Pennsylvania History: A Journal of Mid-Atlantic Studies* 80:3 (Summer 2013): 407.

[33] See v. 32, no. 3 (Nov. 1908) of *The Annals of the American Academy of Political and Social Science* which is largely devoted to the Regulation of the Liquor Traffic.

a drunken man.³⁴ Following a public outcry in 1913, the court threw out all 265 new saloon/tavern applications in Scranton, Pa.,³⁵ a city of some 130,000 inhabitants, including many Slavs.

Obtaining a liquor license was indeed not easy. Local brewers were known for securing liquor licenses for saloon owners, in addition to helping them financially to establish a business. The brewers apparently exercised so much influence that they were able to manipulate local government not only to issue licenses, but also to reinstate ones that had been revoked. All of this came at a price: not only were saloon owners obligated to sell what brewers produced but were also required to give them a cut of the profits.³⁶

Ron Rothbart of the Alcohol Research Center at the University of California at Berkeley argued that although East Europeans were underrepresented in business in general, they were overrepresented in the saloon business.³⁷ Biographies presented in this book support this opinion, as there are among these businessmen forty-six saloon keepers. One of the best-known bars created by a Lemko was Hotz Café in Cleveland, Ohio. John *Hotz, Sr. set up the tavern as a place of comfort, leisure, and fraternity for fellow countrymen and local laborers. His business became a "home away from home" for its blue-collar patrons and when times were bad, he kept his prices low and provided food to struggling neighborhood families. During its early years, amenities at the tavern included a "shoe-shine boy," Blind Robbins brand smoked herring, and such fine cigar brands as White Owl and R.G. Dun. Patrons also gathered to play card games, such as "66." The café attracted such high-profile baseball players as Ty Cobb (1886–1961), Lou Gehrig (1903–1941) and Babe Ruth (1895–1948). Elliot Ness (1903–1957), Cleveland's Safety Director from 1935 to 1940, was a client there and Franklin D. Roosevelt (1882–1945) visited the tavern prior to his election as President in 1932.³⁸

Saloons were only rarely advertised, but businesses such as hotels did advertise their establishments. There are more than forty Lemko hotel owners among the businessmen whose biographies are included in this book. It's quite likely that some or many of these hotels were mainly drinking places with a room or two in the back that could be rented out.³⁹ Olyphant, Pa., alone had half a dozen Lemko hotels!

## Banking

Gmitro *Kapitula, one of the early Lemko immigrants and a businessman, recalled that "we did not know anything about banks then, and therefore did not save our money in them. Each one of us either carried it around with him in his belt, or hid in his mattress, or gave it for safe-keeping to his landlady, who usually took very good care of it."⁴⁰ In addition to boarding house owners, East and South European saloon keepers, grocers, and other entrepreneurs also held deposits that had been left for safekeeping and received

---

[34] "Church News and Personal Notes: Pennsylvania," *The Westminster* 33:27 (Philadelphia, Pa., 1908): 27.

[35] "Kort v Skrentoni vidkynuv vsï pros'by o novi salony-korchmy," *Svoboda* (Jersey City, N.J.), March 20, 1913, p. 1.

[36] Frank Julian Warne, *The Slav Invasion and The Mine Workers: A Study in Immigration* (Philadelphia-London: Philadelphia, London, J.B. Lippincott company, 1904): 114.

[37] Ron Rothbart, "The Ethnic Saloon as a Form of Immigrant Enterprise," *The International Migration Review* 27:2 (summer, 1993): 338.

[38] Tremont History Project and Jim Dubelko, "Hotz Café," Cleveland Historical, https://clevelandhistorical.org/items/show/509

[39] I owe this observation to Richard Custer.

[40] Dmytro Kapitula, "Early Immigrant Life," *Ukrainian Weekly* (Jersey City, N.J.), 8 April 1939, p. 3.

money for transmission abroad.[41] This ethnic banking developed in the 1880s and 1890s. These "bankers" were always ready to handle immigrants' money, writing their letters, receiving their mail, and giving them advice just as every good neighbor would do. Their personal connections with their customers were what gave them an advantage over regular banking institutions.[42] In time, these "bankers" also became important investors and real estate holders active in developing urban ethnic communities within American cities. Such unregulated but advertised banking businesses were run by several Lemkos, including George *Chylak in Olyphant, Pa., and Gabriel *Dziadik of Derby, Conn.

Immigrant "bankers," for the most part, used banks from the old country to transfer money back home. Of the 50 million dollars remitted home by immigrants between 1892 and 1902, almost 39 million dollars went through Austrian banks and the rest via American banks. The Czech Union Bank in Prague alone received six million dollars from America in 1906, one third of which went to Galicia.[43] In 1910 the United States Immigration Commission (Dillingham Commission) composed of members of the House and the Senate concluded that the "failure of the local institutions to meet the needs of the newly arrived immigrant is (…) nowhere more apparent than in the functions of banking."[44] The situation was already changing and mainstream American banks were looking into expanding their operations into immigrant communities. They supported passing laws that spelled the end to unregulated immigrant banking, a process that began around 1907 and concluded in the mid-1920s.[45]

The immigrant response to this effort was twofold. On one hand, some immigrants began to patronize mainstream American banks. On the other hand, some leading immigrant entrepreneurs either created their own ethnic banks or got involved in the management of small, local banks. These actions were responsible for easing the transition of their countrymen to utilizing regulated, modern banks. After all, as Thomas Čapek (1861–1950), a Czech American politician, lawyer, and the President of the Bank of Europe claimed "banks are an unerring barometer of Americanization."[46]

By 1905 it was noted that Slavs were "even reaching higher in the business world. Only recently a banking house has been opened in Shenandoah, conducted exclusively by Slavs.[47] In Mahanoy City, Slavs are also largely interested in one of the banks, and its business is growing rapidly."[48]

One of the early bankers among the Slavs was a Slovak, Michael Bosak (1869–1937).[49]

---

[41]Ivan Light, "The Migration Industry in the United States, 1882-1924," *Migration Studies* 1:3 (2013): 266.

[42]Frederic J. Haskin, *The Immigrant: An Asset and A Liability* (New York: F.H. Revell, 1913): 188.

[43]Immigration Commission, *Immigrant Banks* (Washington, D.C.: GPO, 1911): 80-81.

[44]Immigration Commission, *Immigrant Banks* (Washington, D.C.: GPO, 1911): 25.

[45]Jared N. Day, "Credit, Capital and Community: Informal Banking in Immigrant Communities in the United States, 1880–1924," *Financial History Review* 9:1 (April 2002): 65-78.

[46]Thomas Capek and Thomas Capek, Jr., *The Czechs and Slovaks in American Banking* (New York, 1920): 5.

[47]It is not clear which bank Warne referred to. On Jan. 15, 1902 Shenandoah Trust Company received its charter. The organizers were: Rev. Cornelius Laurisin (the local Greek Catholic priest), M.L. Kemmerer, John Mieldazis, Leon Danowski, and Harry M. Bradigan. Thus, it does not seem that the bank was organized exclusively by Slavs. The entire capitalization of $125,000 was held by the citizens of Shenandoah, a city with a significant Slavic population. "Trust Company Charter," *Republican and Herald* (Pottsville, Pa.), January 15, 1902, p. 1.

[48]Frank Julian Warne, *The Slav Invasion and The Mine Workers: A Study in Immigration* (Philadelphia-London: J.B. Lippincott Company, 1904): 105.

[49]Bosak was born in the village of Okrúhle, Svidník District in the Prešov Region which was inhabited both

He had established Bosak Private Bank by 1897. In 1902 he became involved with the First National Bank in Olyphant, Pa., where he later became the president. In 1912 he established Slavonic Deposit Bank in Wilkes-Barre, Pa., and three years later Bosak State Bank in Scranton, Pa. Bosak's banks were advertised in various Slavic periodicals, including those produced by the Russian Brotherhood Organization, an organization of choice for many Lemkos.

Despite his many achievements, Bosak was not able to enter the upper social class of Scranton or Wilkes-Barre.[50] Perhaps one of the reasons was the fact that his banks were either largely or exclusively run by Slavs.[51] Several Lemkos, who got involved in the banking business, followed a different path but by largely aligning themselves with non-Slavic officers.

Gmitro *Kapitula was one of the founding directors of the First National Bank of McAdoo, Pa., which was established in 1907. John H. Burnard was president and Edward J. Dailey was vice-president.[52] Peter *Basalyga was a promoter and the founding vice-president of the First National Bank of Jessup, Pa. which was established in 1909. The other founding officers of that bank were P.F. Cusick, M.J. Barrett, Fortunato Tiscar, and Chas. M. Carr.[53] George *Chylak was one of the directors of the Bank of Olyphant (est. 1909), and the founding and life-long president was James J. O'Malley (1870-1933), a lawyer born in Olyphant.[54] Peter *Legosh was one of the directors of the People's National Bank of Edwardsville, Pa. This bank was established in 1910 by Sylvester Paukztis, Fred Williams, Jacob M. Lynn, W.O. Washburn, and W.J. Trembath.[55] Especially telling is the involvement of John *Glowa in the creation of the Market Street National Bank (est. 1900). Shamokin was a very large center of Lemko and other Slavic business but, judging by the names, *Glowa was the only Slav among the founders of the Market Street National Bank.[56]

It's obvious that *Glowa's role was to bring in a Lemko and a broader Slavic clientele to the bank. The same role was most likely played by Fortunato Tiscar (1857–1945) in

---

by Slovaks and Rusyns. He immigrated in 1886 and first worked as a breaker boy in Hazleton, Pa. In 1890 he moved to Freeland, Pa. where he worked as an assistant in a store and later for a beer merchant. Both businesses were owned by his kinsmen. Following the usual pattern, he opened a saloon in Olyphant, Pa. and eventually engaged in various financial transactions and sold ship tickets. He also operated a large liquor store and a bottling business. Erwin Dubrowić, *From Central Europe to America 1880-1914* (Rijeka-New York: City Museum of Rijek, 2012): 82-83. For more on him see: Martin Bosák and Rudolf Bosák, *Michael Bosák: An American Banker from Šariš* (Košice: Ibis Publ., 1999).

[50]Burton Folsom, "Like Fathers, Unlike Sons: The Fall of the Business Elite in Scranton, Pennsylvania, 1880–1920," *Pennsylvania History* 46 (October 1980): 305; Rowland Berthoff, "The Social Order of the Anthracite Region, 1825-1902," *The Pennsylvania Magazine of History and Biography* 89:3 (July 1965): 274.

[51]The leadership roster of his banks is given in Thomas Capek and Thomas Capek, Jr., *The Czechs and Slovaks in American Banking* (New York, 1920): 44-45. Among Bosak's leadership there were also Rusyns. His bank in Scranton had George Munchak (1882-1955) serving as a vice-president. (Munchak was a businessman, hotel-keeper, merchant, and the treasurer of the Greek Catholic Union. Artur S. Hamilton, comp., *Statistics. Fraternal Societies* 25 (Rochester, N.Y., 1919): 72). Rev. Nicholas Chopey (1876-1961), a long-lasting pastor of St. Mary's Greek (Byzantine) Catholic Church in Wilkes-Barre was one of directors of Slavonic Deposit Bank. For biographical info on Chopey see: Hon. Daniel J. Flood, "Rev. Father Nicholas Chopey Lauded," *Congressional Record-Appendix*, February 26, 1957, p. A1522-A1523.

[52]"Corporation News Item," *The National Corporation Reporter* 34:7 (1907): 224.

[53]"Commercial and Miscellaneous News," *The Commercial & Financial Chronicle*, December 19, 1909, p. 1576.

[54]"Attorney O'Malley Dies in South Bend," *The Tribune* (Scranton, Pa.), July 20, 1933, p. 10.

[55]"Edwardsville, Pa.," *United States Investor* 21:27 (1910): 1141.

[56]The founders included F. P. Liewellyn, H. S. Zimmermann, M. G. Stelf, G. C. Unger, W. E. Kearney, J. A. Wert, M. G. Reager, W. A. Unger, I. C. Burd, W. H. Zaring, D. E. Shade, George T. Semmonds, and J. P. Haas. "Shamokin New National Bank," *The Philadelphia Inquirer*, April 25, 1900, p. 4

**Market Street National Bank.**—Capital stock paid in, $100,000. Par, $100. Undivided profits, $24,207. Total deposits, $191,424.
Officers: F. P. Lewellyn, Pres.; H. S. Zimmerman, Vice-Pres.; W. M. Tier, Cash. Directors: F. P. Lewellyn, Isaac C. Burd, M. J. Flanagan, M.D., John Glowa, Jos. W. Kessler, H. S. Zimmerman, W. H. Unger, M. G. Stief, J. A. Wert, M. G. Reager, D. S. Shade, J. P. Haas, W. H. Zaring, H. S. Morgan, Geo. T. Semmons.
Correspondents: N. Y., Hanover Nat. Bk.; Phila., Phila., Fourth St. and Corn Exch. Nat. Banks.

2. Market Street National Bank, 1903, 1904.

3. First National Bank of Jessup, Pa, 1918

Jessup as he served as the Italian Vice Consul of Scranton for many years and was widely known among his co-patriots living in the Northeast Pennsylvania.[57]

## Undertakers

Another business area open to immigrants was undertaking. Several Lemko immigrants operated funeral homes. Among them there were: John P. *Chowanes (Shenandoah and Lansford in Pennsylvania), Paul *Holowczak (Cleveland, Ohio), Stephen J. *Jewusiak (Jersey City, New Jersey), Leon *Kowalczyk (Yonkers, New York), Alex Anthony *Rusynyk (Cleveland, Ohio), and John W. *Turko (Olyphant, Pennsylvania). Kowalczyk stood out among them as his sons took over and expanded the business: his sons William, John, and Walter, operated a funeral home in Jersey City, New Jersey. and a fourth son, Harry, operated a funeral home in Auburn, New York. All of these businesses originally operated as Kowalczyk Funeral Home.

## Builders

Building houses and churches in the Lemko Region required the coordinated efforts of a significant group of skillful workers. This experience was transplanted to North America, where several Lemkos distinguished themselves as contractors, while others built their own houses.[58]

Thomas M. *Gamble, after working as a carpenter, opened his own home-building

---

[57]Stephanie Longo, *Italians of Northeastern Pennsylvania* (Charleston, SC: Arcadia Publishing, 2004): 46.

[58]"We also find such Lemkos who built themselves the most modern houses fit for millionaires, while maintaining jobs in factories. Take, for example, Vladymyr Hnatovych in Stamford, Conn., Mykhayl Ksenych in Balston Spa., N. Y., Osyf Dziamba in Cleveland, and there are even more such builders." "Riz'biarstvo pryneslo schast'e i slavu," in *Karpatorusskyi kalendar' Lemko-Soiuza 1960* (Yonkers, N.Y., 1960): 134.

business in Lakewood, Ohio. Similarly, Charles D. *Grucelak, from approximately 1909, worked as a carpenter/home builder in Scranton, Pa. Alex C. *Chylack also had a carpentry and house construction business in St. Clair, Pa. Daniel *Shost, since 1915, was listed as a builder/carpenter in Yonkers, N.Y. He either built or renovated houses. Lazor Sirotiak, after a stormy career in real estate and banking, made a name for himself as a carpenter/building contractor in Yonkers, N.Y. John *Korbelak, from 1920 and through 1930, was listed as a painter/contractor in Bayonne, N.J., working on his own account and employing people.

Alex *Kowalchik, from 1909, worked independently as a plumber and tinsmith in Olyphant, Pa. From 1920 to his death, he owned a hardware/furniture store at 116 (later 112-116) Grant Street. In the 1920s he advertised as a dealer of "Pratt & Lumber Varnish Products." Peter *Basalyga, in addition to running his general and grocery stores, purchased fifty acres of land to the north of Winton, Pa., which he then divided into acres, erected numerous dwellings and sold them to new settlers. He also sold them plots.

Perhaps the most unique life path was that of Michael *Stefansky, who moved from one place to another while working in construction. In 1899 he moved his family to Detroit, Michigan, where he was the first Lemko (and is also remembered as the first Ukrainian) in town and settled among the Germans on the city's East Side. In a few years, he began building homes on Detroit's west side where he also moved his family. In addition to owning a general store, beer garden, meat market and grocery, he was also listed as a carpenter. In 1911 he filed articles of association for the American Building Club, of which he was the principal stockholder, and which had capital of $1,000. Stefansky, who retired by 1930, also helped to establish two Detroit churches: St. John's Greek (now Ukrainian) Catholic Church, which he built with his sons on land donated to him by the Webber Lumber Co., as well as Saints Peter and Paul Russian Orthodox Cathedral.

## Unusual and Rare Lines of Business

A few Lemko businessmen ventured into other lines of business. Let's list a few of them.

Daniel *Bavolack, before opening his general store, first had a horse-drawn wagon taxi, which he used to transport newcomers from Hazleton Junction, Pa., to where they were going to settle, while also selling them what they needed to make beds, set up a kitchen, etc.

Damian "Demko" *Broda, by 1910 bought a carpet cleaning business in Newtown, N.J. When cars became more prevalent, he opened a garage, becoming the first automobile mechanic in Sussex County and was credited with staying ahead of the demand by modernizing and completely re-outfitting his repair shop.

Joseph Harry *Fekula immigrated at the young age of 12 and graduated from Philadelphia College of Pharmacy (1905) as a distinguished student. In 1907 he received a pharmacist's certificate and subsequently operated his pharmacy in Olyphant, Pa., until 1929.

In 1929, Peter *Filak, in partnership with Henry Zimmer, opened the Yonkers Perfect Laundry. In 1934 an investment of $69,000 was made to purchase machinery and by 1940 the laundry employed forty-one people and had ten trucks. In 1943, the laundry was sold to Philip Scheiner and Sylvia Kandel for $30,000. At that time, it employed about twenty-five workers and had six trucks.

Victor P. *Hladick is known as a leader of the Lemko community who was also a businessman and founder of several newspapers. One of them, *Pravda*, was sold to the

Russian Brotherhood Organization for $400. For at least two years, 1908–1909, he was listed as a steamship and insurance agent at 59 Morris Street, Jersey City, N.J. In the late 1920s he organized and managed several recordings of Lemko folk and Orthodox religious music for mainstream American companies, including Columbia and Okeh, which garnered commercial success. Hladick was also involved in the distribution through the mail of recordings sent out from his apartment at 418 East 69th St. in New York City.

Orest *Hyra[59] worked as a barber for five years (Yonkers, N.Y.) before moving to the grocery business.

Charles *Kasych worked as an independent businessman from 1940. First, he operated a gas station, Kasych Service Station on MacArthur Road and Schadt Avenue in Allentown, Pa., and later he operated, with his son, the Highway Army and Navy Store, also on MacArthur Road.

## Most Successful Businessmen

Several of the Lemko businessmen mentioned in the present work achieved larger commercial success.

Nicholas W. *Fedorko operated many businesses. After starting a grocery/butcher shop in Stratford, Conn., and another butcher shop in Bridgeport, Conn., he became the treasurer of Flour, Grain, and Feed Co. (later known as Farmers Flour and Grain Co.) in Stratford and established a mineral water manufacturing company under the name Fedorko and Son, later known as Stratford Bottling Works. He also owned a real-estate company in Stratford, where he also ran a liquor dealership. He was also involved with Barnum Coal and Fuel Company, albeit only briefly.

Cyril W. *Fedorko was the brother of Nicholas W. and was the president of Farmers Flour and Grain Co. on Sutton St., later at 1167 Stratford Ave. in Stratford, Conn. He ran that company at least until 1944.

In 1925 Alexander P. *Grega and John H. *Guba organized the Potato Chip Manufacturing Co. in Cohoes, N.Y. In 1937, Peter Grega replaced John Guba as treasurer of the named G&G Company. Guba initially opened a hotel/restaurant in Schenectady, N.Y., but returned to Cohoes a few years later, in 1939, to form the Super Crisp Potato Chip Company. Both companies flourished for a time.[60]

Peter S. *Hardy started the very successful Health Developing Apparatus Co. Inc. and received a number of patents for his innovations. In 1938 he, together with Frank J. Karandisevski, founded the Peerless Foundry Co. in Bridgeport, Conn. By 1944 the company shifted its primary focus to the production of aluminum castings. At its height it employed up to 300 people. Hardy, whose imagination in the treatment of aluminum was said to be "uncanny," held the role of the new entity's president and treasurer. While working for the Peerless Aluminum Foundry Co., he received several patents. After Hardy's retirement, his son Myron, led the company, eventually turning it into one of the largest producers of aluminum on the East Coast.[61]

---

[59] He was the grandfather of famous Hollywood star Meg Ryan.

[60] "Potato Chips in Cohoes," *Spindle City Historic Society* 4:4 (winter 2001): [6], http://www.spindlecity.net/NewsLetters/2001-4-Winter.pdf

[61] Anna Whelan, "Of People and Places," *Bridgeport Sunday Post*, 30 November 1958, p. B10; "Peerless Aluminum," The CT Mills - Making Places of Connecticut, https://connecticutmills.org/find/details/peer-

## Cooperatives

In 1910 the American economist and sociologist Emily Greene Balch (1867–1961) noted that "very interesting developments, significant, one may hope, though not yet on a large scale, are various cooperative undertakings among Slavic groups."[62] Father Ivan Wolanski (1856–1926), the first Greek Catholic priest in America, who arrived in 1884, initiated the first cooperatives among Lemkos. In October of 1887 he convinced Mykhal Kushvara and Stephen Yanovich, who each owned a small grocery, to join forces and to establish a cooperative store. Kushvara[63], who was the younger of the two, was sent to Philadelphia to learn how to run a business.[64] Within a few years, with help from Father Wolanski's wife, the cooperative had seven stores: Shenandoah[65], Plymouth, Freeland, Hazleton, Olyphant, Honeybrook, and Jermyn, all in Pennsylvania. They were managed by an association led by Father Wolanski himself. The other officers of this association were: Stephen Yanovich, general manager, and Anthony Wislosky, Michael Kaprowski, and Volodymyr Syminovitch/Simenovych.[66] When Father Wolanski left in 1889, he placed Father Constantine Andruchowicz, also known as Father Andrews (1862–19??), in charge of the association. According to historians the stores could not function properly without Father Wolanski's leadership and were plagued by misunderstandings.[67] However, testimonies of all parties indicate power struggles and perhaps ethnonational conflict.[68]

The Russian Mercantile Association Limited, also known as the Russian Mercantile Company,[69] in Shamokin, Pa., was established in 1889, and incorporated in 1896. Lemkos

---

less-foundry, accessed Nov. 20, 2020.

[62] Emily Greene Balch, *Our Slavic Fellow Citizens* (New York: Charities Publication Committee, 1913): 309.

[63] Perhaps he was related to Andrew Kuswara (1866-1907), who in 1900 was listed as a grocery store owner in Shenandoah, Pa.

[64] Ivan Kashchak, "Biznes i tserkva v seredovyshchi ukraïns'kykh immihrantiv pershoï khvyli u SShA," *Patriiarkhat* no. 4 (2018): 18.

[65] In 1890, it was still run by Stephen Yanovich. The same year the Russian Store Company was dissolved and the stock was purchased by George *Wretik. However, in 1897, Mike Bolton, Jacob Muschick, and Theodore Mislowsky who ran a business in Shenandoah under the name Russian Store Company were arrested for allegedly assigning and disposing of their property with the intent to defraud their creditors. The firm was heavily in debt. They were held on $100.00 bail each. "Heraldings," *Weekly Herald* (Shenandoah, Pa.),1 March 1890, p. 7; "Merchants in Trouble," *Mount Carmel Item* (Mount Carmel, Pa.), Jan. 2, 1897, p. 1.

[66] "Borough Budget. Things the People of Town Talk About," *Weekly Herald* (Shenandoah, Pa.), February 1, 1890, p. 1.

[67] Bohdan P. Procko, "The Establishment of the Ruthenian Church in the United States, 1884-1907," *Pennsylvania History* 42:2 (April 1975): 142; Michael Palij, "Early Ukrainian Immigration to the United States and the Conversion of the Ukrainian Catholic Parish in Minneapolis to Russian Orthodoxy," *Journal of Ukrainian Studies* 8, no. 2 (Toronto, 1983): 25; Federico Marti, "The Ruthenians in America: Genesis of the Most Important Case of Oriental Catholic Diaspora in the West," in: Lorenzo Benedetti, Bianca Maria Cecchini, Marco Gemignani, and Tommaso Maria Rossi, eds. *"Tuitio Fidei et Obsequium Pauperum." Studi in onore di Fra' Giovanni Scarabelli per i cinquant'anni di sacerdozio* (Viareggio: La Villa, 2019): 283.

[68] "Borough Budget. Things the People in Town Talk About," *Weekly Herald* (Shenandoah, Pa.), February 1, 1890, p. 1.

[69] In advertisements in the Ruthenian/Ukrainian National Association's almanacs, the name evolved as follows: "ruskii stor" (1903), "Shamokin'ska Ruska Torhovlia / Shamokin Russian Store" (1907), "rus'kyi shtor" (1912), and "ukraïns'kyi shtor" (1920). Richard Custer, "The Influence of Clergy and Fraternal Organizations on the Development of Ethnonational Identity among Rusyn Immigrants to Pennsylvania," in Bogdan Horbal, Patricia Krafcik, and Elaine Rusinko, eds., *Carpatho-Rusyns and Their Neighbors: Essays in Honor of Paul Robert Magocsi* (Fairfax, Va.: Eastern Christian Publications, 2006): 67.

Іван ГЛОВА, предс.   М. Пеляк, кас.
М. Сметана, секретар
**RUSSIAN MERCANTILE ASSOC'N**
найстарший руський штор в Америці має завсїгди доволї сьвіжого товару та продає по дуже умїркованих цїнах. Повилає також гроші і продає шифкарти до всїх частий сьвіта. Обертає місячно сумою $7.500.   Заряд М. Пеляк.

4. Russian Mercantile Association, 1914

were the leaders of this enterprise, including Max *Pelak, Marko *Smetana, John *Glowa, and Vasyl'Peiko. The year it was incorporated it purchased a building at 327 N. Shamokin St. for $18,000. In 1898, the building was enlarged and remodeled and was said to house the largest Rusyn company store in America.[70] Monthly cash flow grew from $2,000 in 1897 to $4,000 in 1903. In 1905 the Russian Store Company, which at that time also had a store in Excelsior, Pa., purchased a property at Shamokin and Independence Streets owned by the estate of Johnand Mrs. G. B. Fisler. The cost was $20,000.[71] By 1914 the monthly cash flow was $7,500 and in 1920 it reached $10,000.

In 1922, its store was burglarized.[72] In 1924 a bid was made by a group of Scranton investors to purchase the building and the land owned by the Russian Mercantile Company in order to build a modern theatre for the staging of vaudeville presentations and other attractions. The price was reported to be attractive, but the shareholders refused to sell.[73] This decision was no doubt soon regretted. In 1925 the store was offering their covered wagons, horses, and harnesses for sale,[74] which clearly indicated financial difficulties. At the beginning of 1926, the company filed for bankruptcy when, after a strike, its assets were only $5,100, while its liabilities stood at $19,000. The company was led at that time by Michael Kolynack and had several hundred small creditors.[75] In 1927 the *Kulanda brothers bought the store.[76]

In 1910, also in Shamokin, the Ruthenian Store Company was incorporated.[77] It was established with the capital of $5,000 (a hundred $50 shares were sold) with the goal of "conducting and carrying on a general retail mercantile store for the buying and selling dry goods, groceries, provisions, general household goods, wearing apparel, mining tools and supplies, at retail."[78] Organizers and directors of this corporation were Lemko businessmen: George Dziobko (Excelsior, Pa), Dennis *Kulanda (Shamokin, Pa.), Theodore Wyshowsky (Shamokin, Pa.), Simon *Horoshchak, (Shamokin, Pa.) and Nicefor *Habura (Excelsior, Pa.). As noted in the incorporation document,[79] the corporation was to exist for a term of 100 years, but its later history requires more research. It was still in business in 1919.[80]

---

[70]"Velykii kompanichnyi stor," *Svoboda* (Mount Carmel, Pa.), September 14, 1899, p. 4.

[71]"Shamokin Property Deal," *Mount Carmel Item* (Mount Carmel, Pa.), November 3, 1905, p. 4.

[72]"Looking Backward," *Shamokin News-Dispatch* (Shamokin, Pa.), April 25, 1947, p. 6.

[73]"Plans of Backers of Venture Revealed When It Was Learned They Had Failed in an Attempt to Purchase Property of the Russian Mercantile Company on Shamokin Street…," *Shamokin News-Dispatch* (Shamokin, Pa.), December 31, 1924, p. 1; "A New Theatre at Shamokin," *The Plain Speaker* (Hazleton, Pa.), January 15, 1925, p. 8.

[74]"For Sale. Covered Wagons," *Shamokin News-Dispatch* (Shamokin, Pa.), March 11, 1925, p. 4.

[75]"Russian Mercantile Company is Bankrupt," *Shamokin News-Dispatch* (Shamokin, Pa.), January 11, 1926, p. 4.

[76]"$318 Damages Awarded for Boy's Injury," *The Daily Item* (Sunbury, Pa.), January 9, 1940, p. 1.

[77]"Changes in Business the Last Week," *Boot and Shoe Recorder* (Boston, Mass.), 25 October 1911, p. 95.

[78]*List of Charters of Corporations Enrolled in the Office of the Secretary of the Commonwealth* 1909/1911 (Harrisburg, Pa., 1911): 161.

[79]Transcribed by Suzanne Cesari and posted at http://files.usgwarchives.net/pa/northumberland/xmisc/ruthenianst.txt

[80]"Mercantile Appraisal List," *Mount Carmel Item*, 5 June 1919, p. 5.

Emily Greene Balch specifically mentioned that in Yonkers, "under the leadership of a public-spirited Ruthenian priest, a model tenement was built on a co-operative plan, and other co-operative enterprises were started."[81] The store that Balch talked about was the Little Russian Cooperative Association, also known as the Little Russian Corporation, which was established in 1901 from the sale of $25 shares, which were initially purchased by fifty people. A local Greek Catholic priest, Fr. Pavlo Tymkevych (1872–1930), was instrumental in the creation of this cooperative.[82] Its founding leadership included: Aleksander Trembach (president), Ivan Sabat (secretary), Stefan Radko (cashier, and later president and controller for 25 years), as well as Dennis Harems, Samuel Fecko, and Sylvester Patrycia.[83] The cooperative purchased two buildings with two lots of land at 355 and 357 Nepperhan Ave. for a total of $18,000 and opened two stores, a grocery and a clothing store, which were sold after two years. The buildings included apartments upstairs, which were rented. In 1903, a new building was constructed on the existing lots at a price of $30,000 and a grocery/butcher shop was opened there. In 1908 the cooperative purchased six lots of land. By 1913 it had 100 members and capital of $40,000. Three people worked at the store and generated a $700 weekly cash flow. The cooperative's property was valued at $80,000, while it owed $27,000 on an outstanding loan to be paid off.[84] Despite two fires (1921 and 1928)[85] the cooperative continued to grow.

Домы и нıторы Народной Сполки въ Yonkers, N. Y.

5. Buildings owned by the Little Russian Cooperative 355 and 357 Nepperhan Ave., Yonkers, N.Y., 1903

---

[81] Emily Greene Balch, *Our Slavic Fellow Citizens* (New York: Charities Publication Committee, 1913): 309.

[82] "Three More Directors," *The Yonkers Statesman* (Yonkers, N.Y.), December 17, 1901, p. 4. Fr. Tymkevych arrived in America in 1898 and first went to Canada. He served in Yonkers, N.Y. (1898-1905) and later in Lyndora, Pa. (1908-1911) before returning to Galicia. Dmytro Blažejovskyj, Ukrainian Catholic Clergy in Diaspora (1751-1988): Annotated List of Priests Who Served Outside of Ukraine (Rome: [s.n.], 1988): 237.

[83] "Three More Directors," *The Yonkers Statesman* (Yonkers, N.Y.), December 17, 1901, p. 4.

[84] "Dim 'Rus'koï Spilky'," *Kalendar Rus'koho narodnoho soiuza v Amerytsï* 1914 (Jersey City, 1913): 238.

[85] In 1921, children playing with matches were the cause of a fire in the four-story double brick apartment at 361 Nepperhan Avenue, owned by the Little Russian Corporation. The bedroom and kitchen on the third floor; the rooms directly over, in the apartment on the fourth floor, and part of the roof, were badly burned with the estimated loss $3,500. "Four Story Flat Damaged by Fire" *The Yonkers Statesman* (Yonkers, N.Y.), February 7, 1921, p. 1. In 1928, a fire of unknown origin damaged a five-story store and apartment building at 355 Nepperhan Avenue costing $9,000. The loss was sustained by the Little Russian Corporation and the

Among the prominent members of this cooperative were a number of Lemko businessmen: Andrew *Dragan (founding director), Walter *Honcharik, Leon *Kowalczyk (president), Dennis *Merena (secretary), Aftan *Pupchyk (president, 1947–1951), Lazor *Sirotiak (founding director), John *Spiak (treasurer, 1905–1935), Awksenty *Telep (founding director), and Jacob *Wandzilak (director).

In 1906 there were six meat markets in Seymour, Conn., a city of 4,500 people. Two of them were run by Lemkos, *Dziadik and *Smey. The other four were owned by: Baldwin & Miles, Buckingham, Coleman, and Mahoney. In 1911 there were eight meat markets in Seymour, whose population was reaching 5,000 people. Three of these markets were run by Lemkos: *Powanda and Adamovich, *Dziadik, and *Smey. The other five were owned by: Adsager, Baldwin & Miles, Coleman, Trewhella, and Mahoney. The meat business landscape got even more crowded in 1913 when, the Seymour Russian Company was organized with nominal capital stock of $4,000 divided into 160 shares of $25 each.[86] The incorporators were Lemkos: Wasil Wan, Amros Yarosh and Peter Brenia, all of Seymour. The company purchased land on Third Street and conducted a grocery and meat business there.[87]

There were probably other cooperatives among Lemkos in the United States.

## Conclusions

Contemporary research shows that first generation immigrants start businesses at nearly twice the rate of their children's generation, and at a rate 27 percent higher rate than that of Americans who are not immigrants. Among those in the first generation, 16.4 percent start businesses, compared, to 8.9 percent in the second generation, and 12.9 percent for entrepreneurs who are not immigrants.[88]

At the turn of the 19th and 20th centuries Lemkos were nowhere close to these numbers. However, that was a much different world than the one in which we live today. Now there is a good deal of assistance from both the government and NGOs for small businesses. People in many countries learn English before they arrive in the United States, and if they do not know English, in large cities like New York they can receive information and help in many languages. When the first Lemko immigrants arrived in the United States, they got little or no help starting businesses and often faced a hostile environment in which it was difficult to make ends meet. Emily Greene Balch observed that

"(…) It seems remarkable that the Slavs, who have been so often accused of lack of individual initiative, and who many of them are commercially very primitive, lacking in all business experience and too often accustomed to being patiently exploited by middlemen (…) have here succeeded as well as they have done in commercial undertakings. Their honesty, and a strongly marked vein of shrewdness, are probably their best assets. One constantly hears praise of Slavs in business dealings, especially for

---

Hudson Valley Confectionery Company, respective owners and occupants of the building. "City Fire Loss $16,442 Higher Than Last Year" *The Yonkers Statesman* (Yonkers, N.Y.), December 31, 1928, p. 3.

[86] Among stockowners there were: Dimitry Karlak (Karliak), Peter Brania (Brenia), Wasyl Wan, Amros Yarosh, Dimitry Gelato (Galeta), Harry Wencko (Winsco), Steve Wislocki, Peter Sakol (Sokol), and Steve Potoski. Information from Robert Klancko.

[87] "Local and Personal," *The National Provisioner* 48:18 (1913): 40.

[88] Elaine Pofeldt, "First-Generation Immigrants Dive into Entrepreneurship," *Forbes*, June 26, 2013, https://www.forbes.com/sites/elainepofeldt/2013/06/26/first-generation-immigrants-dive-into-entrepreneurship/#2b398a1674d8 .

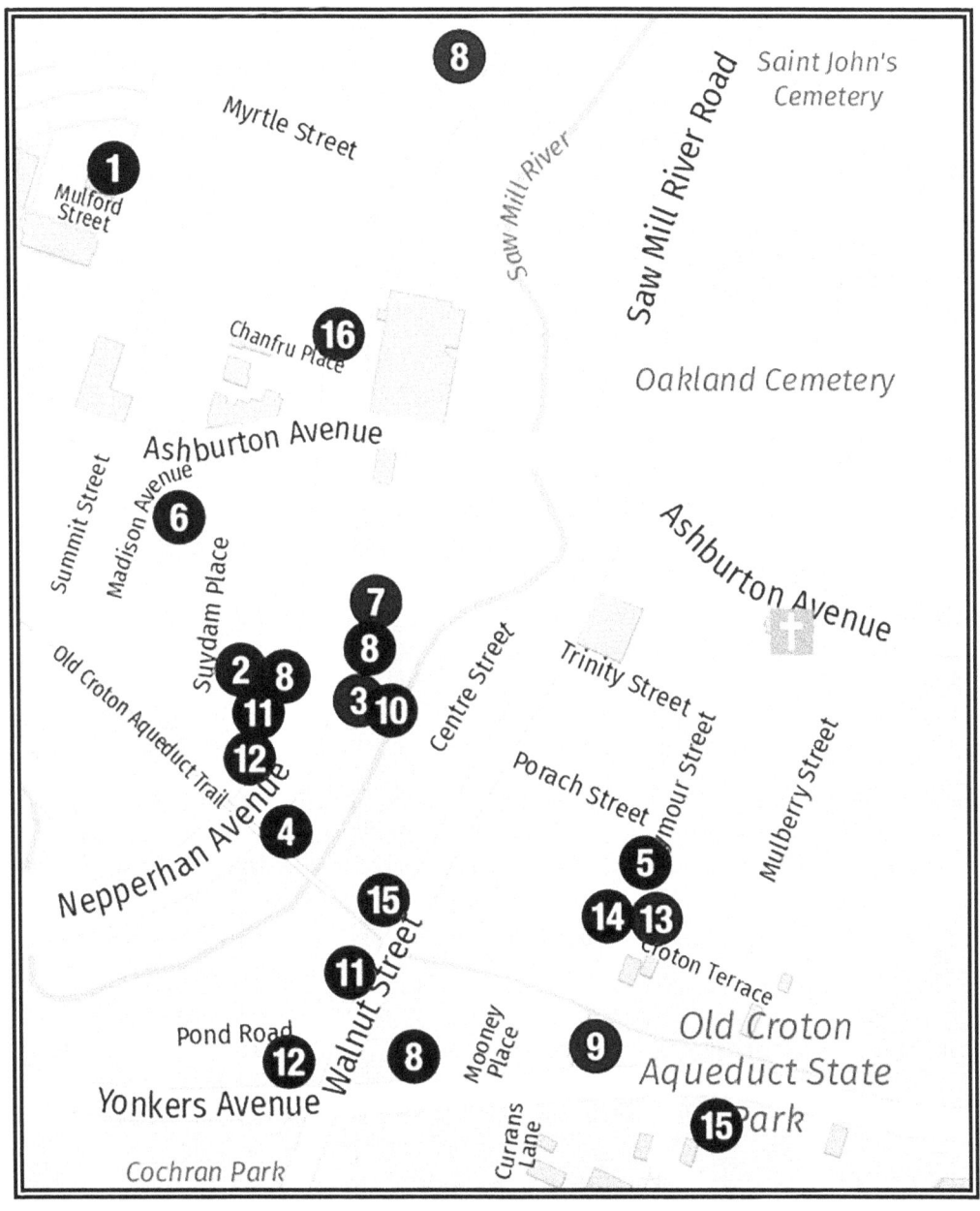

### 6. Yonkers, New York

Distribution of Lemko businesses in the central part of Yonkers.

1. Oscar Ciuryk
2. Andrew Dragan
3. Mitro Fesch
4. Peter Filak
5. Stephen Hodio
6. Michael Karell
7. Jacob Kowalczyk
8. Leon Kowalczyk
9. John Malutich
10. Damian Merena
11. Dennis Merena
12. Aftan Pupchyk
13. Nicholas Symochko
14. Simon T. Turchick
15. Jacob Wandzilak
16. Nicholas M. Washienko

being prompt and sure in payment. (…)"[89]

The largest concentration of Lemko businesses was in Yonkers, N.Y. Other significant centers of Lemko business were in Ansonia, Conn., Shamokin, Pa.,[90] Bridgeport, Conn., Clifton, N.J., and Olyphant, Pa. These numbers are based on 221 biographies of Lemko entreprenours presented in this book.

While Lemko immigrants engaged in various lines of business, the most common among them was keeping boarders, as well as operating a bar/saloon/hotel or a grocery/meat store. In most instances these mom-and-pop businesses relied heavily on labor provided by family members, and some were run in addition to the owner's daytime job (often at a mine or a factory).[91]

Wives were often instrumental in running businesses by working as salespersons or cooks. Several Lemko women distinguished themselves by taking over businesses after their husbands died. Among them there were: Tekla (Paul) *Comcowich, Anna (Paul) *Holowczak, Theodosia/Tevdozka (Alexis) *Horbal, Anna (Simon) *Horoshchak, Fotina (Cost) *Koban, Kathryn (Alex) *Kowalchik, Anna (Elias) *Smerek, and no doubt numerous others who are not mentioned in this book.

After Nicholas *Wartella [Vorotyla] died, his son Stephen became the head of the household but it was Wartella's wife, Mary who became the matriarch of the Wartella family. "A strong and proud woman" she felt was successfully established in the community, though it was said she could not speak English. She had a chauffeur to drive her around in her expensive car, to emphasize her status.[92]

Fannie *Stoppi is the only Lemko woman who has a self-standing biography in this book. She settled in Frackville, Pa., where she was first married to Metro Ritzko (1890–1918) and later Joseph Stoppi (1888–1933). Both men were miners. Probably after her second husband died, she opened a café, first noted in 1934, at 433 W. Pine St., later located at 402 S. Lehigh Ave,, and again at 433 W. Pine St., where she was still in business in 1953.

Lemko businessmen were often leading activists in their ethnic communities, and held leadership positions in ethnic and fraternal organizations not only locally, but on a national level as well. Among these organizations were: the Lemko Association,[93] the Providence Association of Ukrainian Catholics in America,[94] the Russian Brotherhood Organization,[95]

---

[89] Emily Greene Balch, *Our Slavic Fellow Citizens* (New York: Charities Publication Committee, 1913): 307-308.

[90] Bohdan Horbal' and Richard Kaster, "Shamokin, Pennsylvania: Pershyi Tsentr Lemkivskoho Biznesu v Amerytsi," in: *Richnyk Ruskoi Bursŷ / Rocznik Ruskiej Bursy* 2015 (Gorlice, 2015): 59-77.

[91] One such business whose owner is not listed in this book was run by Harry Klemash/Klimash (1891-1968). Out of his home at 72 Cleveland St., Hudson, Pa., he offered costumes for very popular theatrical performances staged by Lemkos in various cities. He advertised his business in the early 1930s but his day job was first at the Delaware and Hudson Coal Company and later at the Delaware and Hudson Railroad where he worked as a car inspector until his retirement. "Harry Klemash Dies at Plains," *Times Leader: The Evening News* (Wilkes-Barre, Pa.), June 19, 1968, p. 60.

[92] "Mary Senko Wartella (1878-1956)," Wartella Geneology, http://wartella.com/mary-senko-wartella-1878-1956/.

[93] Walter *Honcharik.

[94] John Boroshovich.

[95] Anthony W. *Homick, Alex *Kowalchik, George *Retick/Wretic/Vretyk, Alex/Aleksii *Shlanta, and Simon T. *Turchick.

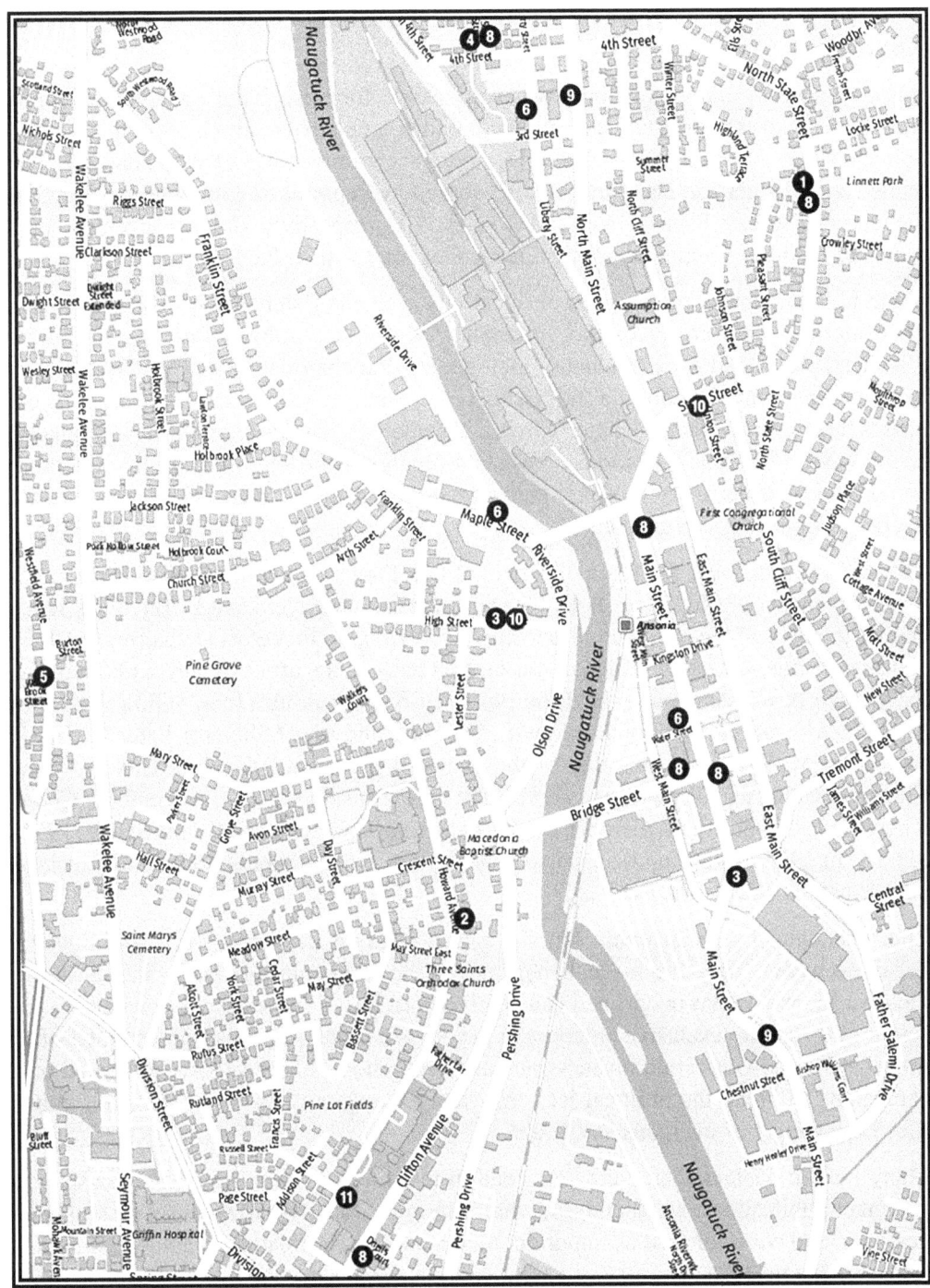

7. Ansonia, Connecticut
Distribution of Lemko businesses in Ansonia.

1. Sidor Cirkot
2. Theodore Cikoth
3. Joseph Comcowich
4. Paul Comcowich
5. Dennis Merena
6. Andrew Pedbereznak
7. Dimitro Pelesh
8. Peter T. Pelesh
9. Charles Powanda
10. Dimitro Sydoriak
11. Joseph Waniga

and the Russian/Little Russian/Ruthenian National Union (later Ukrainian National Association).[96]

Business success and engagement was responsible for raising not only the economic status of Lemko entrepreneurs within their broader, municipal communities but also their political status. Michael *Shostak was Democratic committeeman of West Hazleton, Pa., while John *Holda and Damian *Merena served as Republican committeemen of Diamondtown district in Pennsylvania and Cohoes, N.Y., respectivly. Holda was remembered as one of the most prominent political leaders of Mt. Carmel, Pa.

Some Lemko businessmen served on local city councils (Nicholas W. *Fedorko, Alex *Kowalchik, Onufer *Kowtko, Seman *Metrinko, John *Puschak, Andrew *Skwier/Skweir, and Alex *Shlanta), including as the chairman (Theodor *Wachna) or the president (Gmitro *Kapitula and Nicholas *Yackanicz). Others served on local school boards (Daniel *Bavolack, George *Chylak, Theodore P. *Chylack, Michael N. *Halkowicz, and Alex *Shlanta). Theodosy *Wachna organized the Municipality of Stuartburn and served as its secretary-treasurer and magistrate. He also served as a secretary of the twelve schools he had organized.

Mitrofan *Gambal was the first policeman of Old Forge, Pa., while Gmitro * served as the commandant of McAdoo's Police Department for a decade. Daniel *Bavolack was a charter member of the McAdoo Fire Company (1921), its first elected chairman (1925), and later its trustee. George *Chylak was elected twice to the office of mayor of Olyphant, Pa. Lemko businessmen also held the positions of postmaster (John *Glowa, Nicefor *Habura, Michael N. *Halkowicz, John L. *Merena, and Alex *Shlanta). Peter S. *Hardy served as president and chairman of the board of trustees of the Park City Hospital, Trumbull, Conn. to which he donated $25,000 for expansion in 1957. In Trumbull, Conn., where he lived, he was a member of the Industrial Development Commission (1956–1966?). In 1955 he gave up his land so that a new Town Hall could be built and in 1966 he was named "Citizen of the Year."

This engagement in mainstream American civil affairs is definitely worth highlighting, because it was not easy to achieve. In her study of the immigrant community in Johnstown, Pa., Eva Morawska has underlined that "native-born East Europeans were evidently conscious of the ethnic-exclusive practices in the city's politics." She also added that a small group of second-generation businessmen and professionals in the 1930s embarked on a campaign "to break the political ice" that kept "foreigners" out of mainstream public life. They were, however, unsuccessful.[97]

Many Lemko businessmen were described in mainstream, local American newspapers and other publications, whether during their lifetime, or in obituaries, as successful businessmen, and were admired as important members of their broader communities. Below are some examples.

- Peter *Bohaczyk (Mt. Carmel, Pa.) was described as "one of the community's most successful businessmen."

- John *Chylack (St. Clair, Pa.) was remembered as a "well-known retired businessman."

---

[96]George *Chylak, John *Glowa, Gmitro *Kapitula, Cost *Koban, John *Parylak. Alexis *Sharshon, and Teodozii/Theodore *Talpash.

[97]Ewa Morawska, "East European Labourers in an American Mill Town, 1890-1940: The Deferential-Proletarian-Privatized Workers?" *Sociology* 19:3 (August 1985): 377

## 8. Shamokin Pennsylvania

### Distribution of Lemko businesses in Shamokin.

1. Nicefor Habura
2. Paul Homiak
3. Teodozii Homiak
4. Simon Horoshchak
5. Julian Kopyscianski
6. Dennis A. Kulanda
7. Nicholas Kulanda
8. Phillip Kulanda
9. Peter C. Kuzmicz
10. Efrem Luczkovec
11. Gabriel Maliniak
12. Max Pelak
13. Alexis Sharshon
14. Marko Smetana
15. Teodozii Talpash
16. Michael Tehansky
17. Theodore Worhacz

- Jacob *Gambal (Olyphant, Pa.) was described as "a well-known merchant."
- John *Glowa (Shamokin, Pa.) was described as "a self-made man, one whose excellent judgment and well directed executive ability have made him successful in his various undertakings."
- "Among the people he served so capably, Postmaster *Halkowicz was a beloved official and was known well in Mount Carmel and other surrounding towns as he was in his own community."
- Thomas *Hatala (Garfield, N.J.) was lauded for his meat and provision business "in which undertaking he met with immediate and marked success. He was also identified with the social and moral interests of the neighborhood."
- Akim *Hawran (Simpson, Pa.) was remembered as "one of the most prominent residents of Simpson."
- Thomas *Hawran (Simpson, Pa.) was remembered as "one of the most prominent residents of Simpson who was well known throughout the upper valley."
- Theodore *Homiak (Mt. Carmel, Pa.) was described as "one of our town's best-known hotel men and was remembered as an industrious man and was held in high regard by everyone. He took active interest in community affairs."
- Peter *Horoschak (Mt. Carmel, Pa.) was "ambitious and energetic and was successful as a businessman. He was a charter member of the St. Demetri Society of the Greek Catholic church and was well known in this section among men of all nationalities."
- Simon *Horoshchak was remembered as "one of Shamokin's best-known merchants and most highly-esteemed residents."
- Peter C. *Kuzmicz (Shamokin, Pa.) is "making a substantial position for himself as a high-class tailor and has prospered by hard work and satisfactory service. (…) His customers include some of the best people in Shamokin. He has a high reputation for satisfactory work and is conscientious in filling orders of all kinds; his skill and neatness winning and holding custom being his best recommendation. He is good citizen of his adopted home, industrious and thrifty, and has a good standing among his fellow countrymen in Shamokin."
- Peter *Legosh was remembered as "widely known throughout the valley and for many years (…) a prominent Edwardsville business man."
- Onufry Joseph *Murdza (Shamokin, Pa.) was remembered as an "esteemed resident and churchman."
- Jacob *Onuschak (Northampton, Pa.) was remembered as a "prominent businessman and fraternal man who took quite an interest in his fellow men."
- Max *Pelak (Shamokin, Pa.) was remembered as a "well-known resident."
- John *Repa (Wilkes-Barre, Pa.) was described as a "prominent citizen, for many years active in the business life of Wilkes-Barre."
- Teodozii *Talpash (Shamokin, Pa.). In 1911 it was noted that "his cafe and hotel are well managed, and he has a profitable patronage, built up by excellent business methods and successful catering to the wants of his customers. His reputation as a citizen and

businessman has always been above reproach."

Although Emily Greene Balch observed that "one does not often hear, I think, stories of defaulting bankers" among the Slavs,"[98] the lives of Lemko businessmen were not always smooth. Some worked without necessary licenses, and a few were investigated and even indicted in bootleg scandals, but it is not clear whether they were sentenced. Some failed as businessmen. Still, many Lemkos who entered business were successful, and they even drew this type of praise from a Ukrainian businessman:

"When our older immigrants started a business, they most likely had one idea: to take money to the bank. However, Lemkos or Transcarpathians did not do this, they practiced business, they grew with it materially and spiritually, and that's why today one can see (...) Lemkos, who have not only respectable businesses, but also big industry. These Lemko businessmen provided their children with higher education, (...) and there is a big difference between Lemkos and other Galicians in this matter."[99]

---

My interest in Lemko entrepreneurs eminated from business advertisements that appeared in almanacs, primarily those by the Lemko Association and the Russian Brotherhood Organization. At first I was interested in the wording used and was excited to see the villages of origin of some of the businessmen. When I worked at the Science, Industry and Business Library of the New York Public Library (2003–2018), I learned more about and developed an appreciation for small-business owners.[100]

Providing biographical information of Lemko businessmen in the United States was challenging for many reasons. Establishing the correct year of birth was almost always a problem. One might argue that most immigrants went with a wrong date of birth or simply did not know their real date of birth. Also, many had different dates of birth on different documents. One could check metrical books of Lemko parishes that have been digitized, but this cannot be done for everyone. On the other hand, if one used an incorrect date of birth throughout his/her life in the United States, isn't that one the date that actually matters the most?

Trying to help me, Rich Custer, the founder and moderator of the Facebook group Lemko Rusyns and Friends posted two calls in the summer of 2020 in his group to "European records whizzes" to help establish dates of birth of thirty-six Lemko businessmen in America. As of September 12, 2020, these calls generated seventy-six comments and five shares. With help from several people[101] who used digitized metrical books from various Lemko villages, true dates of birth and places of birth were established for ten Lemko businessmen.[102] These dates might very well be the only true dates of birth given in all the biographies in this book.

Establishing places of birth was also a significant challenge. Some had obituaries (which

---

[98] Emily Greene Balch, *Our Slavic Fellow Citizens* (New York: Charities Publication Committee, 1913): 309.

[99] Platon Stasiuk, *V Novomu Sviti. Spomyny i dumky byznesmena* (N'iu-Iork: [s.n.], 1958): 38.

[100] I'd like to thank my colleague at the Science, Industry and Business Library, Madeleine Cohen for her help with this text.

[101] Mostly from John Senick, but also Kim Krett and Scott N. Sandy Oliver.

[102] John Bochnewicz, Peter Horoschak, George Dudycz, Ozym Dzwonczyk, Mitrofan Gambal, Wasco Gambal, Walter Honczaryk, Aftanazy Koblosh, Seman/Simon Metrinko/Mitrenko, and Theodor Wachna.

did not always mention their place of birth) published in local newspapers or Lemko publications; in some cases, short biographical articles appeared in Lemko publications. Ancestry.com was of some help as well. When all standard sources of information were exhausted, the only thing left was to turn one more time to Richard Custer, who through many years of researching Carpatho-Rusyn/Lemko immigrant communities in the United States compiled an extensive volume of data from Byzantine/Greek Catholic and Orthodox churches and fraternal benefit society sources dealing with their members. Much of this data included village and county of birth, and through Custer's various strategic search exercises, yielded birthplaces for a large number of the Lemko entrepreneurs included herein.

The year of immigration when taken from census records was also a problem. In many instances the census of 1910 gave a different date than the census of 1920 for the same person. Ship manifests can't always be located. I usually gave the date from the oldest census that I was able to locate, unless a ship manifest was located.

There is also an issue with the spelling of names. As noted before, I learned about many of these businessmen from ads in Lemko almanacs that were published in Cyrillic script. In some instances, a Romanized version of the names was the one that was used in Latin script, but in many others the spelling of the name in Latin script was different, sometimes significantly so, from the Cyrillic original. There were also many inconsistencies in spelling of the same names across time. For example, Калістрат Цідило (Kalistrat Tsidylo[103] aka Kalistrat Cidyło[104]) was noted in Latin script as

   Chedello (1914 marriage record)
   Chidelo (1917 World War I draft registration card)
   Chidilo (1924 naturalization record)
   Cidylo (1930 census)
   Chdylo (1940 census)
   Chidyllo (1942 World War II draft registration card)

Six different spellings for one person!

Hardly anybody had their names changed on Ellis Island, despite a widespread conviction that it was the place where immigrants were given changed/misspelled names.[105] Immigration officials at Ellis Island worked with ship manifests. In some cases, immigrants legally changed their names later on, trying to adjust the spelling to preserve the pronunciation by an English-speaking majority or trying to better fit into an English-speaking society. For example, Pearl, Julian, Mary, Anna, Helen, Jeannie, Sally, and Joseph Olesnewicz of Shamokin, Pa., who were most likely adult children of Lemko immigrants, successfully petitioned a local court to have their last name changed to Oless. The reason for the change was reported as follows: "They are desirous of changing their name because it is burdensome and inconvenient, is generally mispronounced and misspelled, causing annoyance in business and social and private transactions."[106]

There is one more piece of information that I owe to Richard Custer. He observed that

---

[103]Romanized according to the Library of Congress Romanization table for Carpatho-Rusyn, https://www.loc.gov/catdir/cpso/romanization/rusyn.pdf .
[104]His name expressed using Polish orthography.
[105]Philip Sutton, "Why Your Family Name Was Not Changed at Ellis Island (and One That Was)," NYPL Blogs, July 2, 2013, https://www.nypl.org/blog/2013/07/02/name-changes-ellis-island .
[106]"Petition Court to Have Names Changed," *The Daily Item* (Sunbury, Pa.), Sept. 26, 1938, p. 9; "Shamokinites Allowed to Change Their Name," *The Daily Item* (Sunbury, Pa.), December 3, 1938, p. 12

Rusyn businesses advertised in publications of both Ukrainian and Russian orientation, even varying their self-ethnic orientation to suit their audience. He gave the example of John W. *Turko, an undertaker in Olyphant, Pa., who advertised his business both as "ukraïns'ke pohrebnyche zavedennia" and "russkii pohrebnyk."[107]

## Sources of information

Biographical data about early Lemko immigration is not only scarce but also often contradictory. While a historian normally looks forward to utilizing a variety of sources, in this case a new source sometimes introduced conflicting data. It is thus quite possible that some biographies included in this work will need to be revised when additional sources of information become available.

I have worked with everything that ancestry.com has to offer, including ship manifests, census results, city directories, etc. as well as family trees. I have also utilized the newspapers.com database where I was able to find newspapers such as: *Shamokin News-Dispatch*, *Mount Carmel Item*, and *The Plain Speaker* (Hazleton, Pa.), to name just a few.[108] I have also worked with the freely accessible Library of Congress' Chronicling America[109] database as well as FultonSearch,[110] in which, of special interest, is *The Yonkers Statesman*. For pre-1925 research HathiTrust is invaluable. Also rich in information about the history of early Lemko immigration to the United States is the fully digitized *Svoboda*,[111] the official organ of the Ukrainian National Association, along with its almanacs[112] and its English-language organ *Ukrainian Weekly*.[113]

The Lemko Association has created a database with digitized issues of its flagship publications Lemko and Karpatska Rus'[114] while its almanacs were digitized by Walter Maksimovich.[115] Roland Anderson's Carpatho-Russian Almanacs[116] site presents digitized content from many kalendarŷ issued by several émigré organizations.[117] All of the above publications include business advertisements and, in some instances, biographical information on Lemko businessmen.

Another online, rather unconventional but rich, source of information is a Facebook group that I have already mentioned, Lemko Rusyns and Friends.[118] This is mostly thanks

---

[107] Richard Custer, "The Influence of Clergy and Fraternal Organizations on the Development of Ethnonational Identity Among Rusyn Immigrants to Pennsylvania," in Bogdan Horbal, Patricia Krafcik, and Elaine Rusinko, eds., *Carpatho-Rusyns and Their Neighbors: Essays in Honor of Paul Robert Magocsi* (Fairfax, Va.: Eastern Christian Publications, 2006): 83-84.

[108] Both available at the New York Public Library.

[109] https://chroniclingamerica.loc.gov/.

[110] https://fultonsearch.org/.

[111] http://svoboda-news.com/svwp/.

[112] https://svoboda-news.com/svwp/.

[113] http://www.ukrweekly.com/uwwp/.

[114] https://lemkoassociation.org/cgi-bin/lemkosearch.

[115] https://www.lemko.org/books/index.html.

[116] http://carpatho-russian-almanacs.org/.

[117] Including the Russian Brotherhood Organization (RBO), the Russian Orthodox Catholic Mutual Aid Society (ROCMAS), the United Russian Orthodox Brotherhood of America (UROBA), the Lemko Association and the Ukrainian National Association (UNA).

[118] https://www.facebook.com/groups/lemkorusyns/.

to the hard work of its founder and moderator, Richard Custer, who has shared hundreds of posts that are rich in data and have been discussed and supplemented by some of the group's 3,700 members (!).

I have also consulted standard American business and finance reference sources, including *Rand-McNally Bankers' Directory and List of Attorneys* (publ. 1876–1954), which was continued by *Rand McNally International Bankers Directory* (1955–1990), as well as the long-running *The American Bank Reporter*. Also of some use were *Moody's Manual of Railroads and Corporation Securities* (1900–1924) and *Moody's Manual of Investments; American and Foreign* (1909–1954). Several trade journals were also utilized.

Finally, I consulted some early county and city histories to learn about Lemko entrepreneurs and to get an overall picture of the economic development of places where Lemkos settled, including Scranton, Pa.,[119] Schuylkill County, Pa.,[120] Northumberland County, Pa.,[121] and the Wyoming and Lackawanna Valleys in Pennsylvania,[122] as well as Passaic, Clifton, Garfield, and Wallington, all located in New Jersey.[123]

In addition to Richard Custer, whom I have mentioned before and who helped in other ways, I would also like to thank Stephen Brewer, Michael Decerbo, Robert Klancko, Madeleine Cohen, and Evelyn Kormanik for reading the manuscript and offering their comments, as well as Jeffrey Paison for the book layout.

New York, July 30, 2023

---

[119] Frederick L. Hitchcock, *History of Scranton and its People*, 2 vols. (New York City: Lewis Historical Pub. Co., 1914).

[120] Adolf W. Schalck and D. C. Henning, eds., *History of Schuylkill County, Pennsylvania ... Including a Genealogical and Biographical Record of Many Families and Persons in the County* ([n.p.]: State Historical Association, 1907).

[121] *Genealogical and Biographical Annals of Northumberland County, Pennsylvania* (Chicago, Ill.: J. L. Floyd & Co., 1911).

[122] Horace Edwin Hayden, Alfred Hand, and John W. Jordan, eds., *Genealogical and Family History of the Wyoming and Lackawanna Valleys, Pennsylvania*, 2 vols. (New York, Chicago: The Lewis Publishing Company, 1906).

[123] *History of Passaic and its Environs: Historical, Biographical*, 3 vols. (New York: Lewis Historical Pub. Co., 1922).

## УКАЗАТЕЛЬ НАШИХЪ АМЕР. РУССКИХЪ БИЗНЕССМЕНОВЪ

### NOTARY PUBLIC & AGENTS

GREGORY KUNASHEVSKY,
179 E. 3rd St., New York, N. Y.

M. N. HALKOWICZ,
P. O. Box 45, Mt. Carmel, Pa.

GEORGE CHYLAK,
111-113 Grant St. Olyphant, Pa.

### GROCERIES & DELICATESSEN

STEPHEN M. FEDORCHAK,
342 E. 71 St., New York, N. Y.

DANIEL STAFINIAK,
250 Ridge St., Coaldale, Pa.

SIMEON CUCURA,
1209 Crest Ave., Charleroi, Pa.

JOHN RENCHKOWSKY,
1113 Crest Ave., Charleroi, Pa.

JOHN F. BOCHNEWICH,
46 Wash. St., Yonkers, N. Y.

ELIAS J. THIER,
Cohoes Road & Craig Street,
Watervliet, N. Y.

STEPHEN RADKO,
481 Nepperhan Ave., Yonkrs, N.Y.

ANDREW KASYCH,
725 Starkweather Avenue,
Cleveland, O.

JOHN S. GUBIK,
146 East Jersey Street,
Telephone 2011 W. Elizabeth, N.J.

JACOB GAMBAL,
120 Lincoln St., Olyphant, Pa.

### UNDERTAKERS.

JNO. J. SWALLOW,
Cor. 17th and Newport Avenue,
Northampton, Pa.

WILLIAM C. STINE,
130 Grant St., Olyphant, Pa.

### GENERAL MERCHANDISE, DRY GOODS, ETC.

DANIEL M. KUREY,
1430 Newport Avenue,
Northampton, Pa.

HARRY ONUSHCHAK,
1054 — 3rd St., Catasaqua, Pa.

TIMOFEY KOSHIK,
Cokeburg, Pa.

### REAL ESTATE & INSURANCE

JOSEPH OLCHOWSKY,
P. O. Box 175, Manville, N. J.

### WHOLESALERS BEVERAGES AND BOTTLERS

JOSEPH GERCHAK,
213-215 Laurel St. Minersville, Pa.

T. N. WASYLKOFF,
417 Willing St., Tamaqua, Pa.

THEODORE WORHACH,
326 Franklin & Spurzheim Sts.,
Shamokin, Pa.

JOHN HARWILLA
215 North St., Minersville, Pa.

ALEXANDER LUPACH,
48 Box Street, Brooklyn, N. Y.

### RESTAURANTS & HOTELS

GABRIEL BLANIAR,
114 River Ave., Olyphant, Pa.

N. YACKANICZ AND SON
Box 85, Beaver Meadow, Pa.

JOHN NOVAK,
Commerce St., Shamokin, Pa.

D. M. KOROPCHAK,
100 Girat St., Atlas, Pa.

MICHAEL HUDOCK,
42 S. Wyo. Str., Hazleton, Pa.

9. Directory of our Russian-American businessmen, 1921
Most of these people were Lemkos

# BIOGRAPHIES

**Jacob Adamiak** was born in July of 1869 in the Lemko village of Banica, Grybów County, Austro-Hungarian Empire [present-day Poland] into the family of Isidore and Melania (née Fedorczak). He immigrated in 1883 and settled in Mayfield, Pa., where by 1896 he operated a hotel at the corner of Maple and Hill Streets. In 1899 his application to expand there and to build a house was opposed. In 1900, he was listed as a hotel owner and in 1910 as a saloon owner. He was among the charter members of the Russian Orthodox Greek Catholic Church of St. John the Baptist in Mayfield, Pa. (1902). Adamiak was married to Efrozima/Iefroska [Charnansky/Chyrnian'ska, 1866–1939) with whom he had: John, Peter, Rose, Olga, Vladimir, Constantine, and Stefania. Adamiak died on December 10, 1914, and was buried in St. John's Russian Orthodox Cemetery, Mayfield, Pa. It appears that his business was continued by his son-in-law.

---

```
Phone: Mulberry 4894
РУССКІЙ ГРОССЕРНИКЪ
АЛЕКСАНДРЪ БАРНА
— Значый тутъ отдавна —
Тутъ гроссерня и всѣ мяса, а
найлучша есть колбаса.
— ЧЛЕНЪ О. Р. Б. —
293 Oliver Str., Newark, N. J.
```

10. Alexander C. Barna, 1930

```
BARNA'S BAR
271 SHERMAN AVENUE
NEWARK, N. J.
ALEX BARNA          STEVE BARNA
Prop.                      Mgr.
```

11. Alexander C. Barna, 1940

**Alexander C. Barna** was born on March 28, 1891, in the Lemko village of Klimkówka, Gorlice County, Austro-Hungarian Empire [present-day Poland] and immigrated in 1909. He settled in Newark, N.J., where he worked as a molder. By 1922 he had a grocery store at 293 Oliver St., which he operated until 1936. In 1937 he moved to Maplewood, N.J., but the next year he was back in Newark where he opened a tavern at 271 Sherman Ave. As of 1943 his tavern was located at 212 Elizabeth Ave. and operated at that location at least until 1957. He was married to Ksenia/Sadie (née Fylak, 1891–1936) with whom he had: Stephen, Peter, Olga Balint, and William. Barna died on February 4, 1958, and was buried in Evergreen Cemetery, Hillside, N.J.

---

**Peter Barna** was born on July 12, 1867, in the Lemko village of Kamionka, Sanok County, Austro-Hungarian Empire [present-day Poland] and immigrated in 1883. By 1910 he had a hotel at 745 Main St. in Edwardsville, Pa. In 1912 his business was opposed because it was too close to a school, but the judge ruled in his favor. In 1919, he purchased a property for $1,200. In 1920 he was listed as a miner. He was married to Piza/Paiza (née Vatrolick or Sukawatski, 1865–1923) with whom he had: Paul, Anna Pietruszewski, Mike, Julia Gola, and Eva. Barna died on February, 21 1923, and was buried in St. John's Russian Cemetery, Pringle, Pa.

```
КТО ДО ЭДВАРДСВИЛЛЪ ПРІЪЗЖАЕ,
——» нехай до ПЕТРА БАРНЫ адресъ мае. «——
       Онъ велики погары пивомъ наливае,
          и добру виску и сигары мае.
PETER BARNA,        745 Main St.,        Edwardsville, Pa.
```
12. Peter Barna, 1913

**Theodore Barna** was born on November 14, 1891, in the Lemko village of Kamionka, Sanok County, Austro-Hungarian Empire [present-day Poland]. Not much is known about his early years in the United States. In 1913 he lived in Nanticoke, Pa., and in 1930 was noted as a laborer in Jersey City, N.J. In 1942, he was employed by the Federal Shipbuilding and Drydock Company at Kearny Point, N.J. By 1950, he operated Barna's Tavern at 85 Center St., Clifton, N.J. He was still in business in 1960. He was married to Mary (née Fesh, 1889–2000) with whom he had Anna Chomiak. Barna died on May 23, 1966.

13. Basalyga Family

**Peter Basalyga** was born on January 1, 1867, in the Lemko village of Stawisza, Grybów County, Austrian Empire [present-day Poland] into the family of Onufrii and Eva (née Stachura). He immigrated in 1884 and first settled in Scranton, Pa., where he eventually opened a general store and bought land. He later moved to Winton, Pa., and conducted his business in nearby Jessup, Pa. By 1893 he had a grocery store there at the corner of Delaware Avenue and Hand Street and later purchased 50 acres of land to the north of the city. He then divided the land into acres and either erected numerous dwellings, which he sold to new settlers, or sold plots. In 1912 he sold five plots on Hill Street for a total of $2,000. The whole area was known as Basalyga's Plot and one of the streets in the city was eventually named after him. In 1912 he also bought land in Winton, Pa., for $35,000 and sold a plot in Scranton, Pa., on Basalyga Avenue for $350.00. In 1920, he was listed as a merchant (iron store). He was also one of five promoters of the First National Bank of Jessup, Pa., which was established in 1909 with capital of $50,000. By 1913, when Basalyga was vice-president, the bank had total resources of $422,178, and in 1921, when Basalyga

14

was still vice-president, the bank's total resources had grown to $1,220,000. He was a founding member of the Holy Ghost Greek Catholic Church in Jessup, Pa., and for several terms occupied the office of the treasurer of the local Greek Catholic Fraternal and Beneficial Society of Winton (est. 1897). In 1929, he lost $60,000, filed for bankruptcy, and announced his retirement from business and public service. Since 1925, he had owned several hundred acres of land in Florida. He moved to Miami and in 1929 started opening small stores. By 1933 he had become vice-president of Florida 5 & 10 Stores Inc., and by 1936 he was president. In 1954 the company had seven department stores in Miami, and Basalyga was worth over a million dollars. He was married to Mary (née Warasicka, 1877–1967) and they had eleven children, one of whom continued to operate his store in Jessup. Two sons worked at Florida 5 and 10 Stores Inc. Basalyga died on May 9, 1960, in Miami and was buried in the Holy Ghost Greek Catholic Cemetery, Jessup, Pa.

**New National Banks.**
Washington—Certificates have been issued authorizing the following national banks to begin business:
The First National Bank of Lordsburg, Cal., capital $25,000. Henry L. Kune, president; Lewis L. Lostutter, vice-president; W. D. Frederick, cashier.
The First National Bank of Jessup, Pa., capital $50,000. P. F. Cusick, president; M. J. Barrett, Peter Basalyga, and Fortunato Tiscar, vice-presidents; Chas. M. Carr, cashier.

15. First National Bank, 1909

Resources Over a Million Dollars.

Member of Federal Reserve System.

Under the Supervision of the U. S. Government.

# The First National Bank

### Jessup, Pa.

Capital, $50,000.00    Surplus, $30,000.00

M. J. BARRETT, President.
PETER BASALYGA, Vice President.
EDW. H. FORD, Vice President.
P. J. O'MALLEY, Cashier.

16. First National Bank, 1923

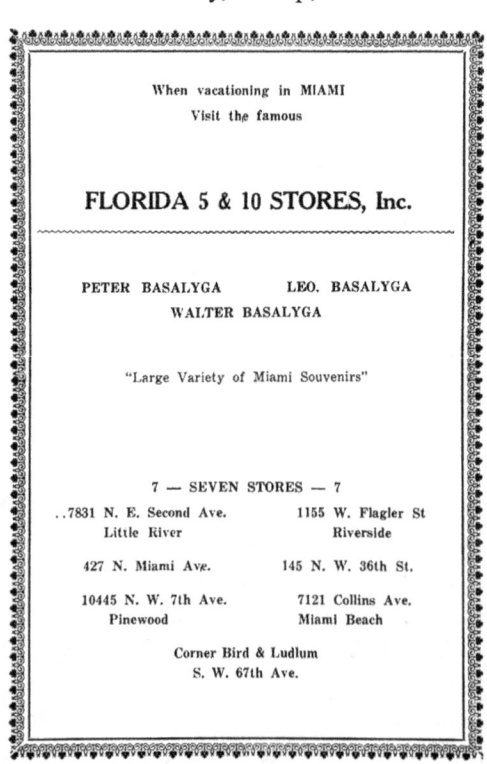

17. Peter Basalyga, 1954

```
КЛИФТОН, Н. ДЖ Phone: PAs. 2-4990

БУЧЕРНЯ И ГРОСЕРНЯ
Симеона Басалыги
В КЛИФТОНІ

На корнері Центер стриты,
Красный Штор, ест што видіти!
Свіжий товар першой кляссы
Куркы, гуси и колбасы.

74 CENTER ST. — CLIFTON, N. J.
```

18. Simeon Basalyga, 1936

```
TEL. PAssaic 2—4990

БУЧЕРНЯ И ГРОСЕРНЯ
СИМЕОНА БАСАЛЫГЫ

На корнері Центер стриты,
Красный штор, ест што видіти!
Свіжий товар першой кляссы
Гросерня и колбасы.

GROCERY & MEAT MARKET
74 CENTER ST.,        CLIFTON, N. J.
```

19. Simeon Basalyga, 1942

**Simeon Basalyga** was born on May 10, 1893, in the Lemko village of Stawisza, Grybów County, Austro-Hungarian Empire [present-day Poland] and immigrated in 1914. He settled in Clifton, N.J., where by 1925 he had a grocery/butcher store. It was first located at 85 Centre St., later at 74 Centre St., and finally at 76 Centre St. He was still in business in 1960. He was married to Pearl/Paraska (née Chomiak, 1897-1954) with whom he had: Olga Yaskowsky, Peter, and John. Basalyga died on May 24, 1967, and was buried in East Ridgelawn Cemetery, Clifton, N.J.

---

**Daniel Bavolack** was born on December 31, 1859, in the Lemko village of Świerżowa Ruska, Jasło County, Austrian Empire [present-day Poland] into the family of Vasyl' and Anna (née Daniliak). He served in the Austro-Hungarian Army (1883–1886), immigrated in 1887, and settled in McAdoo, Pa. Until 1890 he worked for the Lehigh and Wilkes-Barre Coal Company and later followed in the footsteps of his cousin Andrew Skweir. Bavolack first had a horse-drawn wagon taxi which he used to transport newcomers from Hazleton Junction, Pa., to where they were going to settle, also selling them beds, what they needed to set up a kitchen, etc. By 1900, he built a house – a combination of living quarters and business spaces for a general store, which he operated until his death. Bavolack, who was described as "one of the town's most prominent citizens and businessmen" was a charter

```
Даниїл Баволяк

Найбільша і най-
старша руська
гросерня, і добір-
ний стор (у влас-
нім домі). Про-
дає полотно, со-
рочки, чоботи і
всьо потрібне до
убраня, обутя і
їди. А навіть
сьвіже пиво, старе вино і паху-
чі цигара можна у нього дістати.

Чи може бути де ліпше, як
у Д. Баволяка?

Cor. Tomaqua & Sharmon Sts.,
McADOO, PA.
```

20. Daniel Bavolack, 1912

member of the American Legion (1919) and a charter member of the McAdoo Fire Company (1921), of which he was the first-elected chairman (1925) and later a trustee. He also served on the McAdoo School Board as treasurer. Bavolack was also the founding president of the Miners' Bank of McAdoo, which was organized in 1927 and did business in the Bruno Building on the corner of Blaine and Tamaqua Streets. He was married to

21. Bavolack living quarters and general store

Anastasia (née Cirkot, 1867–1957) with whom he had: Julia, Daniel Jr., Dmitro, Adam, and Vasil. Bavolack died on September 23, 1927, and was buried in St. Mary's Ukrainian Catholic Cemetery, McAdoo, Pa.

**PRESIDENT**

DANIEL BAVOLACK, SR.

## Businessman Is Head Of New Bank

Daniel Bavolack, Sr., president of the Miners' Bank of McAdoo, is one of the town's most prominent citizens and businessmen.

Born in Austria Galacia, in the year 1859, Mr. Bavolack prepared himself with a rudimentary education in his native land and at the age of 24 years he enlisted in the Austrian Army, serving his native land from 1882 to 1886. Imbued with the spirit of progress, he emigrated to America and settled in Kline township, the section which is today McAdoo borough. This was in the year 1887 and since that time until the present he has been one of this community's residents.

Mr. Bavolack's first position here was with the Lehigh and Wilkes-Barre Coal Company, with whom he remained until 1890, when he embarked in business on a small scale in McAdoo. His thorough business methods and his standing in his home town soon gained for him a wide clientele and with the passing of the years he expanded his business to such an extent that today he is one of the South Side's most successful and best known merchants.

22. Daniel Bavolack, 1926

23. Anastasia and Daniel Bavolack, 1942

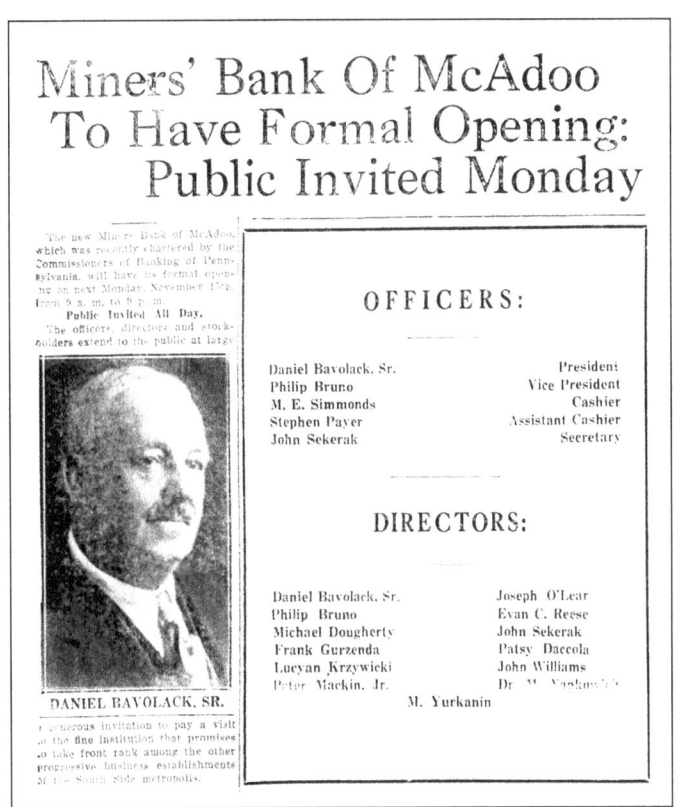

24. Daniel Bavolack, 1926

**Theodore Bihuniak** was born on June 4, 1889, in the Lemko village of Nowica, Gorlice County, Austro-Hungarian Empire [present-day Poland] into the family of Vasyl'and Fatima (née Oseniak). He immigrated in 1907 and by 1917 operated a grocery/butcher shop in Brooklyn, N.Y., at 147 North 6th St. He was still in business in 1930 but by the late 1930s became an employee in the wool/textile industry. He was married to Tessie (née Parahus, 1895–1952). They had a daughter, Justina Chandler. Bihuniak died on June 21, 1958, and was buried in S.S. Peter and Paul Orthodox Cemetery, Saddle Brook, N.J.

25. Theodore Bihuniak, 1930

---

**William "Wasil" Bincarowsky** was born on October 15, 1879, in the Lemko village of Polany, Grybów County, Austro-Hungarian Empire [present-day Poland] and immigrated in 1898. He settled in Yonkers, N.Y., where by 1909 he had a butcher shop/grocery in partnership with a fellow Lemko, Oscar Ciuryk. In 1911 he left this business to establish his saloon at 1 Mulberry St., which lasted at least until 1914. In 1917 he was listed as a motorman. By 1920 he moved his family to Mauch Chunk, Pa., where he was listed as a miner. In 1930 he was listed as a butcher and in 1940 as a machinist working in a coal mine. He was married to Suzanna (née Sheer, 1880–1957) with whom he had: Peter, John, Joseph, William, Helen, and Andrew Benson. Bincarowsky died on August 4, 1954, and was buried in St. John's Russian Orthodox Cemetery, Nesquehoning, Pa.

26. William Bincarowsky, 1910

**Alexander Bischak** was born in 1894 in the Lemko village of Banica, Grybów County, Austro-Hungarian Empire [present-day Poland] and immigrated in 1912. By 1927 he had a grocery/butcher store at 40 Van Winkler Ave., Garfield, N.J. By 1935 he was listed as an owner of a liquor store. He was still in business in 1940. He was married to Olga (née Osterjohn? 1901–1958) with whom he had: Theodore, Alexander, William, Robert, Joyce Formas, Julius, and Richard. Bischak died on December 20, 1949, and was buried in Cedar Lawn Cemetery, Paterson, N.J.

```
ПЕРВОРЯДНА БУЧЕРНЯ И ГРОССЕРНЯ
         АЛЕКСАНДРА БИЩАКА
           Александра Бищака
           Краяна изъ Баницы
           Знаютъ русски люде
           Въ Пассайкѣ — околицѣ
           Знаютъ го зъ доброй страны
           Якъ бучера доброго,
           знаютъ го, якъ каждого
           Бизнессмена честного...
      MEAT MARKET AND GROCERY
  40 Van Winkle Ave.      Garfield, N. J.
```
27. Alexander Bischak, 1930

**John Bochnewich** was born on January 2, 1894, in the Lemko village Leszczyny, Gorlice County, Austro-Hungarian Empire [present-day Poland] into the family of Fotii and Mary (née Wojtowicz). He immigrated in 1909 and settled in Yonkers, N.Y., where he first worked at the Alexander Smith and Sons Carpet Company. By 1921 he had a grocery/butcher store at 46 Washington St., which in the mid-1920s moved to 53 Clinton St. He was still in business in 1942. He was married to Eva (née Paranich, 1895–1958) with whom he had John, Michael, Paul, Kirill, Olga Pagkos, Therese, and Vera Colgan. Bochnewich died in October of 1972, and was buried in St. Joseph Cemetery, Yonkers, N.Y.

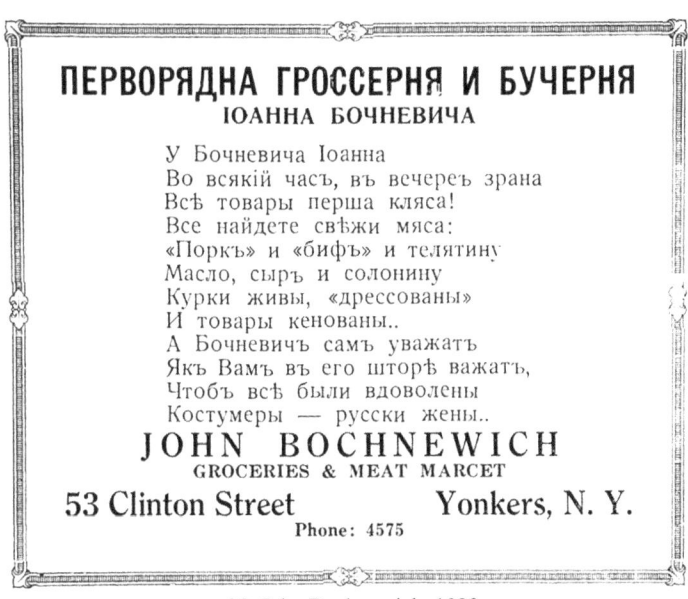

28. John Bochnewich, 1929

**Peter Bohaczyk** was born on May 4, 1884 in the Lemko village of Wawrzka, Grybów County, Austro-Hungarian Empire [present-day Poland] into the family of Daniel and Mary (née Worobel). He immigrated in 1902. He lived on a farm in Elysburg, Pa. for five years. By 1917 he had a grocery store at 311 E. Center St. in Mt. Carmel, Pa., where he lived for seven years. By 1930 he had moved to Kulpmont, Pa., where he lived for 22 years and was described as "one of the community's most successful businessmen." He had a store in Kulpmont, first at 1225 Scott St., and as of 1931 at 1201 Scott St. By 1939, his store was located at 1023 Chestnut St. He also had a farm. He retired by 1955 and moved to Daytona Beach, Fl. He was married to Anna (née Pecushak, 1894–1976) with whom he had: Andrew, Tillie Pelak, Mary Maurer, Anna Pursel, Stella Melia, Delores Stewart, Melanie Way, Olga Wolf, and Peter. Bohaczyk died on August 24, 1972, and was buried in Saint Michael's Orthodox Cemetery, Mt. Carmel, Pa.

29. Peter Bohaczyk

30. Peter and Anna Bohaczyk

**John Boroshovich** was born on June 17, 1874, in the Lemko village of Bartne, Gorlice County, Austro-Hungarian Empire [present-day Poland] into the family of Leshko and Maryia (née Smarz). He immigrated in 1897 and spent two years in Olyphant, Pa. He later moved to Ansonia, Conn., where by 1904 he had a grocery store with Frank Cirkoth at 24 Jersey St. Since 1905 he was listed as a saloon keeper at 20 Jersey St., later at 86 Jersey St., and later at 2 Railroad Ave. In 1910 he was listed as the owner of a grocery store in Philadelphia, Pa. He was married to Paiza/Pelagia (née Gbur, 1881–19??) with whom he had at least four children: Nicholas, Mary, Pauline, and Walter. He was active in the Ukrainian community, serving as the national treasurer of the Providence Association of Ukrainian Catholics in America, as well as managing for many years the Ukrainian Home in

**Іван Борошевич**

Ансонійці памятайте, Борошевича не минайте; в нього добре пиво, віска, а до того ще й закуска. Сальон його коло дипа. 2 Rail Road Ave., Ansonia, Conn.

31. John Boroshovich, 1909

Philadelphia, Pa. Boroshovich died on November 11, 1944 and was buried in St. Mary's Ukrainian Cemetery, Fox Chase, Pa.

32. John Boroshovich, 1907

**Damian "Demko" Broda** was born on November 2, 1861, in the Lemko village of Stawisza, Grybów County, Austrian Empire [present-day Poland] and immigrated in 1880. He went to work in Franklin, N.J., and later at a nearby farm, where he learned English. He eventually settled in Newtown, N.J., where by 1900 he worked as a carpet cleaner and by 1910 had bought that business. In 1910, he was listed as a carpet mender working on his own account. When cars became popular he opened a garage, becoming the first automobile mechanic in the county of Sussex. In 1920 he was listed as a machinist working for himself and employing others. Broda was credited with staying ahead of the demand by modernizing and completely re-outfitting his repair shop at 62 Water St. He had retired by 1930. In his native village, he built a sawmill after bringing the machinery from the United States. He was married to Sarah

33. The Brodas, 1928

Ann (née Howell, 1872–1940) with whom he had: Mabel Coriell and Frances Goldsmith. Broda died on March 13, 1943, and was buried in Newtown Cemetery, Newtown, N.J.

Damian Broda sits proudly behind the wheel of an open Ford touring car while his assistant looks on in this photograph taken about 1907. As the owner of the first automotive repair shop in Sussex county, Broda had the opportunity to work on a wide variety of horseless carriages. If you look on the back wall of the garage, you can see that the tradition of decorating workshops with pin-up girls has been around for many years. The car in the background is standing where the central bar of the County Seat Restaurant stands today.

Photo and caption: Kate Gordon and Wayne T. McCabe, *Newton*, Charleston SC: Arcadia, c1998

**Andrew Bybel** was born on December 6, 1878, in the Lemko village of Banica, Gorlice County, Austro-Hungarian Empire [present-day Poland] into the family of Petro and Anna (née Szkymba). He immigrated in 1901 and first lived in Lansford, Pa., where he worked as a miner. By 1910 he had moved to Coaldale, Pa., where until 1919 he was listed as a miner but due to sickness left that profession. In January 1920 he was listed as a butcher working on his own account (meat market). In May 1920 he was back working as a miner. He was married to Mary Florence (née Matika, 1884–1963) with whom he had: Peter, Anna, John, Stephen, Andrew, Harry, William, Paul, and Eva. Bybel was killed in a mining accident May 4, 1923, and was buried in St. Mary's Russian Orthodox Cemetery, Summit Hill, Pa.

35. Andrew Bybel with family, 1913

36. Frank Bybel

**Theodore / Frank D. Bybel** was born in 1875 in the Lemko village of Krzywa, Gorlice County, Austro-Hungarian Empire [present-day Poland] into the family of Ivan and Eva (née Kycej). He immigrated in 1887/1889 and settled in Yonkers, N.Y., where he operated a grocery/butcher shop at 20 Croton Terrace for 25 years, until 1933. He was among the organizers of the Holy Trinity Russian Orthodox Church in Yonkers. He was married to Anna (née Pac, 1874–1961) with whom he had: Julia Golowitz, Mary Sura, Alexander, William, Olga Perog, and Elizabeth Meschan. Bybel died on March 11, 1941, and was buried in the Oakland Cemetery, Yonkers, N.Y.

ПЕРВОРЯДНАЯ ГРОСЕРНЯ-БУЧЕРНЯ

**ѲЕОДОРА Д. БЫБЕЛЯ**

20 CROTON TERRACE,             YONKERS, N. Y.

Маю на складѣ найлучшіи, завсе свѣжіи,
съѣстныи товары.

ПОПРОБУЙТЕ РАЗЪ — ДО ДРУГОГО НЕ ПОЙДЕТЕ.

37. Theodore Bybel, 1911

**Kalistrat Cidylo** was born on December 3, 1888, in the Lemko village of Czyrna, Grybów County, Austro-Hungarian Empire [present-day Poland] and immigrated in 1910. He settled in Brooklyn, N.Y., where in 1924 he was listed as a laborer. By 1930, he had a grocery store at 154 Bedford Ave. In 1940 he was listed as an iron chipper and in 1942 as unemployed. He was married to Paraska (née Zabowska, 1895–1989) with whom he had: John, Nicholas, Olga, and Peter. Cidylo died in 1960 and was buried in Mt. Olivet Cemetery, Maspeth, N.Y.

38. Kalistrat Cidylo, 1931

**John P. Chowanes** was born in 1878 in the Lemko village of Tylicz, Nowy Sącz County, Austro-Hungarian Empire [present-day Poland] and immigrated in 1894. He settled in Shenandoah, Pa., where in 1900 he opened a saloon at 400 W. Center St. and, a year later, an undertaking business at 13 W. Center St. In 1901 he acquired a retail license from John Powloskie. In 1906 he advertised his saloon for sale and in 1907 purchased a property on W. Center Street, where he opened a salon (515 W. Center St.) and a grocery store (513 W. Center St.). In 1913 during a fire at his warehouse at the corner of Lloyd and Catherine Streets he suffered losses estimated at $1,500. In 1914 he transferred his retail liquor license to Stanley Lukasik and started a process to acquire a tavern license from William L. Sweeney. In 1915 he purchased the Sweeney Hotel on Reach Street in Lansford, Pa., where he also continued his undertaking business and moved his family. By 1926 he was back in Shenandoah, where he continued to work as a funeral home director at 515 W. Centre St. until his death. In 1943 he was described as a "prominently known Shenandoah undertaker" and at the time of his death as "one of the oldest practicing undertakers in Pennsylvania." Since 1928 he was also one of the directors of the Citizens National Bank of Shenandoah (est. 1908). The bank reached its financial peak in 1930 with

**Chowanes New Place.**
John Chowanes, the enterprising West Centre street business man removed today from the Gilbert street corner to his handsome new store at No. 513 the same street, formerly the Devitt property, which he recently purchased. Mr. Chowanes will sell groceries and continue to conduct his undertaking and livery business. 1t

39. John Chowanes, 1907

$2.8 million in resources. Chowanes held this position until the bank failed in 1934, despite attempts by him and others to reorganize it. He was married to Eva (née Haluschak, 1883–1935) with whom he had: Peter, Mary Harrington, Jean, Anna Vassalo, Nancy, George, Michael, and Helen Kufrovich. Chowanes died on September 7, 1952, in New York City and was buried in St. Michael's Greek Catholic Church Cemetery, Shenandoah, Pa.

**THE CITIZENS NATIONAL BANK (Shenandoah, Pa.):** Chartered under National Bank Act in 1908. Conducts a general banking business. Memberships: Federal Reserve System, American Bankers Assn. and Pennsylvania Bankers Assn. State depository. Number of employees, Dec. 31, 1930, 7.

OFFICERS: S. A. Ramonat, Pres.; E. D. Longacre, 1st Vice-Pres.; Z. F. Rynkiewicz, 2nd Vice-Pres.; G. H. Krick, Cashier, Chenandoah, Pa.

DIRECTORS: Frank Bradley, J. W. Curtin, John Chowanes, G. H. Krick, E. D. Longacre, J. W. Miernicki, Michael Pribula, Z. F. Rynkiewicz, Frank Szalek, P. J. Maher, S. A. Ramonat, E. R. Williams, Michael Wolsky, W. A. Schmidt, Shenandoah, Pa.; W. W. Rynkiewicz, Tamaqua, Pa.

ANNUAL MEETING: Second Tuesday in Jan.

OFFICE: 10-12 South Main Street, Shenandoah, Pa.

COMPARATIVE INCOME ACCOUNT, YEARS ENDED DEC. 31

|  | 1930 | 1929 | 1928 |
|---|---|---|---|
| Gross earnings | $144,325 | $153,806 | $148,932 |
| Expenses, etc. | 105,989 | 107,529 | 99,389 |
| Net profits | 38,336 | 46,277 | 49,543 |
| Dividends | 24,000 | 24,000 | 24,000 |
| Surplus for year | *$14,336 | $22,277 | $29,543 |
| Earned per share | $38.34 | $46.28 | $49.54 |
| Shares outstanding Dec. 31 | 1,000 | 1,000 | 1,000 |
| Dividends to profits | 62.60% | 51.86% | 40.37% |

* Before surplus adjustments.

TREND OF DEPOSITS, AS OF DEC. 31

|  | 1930 | 1927 | 1920 | 1915 |
|---|---|---|---|---|
| Commercial | $256,694 | $302,707 | $328,914 | $178,062 |
| Savings | 1,809,252 | 1,645,998 | 1,080,192 | 479,783 |
| Other | None | 75,000 | None | None |

STATEMENT OF CONDITION, AS OF DEC. 31

| RESOURCES: | 1930 | 1929 |
|---|---|---|
| Loans and discounts | $1,548,290 | $1,677,406 |
| Overdrafts | 1,578 | 1,089 |
| U. S. Government securities | 156,400 | 156,400 |
| Other securities | 714,476 | 717,192 |
| Banking house, etc. | 43,750 | 42,000 |
| Other real estate | 56,709 | 48,159 |
| Cash and reserve | 190,556 | 143,415 |
| Checks and cash items | 4,557 | 9,174 |
| Redemption fund | 5,000 | 5,000 |
| **Total** | **$2,721,316** | **$2,799,835** |
| LIABILITIES: | 1930 | 1929 |
| Capital stock | $100,000 | $100,000 |
| Surplus | 300,000 | 300,000 |
| Undivided profits | 119,791 | 122,072 |
| Reserves | 9,000 | 9,000 |
| Circulation | 100,000 | 100,000 |
| Checks, cashier's etc. | 685 | 3,232 |
| Demand deposits | 257,588 | 336,657 |
| Time deposits | 1,809,252 | 1,736,809 |
| Bills payable, etc. | 25,000 | 92,065 |
| **Total** | **$2,721,316** | **$2,799,835** |
| Book value per share | $519.79 | $522.07 |

40. John Chowanes, 1932

> **Notice.**
> The petition for the transfer of the Tavern License now held by William A. Sweeney, Middle ward, Lansford to John Chowanes has been filed in my office and will be presented to the Court of Quarter Sessions in ten days from this date.
> John J. McGinley, Clerk
> Mauch Chunk, Pa., August 14, 1914

41. John Chowanes, 1914

> **Conducted Funeral Here.**
> John Chowanes, who recently removed to Lansford, where he conducts a hotel and undertaking establishment, was in town today conducting a funeral. He is delighted with his new location and is getting along nicely. He invites his friends to pay him a visit.

42. John Chowanes, 1914

**Alex C. Chylack** was born in 1870 in the Lemko village of Kamianna, Grybów County, Austro-Hungarian Empire [present-day Poland] to Peter and Tekla (née Polefka] and immigrated in 1889. At first he resided in Blackwood, Pa., and later in Lansford and Nesquehoning until 1892, when he went to St. Clair, Pa. He worked in the mines for a few years at Pine Forest P. and R. C. and I. Colliery. In 1900 he was listed as a clerk in a grocery store. Engaging in merchandising, he later operated food markets for a number of years then became the foreign-language salesman for Boone's General Store. By 1910 he was working as a carpenter and as a self-employed builder erected rental homes. By 1946 he had seven in the vicinity of his Park Hotel at the corner of Nichols and Franklin Streets. Chylack retired by 1948 and later his hotel was operated by his son-in-law, Walter Drosdak. Chylack was among the founders of St. Mary's Russian Orthodox parish in St. Clair and the builder of its church. Chylack was married to Anastasia (née Polansky). Together they bore: Theodore and Mary Drosdak. He was later married to Akelena (1878–1938) with whom he had Andrew. Chylack died on August 20, 1951, and was buried in St. Mary's Russian Orthodox Cemetery, Arnots Addition (St. Clair), Pa. His Park Hotel Restaurant was later managed by his daughter.

**John Chylack** was born on February 8, 1875, in the Lemko village of Kamianna, Grybów County, Austro-Hungarian Empire [present-day Poland] to Peter and Tekla (née Polefka] and immigrated in 1895. By 1910, he operated a hotel in St. Clair, Pa. at 909 Wadesville Rd. He was still in business in 1930. He was married to Anna (née Bice/Bajas, 1875-1964) with whom he had: Natalie Gogotz, Michael, Peter, Julia Garland, Harry, Nestor, and Jerome. Chylak died on June 22, 1949 and was buried in Charles Baber Cemetery, Pottsville, Pa. He was remembered as a "well-known retired businessman."

**Theodore P. Chylack** was born in 1865 in the Lemko village of Kamianna, Grybów County, Austrian Empire [present-day Poland] to Peter and Tekla (née Polefka] and immigrated in 1884. He first settled in Shamokin, Pa. and moved to St. Clair, Pa. in 1891. He had a saloon/hotel there by 1899. In 1901, it was located on 3rd Street at the corner of Hancock. He retired in 1932. He was among the founders of St. Nicholas Greek Catholic Church in St. Clair, Pa. and served several terms as a member of the school board in that borough. He was married to Anna (née Warcholak, 1872-1936) with whom he had: Mary, Helen, Anna Hoover, Rosalie, Geraldine, and Leo. Chylak died on November 12, 1947, and was buried in Charles Baber Cemetery, Pottsville, Pa.

**Theodore P. Chylack** was born in 1865 in the Lemko village of Kamianna, Grybów County, Austrian Empire [present-day Poland] to Peter and Tekla (née Polefka] and immigrated in 1884. He first settled in Shamokin, Pa. and moved to St. Clair, Pa. in 1891. He had a saloon/hotel there by 1899. In 1901, it was located on 3rd Street at the corner of Hancock. He retired in 1932. He was among the founders of St. Nicholas Greek Catholic Church in St. Clair, Pa. and served several terms as a member of the school board in that borough. He was married to Anna (née Warcholak, 1872-1936) with whom he had: Mary, Helen, Anna Hoover, Rosalie, Geraldine, and Leo. Chylak died on November 12, 1947, and was buried in Charles Baber Cemetery, Pottsville, Pa.

---

**George Chylak** was born on May 20, 1866, in the Lemko village of Binczarowa, Grybów County, Austrian Empire [present-day Poland] into the family of Kundrad and Annie. He immigrated in 1884, stopping first at Shamokin, Pa., and then proceeding to Olyphant, Pa., and was employed at mine labor in both places. He later became an outside driver, afterward obtaining a position in a store as a clerk. By 1894 he opened a general store himself at 111-113 Grant St.; by 1901 he had opened a hotel and by 1906 he was selling ship tickets, sending money to the homeland, and arranging the purchase of land and farms. He became a notary public in 1907. Chylak was also one of the directors of the Bank of Olyphant, which was established in 1909 with capital of $100,000. At the end of

43. George Chylak, 1894

44. George Chylak, 1897

1913 its resources were $706,508 and during his last year (1928) grew to $3,474,800. By 1924, and until 1931, he was one of the directors and the secretary of the Miner's Savings Bank, which in 1930 had undivided profits of $160,000. In 1920 he was elected president of the St. John the Baptist Beneficial Society in Olyphant, Pa., which belonged to the Ukrainian National Association. He was also the president of

### ЮРІЙ ХИЛЯКЪ,

Агентъ Р. Народного Дому въ Олифантъ, Па. и на околицяхъ.

#### Банковый Бизнесъ.

Тутъ можете послати свои гроші безпечно а оплата дуже тана.

Також продаю шифкарты на всѣ лініи за ту саму цѣну, що и головня компаніи.

Хто хоче дати відложити гроші, чи лите на часъ або на процентъ, або въ старомъ краю въ Банку на процентъ, або хоче позичити грошей на добру заруку, най удасть ся до мене.

#### Офіеъ Адвокатекій.

Хто бы хотѣвъ продати або купити собѣ фармы тутъ, або домъ въ старомъ краю продати або купити ґрунтъ, увольнити си водъ контроле войскового, водъ екавцирки або асентерунку, най прийде до мого офису або менѣ напише.

Гроші посылайте на money order або Bank Draft на адресу:

GEO. CHYLAK
BOX 368, OLYPHANT, PA.

Въ ГОТЕЛЮ ХИЛЯКА найдете всегда свѣже, зимне пиво, імпортовані вина и цигара першои класы.

---

Гей Русины! чи знаете вы дорогу до дешевого и доброго купна? Она веде просто до

### Юрія Хиляка

ВЪ OLYPHANT, PA.

Вы его певно добре знаете. Въ него знайдете одинокій, найдешевшій, найлучшій и наймоднѣйшій сторъ въ убраннями. Купите добре "шифкарту" и скоро а безпечно пôйде вамъ гроші до старого краю. Не гадайте однакъ, що то вже все — нѣ! Вôнъ мае ще найпараднѣйшій салунъ въ мѣстѣ пôдъ назвою:

### Anthracite Hotel.

Тамъ доперва погостите ся, якъ въ рôднои бабки на веселю.

45. George Chylak, 1901

47. George Chylak, 1906

---

## GEORGE CHYLAK, GENERAL STORE,

BOOTS, SHOES, HATS, CAPS, DRY GOODS, GROCERIES AND FRESH MEATS AND POULTRY.

P. O. Box 368.

### STEAMSHIP AGENCY AND MONEY EXCHANGED

Along with conducting a general store where the prices are always right, George Chylak also conducts a steamship agency and a money exchange. Fresh meats and poultry, boots, shoes, caps, dry goods and groceries comprise his main stock.

* * *

46. George Chylak, 1911

---

### ДОБРА РАДА

КТО ХОЧЕ ПОѢХАТИ ДО СТАРОГО КРАЮ, ИЛИ ПОСЫЛАТИ ГРОШИ ДО РОДИНЫ ИЛИ СПРОВАДИТИ СЪ КРАЮ КОГОСЬ ДО АМЕРИКИ

Нехай прійде до офису или напише по інформаціи до:

## ЮРІЯ ХИЛЯКА

30 ЛѢТЪ ЯКЪ ПОСЫЛАЕМЪ ГРОШИ ДО КРАЮ, ПРОДАЕМЪ ШИФКАРТЫ ТА ПОЛАГОЖУЕМЪ ВСЯКИ НОТАРІЯЛЬНЫ СПРАВЫ ЧЕСТНО И СПРАВЕДЛИВО ПО ХРИСТІЯНСКИ.

Если хочете добру пораду, быти честно и совѣстно обслужены удавайтеся или пишите на адресу:

### GEORGE CHYLAK
NOTARY PUBLIC,
FOREIGN EXCHANGE BANK
111—113 GRANT STREET, —:— OLYPHANT, PA.

48. George Chylak, 1920

49. George Chylak, 1923

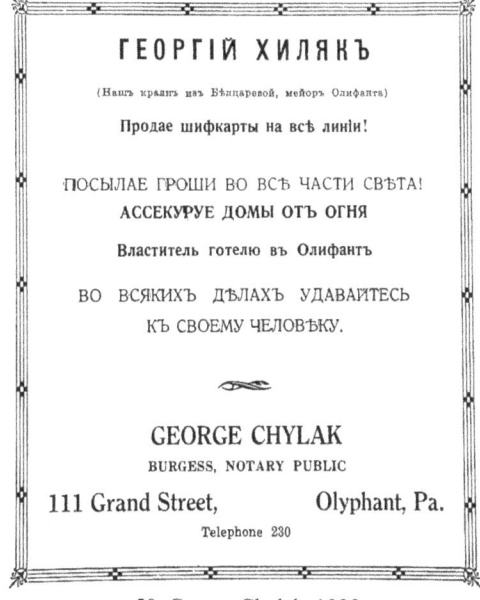

50. George Chylak, 1929

a fraternal order, Concord of Olyphant Societies (est. 1914), which in 1930 had total resources of some $75,000. He was, at one time, treasurer of the Borough of Olyphant, also the mayor (1905, 1925–1930) and as of 1904, he was a member and later the president of the local School Board of Directors. Chylak served as a treasurer (1895–1898) and the president (1898–1900) of the Russian/Little Russian National Union (later Ukrainian National Association). He was married to Julia (née Czar, 1875–1930), with whom he had nine children, of whom only four were alive at the time of his death: Mary, George Jr., Tillie and Nestor. Chylak died on January 23, 1953.

---

**Hnat Cikot** was born in 1872 in the Lemko village of Ropki, Gorlice County, Austro-Hungarian Empire [present-day Poland] into the family of Iakov and Matrona. He immigrated in 1884. By 1905 he had a saloon at 601 W. Centre St., Shenandoah, Pa., and was still in business in 1913. Later on in his life he was listed as a laborer. He was first married to Helen (1874–1916), with whom he had: Simon, John, Steve, Mary, Julia, and Annie. He was later married to Anastasia (née Pirog/Wandzilak, 1875–1949). Cikot died on January 15, 1929, and was buried in St. Michael's Greek Catholic Church Cemetery, Shenandoah Heights, Pa.

---

**Peter Cirko** was born on August 20, 1894, in the Lemko village of Kamionka Rymanowska, Krosno County, Austro-Hungarian Empire [present-day Poland] into the family of Michael and Pearl (née Barna). He immigrated by 1917. He worked at Truesdale Coliery in Lower Askam, Pa., for 42 years, where he was also the proprietor of Blue Arrow Inn at 1 Martin St. He was the founder of the Russian Brotherhood Organization's Lodge 201 in Nanticoke, Pa. (1914). He was married to Anna (née Chomiak, 1901–1976) with whom he had: Peter Jr., Michael, and Mary Antonik. Cirko died on March 20, 1969, and was buried in Oak Lawn Cemetery, Hanover Township, Pa.

---

**Sidor Cirkot** was born on May 18, 1873, in the Lemko village of Bartne, Gorlice County, Austro-Hungarian Empire [present-day Poland] into the family of Osyf and Olena (née Hodio). He immigrated in 1893 and by 1913 had opened his grocery store in Derby, Conn., at 122 Olivia St. By 1917 he had moved his business to Ansonia, Conn., first to 123 N. State St. and by 1920 to 129 N. State St. In 1940 he was still listed as a merchant but retired soon after and moved to Stamford, Conn. He was married to Joanna (née

Stasienko, 1892–1979) with whom he had: Elena, Alex, Olga, and Ruth. Cirkot died on June 15, 1946.

---

**Theodore Cirkoth** (Cirkot) was born on February 22, 1875, in the Lemko village of Bartne, Gorlice County, Austro-Hungarian Empire [present-day Poland] into the family of Il'ko and Maryia (née Gbur). He immigrated in 1893 and settled in Ansonia, Conn., where he had a grocery and butcher store at 24 (later 58 and then 65 Jersey St.) from 1905 until his death. By 1911 he also had another grocery at 96 Howard Ave. He was a charter member of the Saints Peter and Paul Russian Benevolent Society (est. 1894) and the president of the local Greek Catholic parish. He was married to **Irene** (née Dokla, 1876?–1963) with whom he had eight children: Ella Madigosky, Marry Cushon, Anne C. Giffin, Stella, William, Louise D. Klein, Theodore, and John. Cirkoth died on February 11, 1917, and was buried in Saint Peter and Saint Paul Ukrainian Greek Catholic Cemetery, Ansonia, Conn. The businesses were continued by his wife until at least 1918.

**ТЕОДОР ЦІРКОТ**
Знаменито уладжена ґросерня і бучерня з найліпшими товарами. Ансонійці! Йдіть лиш до нього, бо він чесний і чесно Вас обслужить.
**65 Jersey St., ANSONIA, Conn.**

51. Theodore Cirkoth, 1909

52. Theodore Cirkoth and Irene Dokla, 1898

**Oscar Ciuryk** was born on June 26, 1872, in Smerekowiec, Gorlice County, Austro-Hungarian Empire [present-day Poland]. He had a grocery store at 20 Croton Terrace in Yonkers, N.Y., by 1907, which had evolved into a butcher shop/grocery in partnership with a fellow Lemko, William *Bincarowsky, by 1909. The latter, however, soon left and by 1911 Ciuryk was doing business by himself again, running a grocery at 31 Orchard Terrace in a building that he owned. By 1920 the business had again evolved into a butcher shop and by 1931 he was listed as a meat cutter at 18 Mulford St. Ciuryk served as a president and a trustee of the Holy Trinity Orthodox Church in Yonkers, N.Y., but was later affiliated with St. Mary's Orthodox Church. He was married to Anna (née Sarich, 1876–1969) with whom he had: Anthony, Larry, Alexander, Anna Medenek, Mildred Curth, Mary Woytowick, Elisabeth Ross, Olga Shost, Julia and Evelyn Stone. Ciuryk died on July 11, 1943, and was buried in the Oakland Cemetery, Yonkers, N.Y.

53. Oscar Ciuryk, 1909

---

**Joseph Comcowich** was born on May 4, 1894, in the Lemko village of Przegonina, Gorlice County, Austro-Hungarian Empire [present-day Poland] and immigrated in 1900. In 1915 he was listed as a butcher in Jersey City, N.J., and during the last year of the war was in the Army reserves. He was a clerk in 1919 but a year later was working as a manager of National Supply Co. (meat market) at 407 Main St. in Ansonia, Conn. By 1922 he had opened up his own meat market/grocery at 22 High St. in Ansonia. By 1927 he also had a confectionary and ice cream business at 180 Broad St., while from 1928–1931 his business at 22 High St. was listed as a cigar and tobacco store. In 1931 he purchased Warcholic Hall at 160 Broad St., where beginning in 1933 he had a restaurant. He served as supernumerary for the Ansonia Police Department. He was married to Mary (née Zanowiak, 1898–19??), with whom he had three children: Dorothy, Edward, and Lillian. Comchowich died on January 22, 1935. Warcholic Hall was destroyed in a fire in 1955 and the burned-out ruins were demolished after a flood that year, but it is not known whether the Comcowich family still owned the building at that time.

---

54. Paul Comcowich, 1909

**Paul Comcowich** was born in 1864 in the Lemko village of Przegonina, Gorlice County, Austrian Empire [present-day Poland] into the Chomkowicz family. He immigrated by 1893 and settled in Ansonia, Conn., where he worked at Cameron Electrical Manufacturing Co. By 1908 he had a dry goods store at 17 Star St. A year later, he advertised a saloon at the same location but he died later that year and was buried in the St. Peter and St. Paul Ukrainian Greek Catholic Cemetery, Derby, Conn. He was married to **Tekla** (née Tezbir) who was born in 1868 in the Lemko village of Regietów, Gorlice County, Austro-Hungarian Empire [present-day Poland]. She immigrated in 1889 and they had seven children: John, Harry, Thomas, Helen, William, Michael, and Theodore. After Paul's death, Tekla revived their business and by 1912 was running a confectionary store at 21 Star St. By 1918 she was listed as the owner of a dry goods store at 19 Star St., which she ran until at least 1932. Tekla died in 1940 and was buried next to her husband.

---

**Steve Corba** was born on August 10, 1882, in the Lemko village of Leszczyny, Gorlice County, Austro-Hungarian Empire [present-day Poland] and immigrated in 1901. He settled in Carnegie, Pa., where by 1910 he had a grocery store, which in 1919 was located at 221 Jane St. He was still in business in 1940. He was first married to Annie (née Fechosko, 1888–1915), with whom he had: Joseph and Steve. He was later married to Mary (née Bock, 1899–1992), with whom he had: Helen, Vladimir, Nick, Peter, and Harvey. Corba died on August 30, 1952, and was buried in Saints Peter & Paul Ukrainian Orthodox Cemetery, Carnegie / Scott Township, Pa.

---

**Andrew Dragan** was born on December 25, 1874, in the Lemko village of Kłopotnica, Jasło County, Austro-Hungarian Empire [present-day Poland] into the family of Mykhal and Eva (née Luciszyn). He immigrated in 1893 and settled in Yonkers, N.Y. By 1898 he had a saloon at 328 Nepperhan Ave. with a fellow Lemko, Damian *Merena. In 1900 he worked as a hat finisher. In 1901 he was one of the founding directors of the Little Russian Cooperative Association. In 1905 he was listed as a butcher and in 1910 was listed as having his own meat store. By 1914 he had moved to Bridgeport, Conn., where he first partnered with Samuel *Telep to operate a grocery at 705 Hallett St. By 1916 he ran a grocery/meat market with Awksenty *Telep first at 706 Hallett St. and during 1917–1918 at 681 Hallett St. He was married to Fannie/Euphemia (née Koltko, 1875–1955) with whom he had: Elsie, Olga, Mary, Eva, Anna, Stefania, Stella, John, and Vladimir. Dragan died on December 12, 1918, and was buried in St. John the Baptist Greek Catholic Cemetery, Stratford, Conn.

---

**Metro Drosdak** was born on September 29, 1870, in the Lemko village of Bogusza, Grybów County, Austro-Hungarian Empire [present-day Poland] into the family of Isaack and Marianna Drozdiak. He immigrated in 1889 and settled in Mauch Chunk, Pa. [aka Hauto] where, at least until 1910, he worked as a coal breaker. In 1915 he was listed as

ДМИТРІЙ ДРОЗДЯКЪ,
РУССКІЙ ЛЕМКО, ВЪ
**HAUTO, PA.**
Мае добру гросерню.
Свой до свого, — братья Лемки.
ВЪ СОЛИДАРНОСТИ НАША СИЛА!

55. Metro Drozdak

the owner of a cigar store. By 1920 he had opened a grocery store. In 1930 he was reported as a salesman operating his store and in 1940, at the age of 70, he was listed as a wage or salary worker in private work and his occupation was a molder. He was married to Mary (née Warcholak, 1883–1937) with whom he had: Simon, Anna Rusyn, Walter, Helen Diehl, Leo, John, Metro, Alex, Michael, Mary, George, and Joseph. Drozdak died on May 19, 1942, and was buried in St. Mary's Russian Orthodox Cemetery, Summit Hill, Pa.

---

**John Dudra** was born on April 12, 1879, in the Lemko village of Łosie, Gorlice County, Austro-Hungarian Empire [present-day Poland] into the family of Andryi and Anastazyia (née Szlanta). He immigrated in 1905 and settled in Charleroi, Pa. By 1918 he was oper-

40.—Application for Passport.—Naturalized Citizen.  
[Edition of July, 1888.]  
John Polhemus Printing Company, Printers and Mf'g Stationers, 102 Fulton St., New York.

No. _____    Issued _____

# United States of America.

State of _New York_  
County of _Westchester_ } ss:

I, _Andro Dragan_, a NATURALIZED AND LOYAL CITIZEN OF THE UNITED STATES, do hereby apply to the Department of State at Washington for a passport for myself ~~and wife, and my minor children as follows:~~

born at _____ on the _____ day of _____, and _____

In support of the above application, I do solemnly swear that I was born at _Klopotnicza, Austria, Galicia in Europe_ on or about the _25th_ day of _December_ 1874; that I emigrated to the United States, sailing on board the _Bremen Line_ from _Bremen_, on or about the _13th_ day of _July_ (ship not known), 1893; that I resided _16_ years, uninterruptedly, in the United States, from _July 1893_ to _1909_ at _Yonkers, N.Y._; that I was naturalized as a citizen of the United States before the _County_ Court of _Westchester County_ at _Village of White Plains_ the _22_ day of _June_ 1900, as shown by the accompanying Certificate of Naturalization; that I am the IDENTICAL PERSON described in said Certificate; that I am domiciled in the United States, my permanent residence being at _Yonkers_, in the State of _New York_, where I follow the occupation of _Butcher & Grocer_; that I am about to go abroad temporarily; and that I intend to return to the United States _in December 1909_, with the purpose of residing and performing the duties of citizenship therein.

## OATH OF ALLEGIANCE.

**Further**, I do solemnly swear that I will support and defend the Constitution of the United States against all enemies, foreign and domestic; that I will bear true faith and allegiance to the same; and that I take this obligation freely, without any mental reservation or purpose of evasion; SO HELP ME GOD.

Sworn to before me, this _17th_ day of _May_ 1909.

_Andro Dragan_

_M. J. Murin_, Notary Public.

## DESCRIPTION OF APPLICANT.

Age: _35_ years.  
Stature: _5_ feet, _7½_ inches, Eng.  
Forehead: _Broad_  
Eyes: _Gray_  
Nose: _Roman_  
Mouth: _normal_  
Chin: _normal_  
Hair: _Blonde (little bald-headed)_  
Complexion: _Blonde_  
Face: _Oblong_

## IDENTIFICATION.

**I hereby certify** that I know the above-named _Andro Dragan_ personally, and know him to be the identical person referred to in the within described Certificate of Naturalization, and that the facts stated in his affidavit are true to the best of my knowledge and belief.

_Michael J. Murin_

[ADDRESS OF WITNESS.] _326 Nepperhan Ave., Yonkers, N.Y._

Applicant desires passport sent to following address: _Andro Dragan, 455 Nepperhan Ave., Yonkers, N.Y._

One dollar tax, as imposed by law, will be required, in U. S. currency, with each application.  
When husband, wife, minor children and servants expect to travel together, a single passport for the whole will suffice.  
For any other person in the party a separate passport will be required.  
Address "Department of State, Passport Division," Washington, D. C.

56. Andrew Dragan, 1909

ating a butcher shop with John Renchkovsky at 1107 Crest Ave. He was still in business in 1942. He was married to Eva (née Trembacz, 1889–1971) with whom he had: Eva Yeager, Peter, Olga Garofalo, and John. Dudra died on June 18, 1968 and was buried in Belle Vernon Cemetery, North Belle Vernon, Pa.

---

**George Dudycz** was born on May 8, 1879, in the Lemko village of Regietów Nyżni, Gorlice County, Austro-Hungarian Empire [present-day Poland] and immigrated in 1900. He first settled in Yonkers, N.Y., where he worked in a factory. He later moved to Bridgeport, Conn., where by 1916 he partnered with Awksenty *Telep and ran a grocery/meat market first at 706 Hallett St. and until 1920 at 681 Hallett St. During the same time he also partnered with Samuel *Telep and to run a grocery at 133 Caroline St. By 1925 he had his own grocery, which he operated until 1929 on Old Field Rd. in Fairfield, Conn. In the early 1930s he was listed as a peddler and later purchased a farm in Stratford, Conn. In 1942 he was listed as self-employed. He was married to Theodora/Dora (1885–19??) with whom he had: Helen, Peter, Lillian, and another child. Dudycz died on December 1, 1944.

---

**Anthony Durkot** was born on March 1, 1907, in the Lemko village of Hańczowa, Gorlice County, Austro-Hungarian Empire [present-day Poland] and immigrated in 1930 and settled in Yonkers, N.Y. In 1932 he was listed as a store keeper. In 1933 he received a beer license and by 1936 he was operating Seymour Grill Restaurant, but the next year he filed for bankruptcy, which was discharged by the U.S. District Court in New York City. At that time Durkot was listed as a laborer. In 1938 he had a new business at 66 Woodworth Ave., for which he immediately got a beer license and by 1940 it had evolved into Woodworth Restaurant and Bar, with a full liquor license. He operated this restaurant with his wife until his death. Durkot was married to Eva (née Sterzyn/Sturgeon, 1908-2000) with whom he had Michael and Helen Lesko. Durkot died on October 18, 1972, and was buried in the Oakland Cemetery, Yonkers, N.Y. His son Michael was the proprietor of Durkot's Bar and Grill for over 30 years.

57. Anthony Durkot, 1963

U. S. DEPARTMENT OF LABOR
NATURALIZATION SERVICE
ORIGINAL

No. 53941

# UNITED STATES OF AMERICA

## DECLARATION OF INTENTION

**Invalid for all purposes seven years after the date hereof**

State of Pennsylvania,
Western District of Pennsylvania, ss:  In the District Court of the United States.

I, **John Dudra**, aged **39** years, occupation **Butcher**, do declare on oath that my personal description is: Color **White**, complexion **Fair**, height **5** feet **9** inches, weight **150** pounds, color of hair **Black**, color of eyes **Brown**, other visible distinctive marks **None**. I was born in **Losa, Austria Hungary** on the **12th** day of **March**, anno Domini 1 **879**; I now reside at **1107 Crest Avenue, Charleroi**, Pennsylvania.
(Give number, street, and city or town.)
I emigrated to the United States of America from **Bremen** on the vessel **do not know**; my last foreign residence was **Losa, Austria Hungary**; I am **married**; the name of my wife is **Ella**; she was born at **Austria Hungary** and now resides **with me**.
It is my bona fide intention to renounce forever all allegiance and fidelity to any foreign prince, potentate, state, or sovereignty, and particularly to **CHARLES EMPEROR OF AUSTRIA AND APOSTOLIC KING OF HUNGARY** **of the Present Government of Austria Hungary as the case maybe**, of whom I am now a subject; I arrived at the port of **Baltimore**, in the State of **Maryland**, on or about the **12th** day of **March**, anno Domini 1 **905**; I am not an anarchist; I am not a polygamist nor a believer in the practice of polygamy; and it is my intention in good faith to become a citizen of the United States of America and to permanently reside therein: SO HELP ME GOD.

*John Dudra*
(Original signature of declarant)

Subscribed and sworn to before me in the office of the Clerk of said Court at Pittsburgh, Pa., this **20th** day of **December** anno Domini 191 **8**

[SEAL]

**J. Wood Clark**,
Clerk of the District Court of the United States.
By **J. M. Evans**, Deputy Clerk.

58. John Dudra, 1918

59. Anthony Durkot, 1945

---

**Gabriel Dziadik** was born on July 15, 1868, in the Lemko village of Brunary Niżne, Grybów County, Austro-Hungarian Empire [present-day Poland] and immigrated in 1886. He settled in Derby, Conn., and in 1900 was listed as a provisions dealer. His grocery store, up until 1902, was co-owned with Harry *Zuraw, and was located at 152 Main St. He was also a notary public, had a banking business, and sold ship tickets. He was one of the founders of Saints Peter and Paul Greek Catholic Church in Ansonia, Conn., and an active member of the Russian/Little Russian National

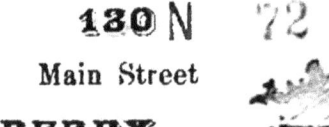

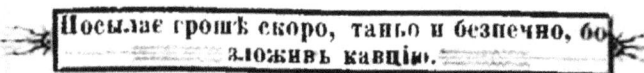

60. Gabriel Dziadik, 1902

61. Gabriel Dziadik with family

Union (later Ukrainian National Association). He was married to Catherine (née Wójcik, 1864–1942) with whom he had: Peter, Olga A. Hess, Stephena Turula, Michael, Stephen, Jaroslawa, Edward, Gabriel, and Mary McGivney. In mid-1919, due to illness, he put his grocery store up for sale, along with a 150-acre farm with a house. Dziadik died on December 15, 1919, and was buried in Saints Peter and Paul Greek Catholic Cemetery in Derby, Conn.

62. Gabriel Dziadik, 1907

63. Gabriel Dziadik, 1908

**Samuel Dziama** was born on September 5, 1890, in the Lemko village of Rozstajne, Jasło County, Austro-Hungarian Empire [present-day Poland] into the family of Dan'ko and Anastazyia. He immigrated in 1910 and settled in Cleveland, Ohio. By 1917 he had a grocery/meat store at 2202 6th St., which by 1920 was moved to 809 Starkweather Ave. and by 1928 to 4204 Bucyrus Ave. In 1930 through 1940 he was listed as a store owner and was still in business in 1942. He was married to Freida/Efroska (née Sudyk, 1895–1969) with whom he had: Raymond, Peter, and Steven. Dziama died on December 20, 1950.

**Nicholas Dzwinchik** was born in 1868 in the Lemko village of Bielanka, Gorlice County, Austro-Hungarian Empire [present-day Poland] and immigrated in 1885. He lived in Shamokin, Pa., In 1909, he applied for a hotel license for his establishment on Belmont St. in Fell Township, Pa. In 1910 he was listed as a grocery store owner on Nanticoke St. in the Hanover section of Nanticoke, Pa. In 1920 he was listed as a hotel owner in Larksville, Pa. In 1921 he sold the property in Larksville for $9,800. He was married to Anna (née Cekleniak, 1864–1922) with whom he had: Alex, John, Mary, Chester, and Olga Capitan. Dzwinchik died on March 1, 1928, and was buried in St. Nicholas Greek Catholic Cemetery, Nanticoke, Pa.

---

**Ozim Dzwonczyk** was born on July 26, 1861, in the Lemko village of Kunkowa, Gorlice County, Austro-Hungarian Empire [present-day Poland] into the family of Mykolai and Anastazyia (née Wojtowicz). He immigrated in 1885 and by 1900 he operated a hotel on Hill St. in Mayfield, Pa. In 1904 he was listed as owner of a retail business. In 1920 he was listed as a hotel owner and in 1930 as a retail merchant. He was married to Domka (née Maksimiak, 1871–1921) with whom he had: Eve, Michael, Vasyl, Victor, Anthony, and Mary Barna. Dzwonczyk died on October 12, 1942, and was buried in St. John's Russian Orthodox Cemetery, Mayfield, Pa.

---

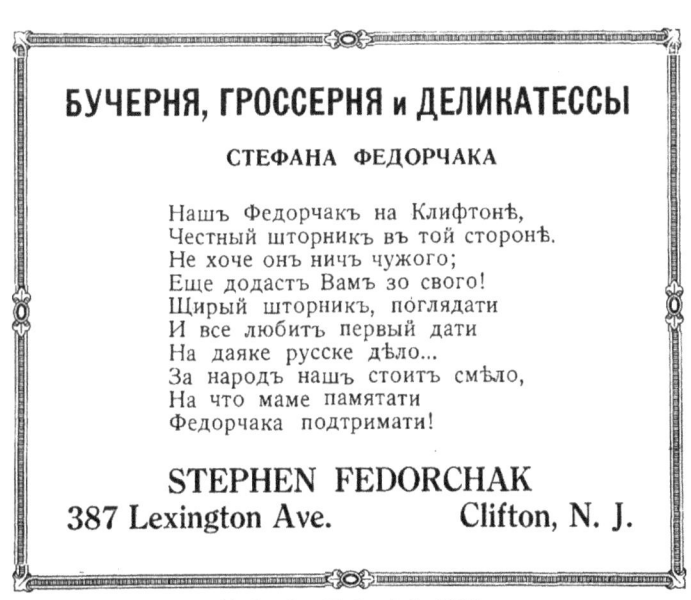

64. Stephen Fedorchak, 1929

**Stephen Fedorchak** was born on May 15, 1881, in the Lemko village of Pielgrzymka, Jasło County, Austro-Hungarian Empire [present-day Poland]. He immigrated in 1902 and settled in New York City. In 1910 he was listed as an oiler in a power house in Manhattan. He eventually opened a grocery store in the city (probably on the Upper East Side). By 1922 he was living in Clifton, N.J., where he purchased a three-story building at 387 Lexington Ave. and opened a grocery/delicatessen. In 1930 he was listed as a meat/grocery store owner. By 1937 he also had a saloon/grill at 2 Kulik St., where he was still in business in 1942. He was married to Pelahia (née Bodin/Bodon, 1887–1969) with whom he had: Helen, John, Jerry, and Theodore. Fedorchak died on May 24, 1943, and was buried in Cedar Lawn Cemetery in Paterson, N.J.

> **СТЕФАНЪ ФЕДОРЧАКЪ**
>
> 387 LEXINGTON AVE. COR. KULIK ST., CLIFTON, N. J.
>
> —— FIRST CLASS MEAT MARKET & GROCERY ——
>
> Федорчака рада така: Якъ хочете здоровы быти, треба свѣжи стравы ѣсти. Свѣже мясо, удженину, чапсы, стейки, курятину, салцесоны, солонину, садовину, зеленину, хлѣбъ, молоко, яйця, масло, сыръ, каву, чай. Того, братку, ся тримай! И Федорчакъ ся тримае — въ своемъ склепѣ Все лемъ свѣже и чистеньке онъ спродае.

65. Stephen Fedorchak, 1930

> **STEPHEN FEDORCHAK GRILL**
>
> Въ Стефана Федорчака все свѣже
> Пиво и вино каждый достане
> Тамъ сой по пріятельски забавлятъ
> И патріотичны бесѣды поговорятъ.
>
> **STEPHEN FEDORCHAK**
>
> 2 KULIK STREET     CLIFTON, N. J.

66. Stephen Fedorchak, 1942

**Cyril W. Fedorko** was born on December 15, 1888, in the Lemko village of Gładyszów, Gorlice County, Austro-Hungarian Empire [present-day Poland] into the family of Vasyl' and Tekla (née Dziubina). It is not known when he immigrated. In 1917 he was listed as a store keeper at 35 Washington Ave. in Yonkers, N.Y. in partnership with his twin

> C. W. FEDORKO     N. W. FEDORKO
>
> **Farmers
> Flour, Grain and Feed Co.**
>
> WHOLESALE AND RETAIL
>
> Phone Stratford 128 from 7:30 A. M. to 6 P. M    Phone Stratford 14 after 6 P. M.
>
> **Foot of Sutton Avenue**     **Stratford, Conn.**

67. Cyril W. Fedorko, 1919

brother, Nicholas. By 1919 he was the president of Flour, Grain, and Feed Co. (later known as Farmers Flour and Grain Co.) on Sutton Street then later at 1167 Stratford Ave., in Stratford, Conn., where Nicholas was treasurer. He ran that company at least until 1944, but it was no longer listed in 1949. He later retired to Hollywood, Fla., with his wife, Helen. They had no children. Fedorko died on July 17, 1973.

**Nicholas W. Fedorko** was born on December 15, 1888, in the Lemko village of Gładyszów, Gorlice County, Austro-Hungarian Empire [present-day Poland] into the family of Vasyl' and Tekla (née Dziubina). He immigrated in 1906 and made a trip back to his homeland in 1913. In 1914 he worked at a meat market, John Hodio and Co., in Yonkers, N.Y. A year later he was listed as an insurance agent in the same city. He later had a store with his twin brother, Cyril, at 35 Washington Ave, Yonkers. By 1917 he had a grocery/butcher shop at 1825 Barnum Ave. in Stratford, Conn. While operating this store, he also opened a butcher shop in 1919 at 425 Catherine St. in Bridgeport, Conn. The same year, he became engaged in business with Cyril as the treasurer of Farmers Flour and Grain Co. located on Sutton St. in Stratford. It appears that by 1923 he turned all his attention to other lines of business. First, he established a mineral water manufacturing company under the name Fedorko and Son, which he incorporated with Peter Deackon and John Miczejewski in 1926 as Stratford Bottling Works. It manufactured and dealt in carbonated beverages and was located at 23 Noble St., Stratford, Conn. Fedorko served as its secretary/treasurer and his wife was vice-president. The company was later led by their sons Peter and William and ceased to exist in 1991. By 1928 Fedorko also had a real-estate company located at 1726 Barnum Ave. in Stratford, where he ran a liquor dealership in the 1950s and 1960s. He was also involved with Barnum Coal and Fuel Company, but probably only briefly. He was active in local politics and served as Stratford's Fourth District councilman. He was married to **Julia** (née Preslovska/Pryslopska, 1894–after 1972) with whom he had two sons: Peter and William. Fedorko died on August 31, 1972, and was buried in St. John the Baptist Greek Catholic Cemetery, Stratford, Conn.

JOSEPH H. FEKULA        Ethelbert, Manitoba, Can.
Born, February 20, 1884; Grammar School; 5 feet 4 inches; 135 pounds; dark hair; brown eyes; Democrat.
*"See thy friend with his hat off before thee attempt to judge his powers."*

68. Joseph H. Fekula, College Graduation, 1905

**Joseph Harry Fekula** was born on August 10, 1884, in the Lemko village of Łosie, Gorlice County, Austro-Hungarian-Empire [present-day Poland] into the family of Hryhoryi/Harry (1844-1937) and Eva (née Yewusiak, 1847–1918). He immigrated in 1896 and graduated from Philadelphia College of Pharmacy in 1905 as a distinguished student. In 1907 he received a pharmacist's certificate and subsequently was affiliated with Dr.

40
No. 40

ORIGINAL

# UNITED STATES OF AMERICA

**Department of Commerce and Labor**
BUREAU OF IMMIGRATION AND NATURALIZATION
DIVISION OF NATURALIZATION

## DECLARATION OF INTENTION
(Invalid for all purposes seven years after the date hereof)

United States of America, } ss: In the Circuit Court
Eastern District of Penna. } of United States.

I, Joseph H. Fekula, aged 23 years, occupation Druggist, do declare on oath (affirm) that my personal description is: Color White, complexion Dark, height 5 feet 4 inches, weight 130 pounds, color of hair dark brown, color of eyes light brown, other visible distinctive marks none. Losie; I was born in Austria, on the 12 day of August, anno Domini 1884; I now reside at 1155 No 20th St Pa I emigrated to the United States of America from Austria on the vessel* unknown Hamburg American Line; my last foreign residence was Losie, Galicia, Austria. It is my bona fide intention to renounce forever all allegiance and fidelity to any foreign prince, potentate, state, or sovereignty, and particularly to Emperor of Austria & Apostolic King of Hungary, Francis Joseph of which I am now a subject; I arrived at the port of Philadelphia, in the State Territory of Pennsylvania on or about the 11 day of July, anno Domini 1906; I am not an anarchist; I am not a polygamist nor a believer in the practice of polygamy; and it is my intention in good faith to become a citizen of the United States of America and to permanently reside therein: SO HELP ME GOD.

Joseph H. Fekula
(Original signature of declarant.)

Subscribed and sworn to (affirmed) before me this 11th

[SEAL.] day of October, anno Domini 1906.

Samuel Bell,
Clerk of the Circuit Court.
By Geo Bradford Jr Deputy Clerk.

*If the alien arrived otherwise than by vessel, the character of conveyance or name of transportation company should be given

11—2526

69. Joseph H. Fekula, 1906

Patrick Kelly Pharmacy in Philadelphia, Pa. In 1910 he opened his pharmacy at 124 Lackawanna Ave. in Olyphant, Pa. After retiring in 1929, he moved to Forty Fort, Pa. and was employed in various drug stores. At his alma mater, now known as the University of Sciences, he endowed the Joseph H. and Anna H. Fekula Memorial Scholarship, to be awarded annually to a worthy upper-class student of good scholarship and character whose circumstances require assistance. He was married to Anna (née Herbut, 1897-1989). Fekula died on December 9, 1967, and was buried in Fern Knoll Burial Park, Dallas, Pa.

70. Fekula brothers. James Fekula's two brothers, Basil and Michael were Orthodox priests

**Mitro Fesch** was born in 1847 (?) in the Lemko village of Banica, Gorlice County, Austrian Empire [present-day Poland] and immigrated in 1886. He settled in Yonkers, N.Y., where he was eventually affiliated with the police department and had a special officer's badge but was deprived of it in 1905. By 1908 he had a saloon at 464 Neppherhan Ave. but that year he ran into legal problems for violating the Excise Law and was held on $1,000 bail. In 1910 he obtained a liquor tax certificate from Helen Lamanyecz and ran his saloon at 351 Nepperhan Ave. At that time he advertised himself as an old businessman who had wide connections in Yonkers and could advise where to get a job. By 1912 he had moved the saloon to 457 Nepperhan Ave. and that year faced more legal problems. In 1914 he was listed as a bartender living at 473 Nepperhan Ave. It appears that he gave up entrepreneurship in his later years. He was a founding director of the Russian National Brotherhood of St. Cyril and Methodius, founded in 1907. He was married to Rose, with whom he had: Eva, Mary, Adeline and Julia. Fesch died on April 19, 1923.

---— Р У С С К І Й   С А Л О Н Ъ -—

## D. FESHA

464 Nepperhan Ave.                    Yonkers, N. Y.

Тутъ Димитрій Фешъ голоситъ  
Всѣхъ Русиновъ красно проситъ:  
Кто перейде попри мене  
Нехай вступитъ, та побачитъ,  
Що у Феша вся порада  
И веселость, та розвада.  
Лѣкъ у него каждый найде  
Кто лишь въ его сальонъ войде.  
Кто терпитъ боль на жолудокъ  
Въ кого корчи, въ кого смутокъ  
Кто примерзне на тѣлѣ  

Нехай зайде до галѣ.  
У мене трунки суть всяки  
Пиво, вино та конякы,  
Горѣвки, румъ та все,  
Що лишь душа забагне.  
Маю галю на митянги,  
Хочь женитись, то еще и нынѣ  
Весѣлье я тобѣ справлю,  
Дуже гарно тя забавлю.  
Всѣ до мене лишь прійдѣтъ,  
Свого Русина попрѣтъ.

71. Mitro Fesch, 1908

## Димитрій Фешъ

351 Nepperhan ave.                    Yonkers, N. Y.

Кто до Юнкерсъ пріѣзжае,  
Най до Феша адресъ мае!  
Онъ каждому дастъ пораду,  
Где достати можь роботу  
И где краянъ вашъ мешкае.  
Бо онъ старый бизнесиста,  
Онъ каждого въ Юнкерсъ знае.  

А кто въ Юнкерсъ вже мешкае,  
Най же Феша не минае:  
Въ него виска, розны вина,  
Но а пиво — якъ сметана.  
Завше свѣжій напой мае,  
Вельки шклянки наливае,  
— каждому.

72. Mitro Fesch, 1910

**Peter Filak** was born on February 15, 1894, in the Lemko village of Banica, Gorlice County, Austro-Hungarian Empire [present-day Poland] to Andryi and Maryia (née Fesh) and immigrated in 1911. He settled in Yonkers, N.Y., and first worked in a carpet shop. In 1929, in partnership with Henry Zimmer, he opened the Yonkers Perfect Laundry. It was first located at 18 Archer Pl. and remained there until 1934, when it was transferred to a larger building at 300 Nepperhan Ave. At that time an investment of $69,000 was made to purchase machinery. In 1940 the laundry employed forty-one people and owned ten trucks. In 1943 it was sold to Philip Scheiner and Sylvia Kandel for $30,000. At that time it employed about twenty-five workers and had six trucks. By 1954, Filak lived in Danbury, Conn., where he died on September 17, 1954. He was married to Mary.

YONKERS PERFECT LAUNDRY, 300 NEPPERHAN AVENUE

73. Peter Filak

ПЕТРЪ А. ФИЛЯКЪ
74. Peter Filak

ЮНКЕРС, Н. Й.

Phone: YOn. 3123.

ЛЕМКОВСКО - РУССКА ПРАЛЬНЯ

**ПЕТРА ФИЛЯКА**

Всі русскы люде в Юнкерс дают свое праня до русской пральні, бо мают добру практику, што там им зроблят чысту роботу на час и не дорого.

●

**Yonkers Perfect Laundry**

300 NEPPERHAN AVE.,
YONKERS, N. Y.

75. Peter Filak, 1937

**Thomas P. Filak** was born on October 27 1889, in the Lemko village ofŁug (?), Gorlice County, Austro-Hungarian Empire [present-day Poland]. He immigrated in 1904 and settled in Jersey City, N.J., with his parents Paul and Justina. By 1910 he ran a saloon/hotel at 141 Essex St., for which he received a liquor license in June of 1913. He was still listed as a saloonkeeper in 1925. In 1930 he was listed as a watchmaker with his own shop. He was married to Mary (née Wysowski, 1889–1978) with whom he had: Stella, Paul, Michael and Peter. Filak died on November 1, 1931.

**РУССКІЙ ГОТЕЛЬ**

# ТИМОФЕЯ ФИЛЯКА

**141 ESSEX STREET, JERSEY CITY, N. J.**

Мае прекрасно зарядженный Готель, где можно выпити все свѣжого **пива**, импортованного и Американского вина, и закурити доброго цигара.

**Напитки достарчаются на пикники, балѣ, весѣлья, крестины до дому.**

**САМЫИ ДОСТУПНЫИ ЦѢНЫ. А НУ ПОПРОБУЙТЕ!**

76. Thomas Filak, 1917

Form 1 20516 REGISTRATION CARD No. 289

1 Name in full Thomas P. Filak 817 Age, in yrs. 29

2 Home address 141 Essex St Jersey City NJ

3 Date of birth Oct 27th 1889

4 Are you (1) a natural-born citizen, (2) a naturalized citizen, (3) an alien, (4) or have you declared your intention (specify which)? Naturalized Citizen

5 Where were you born? Holosko Galicia Austria

6 If not a citizen, of what country are you a citizen or subject?

7 What is your present trade, occupation, or office? Saloon keeper

8 By whom employed? Self

Where employed? 141 Essex St JC

9 Have you a father, mother, wife, child under 12, or a sister or brother under 12, solely dependent on you for support (specify which)? Wife & 3 Children

10 Married or single (which)? Married Race (specify which)? White

11 What military service have you had? Rank ——— ; branch ———

years ; Nation or State

12 Do you claim exemption from draft (specify grounds)?

I affirm that I have verified above answers and that they are true.

Thos P. Filak

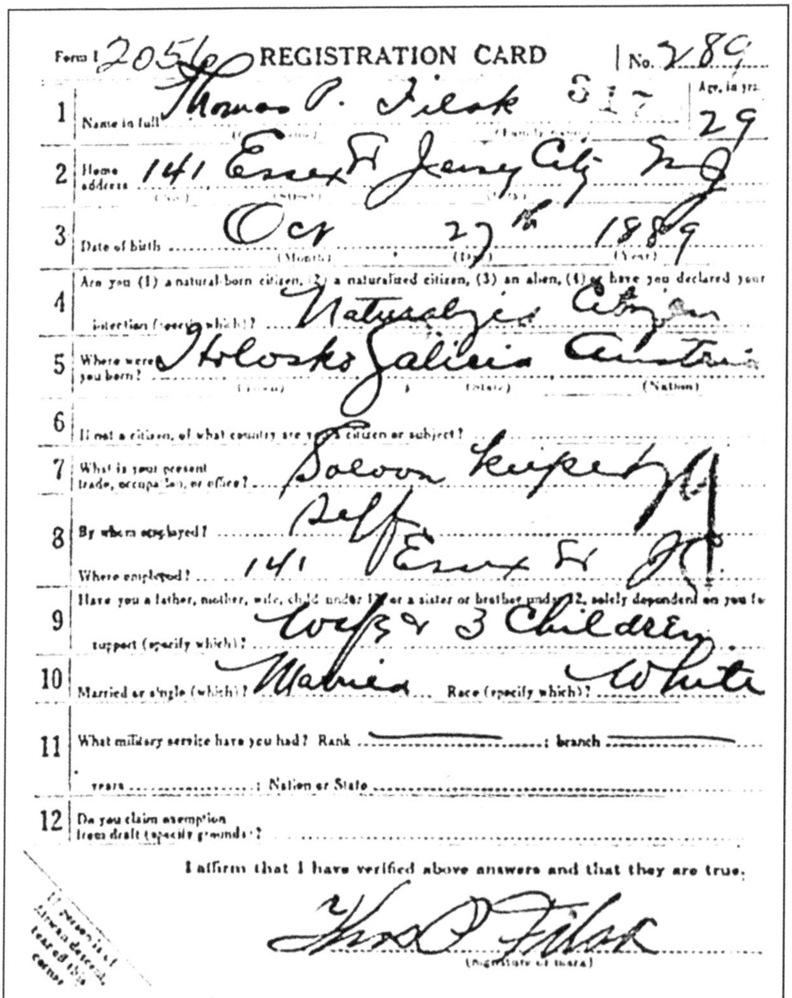

77. Thomas Filak, 1918

**Andrew Fill** was born on December 10, 1886, in the Lemko village of Wołowiec, Gorlice County, Austro-Hungarian Empire [present-day Poland] and immigrated in 1906. He settled in Cleveland, Ohio, where in 1912 he was listed as a laborer. He first owned a bar/tavern called Andy's Place. By 1917 he had a grocery and butcher shop at 4501 Gifford Ave. He was still in business in 1940. He was married to Maria (née Horbal, 1891–1948) with whom he had: Eva, Michael, Steven, Rosa, George, and Raymond. Fill died on October 26, 1953, and was buried in St. Theodosius Orthodox Cemetery, Brooklyn, Ohio.

---

**Kost Furtak** was born in December 1873, in the Lemko village of Łosie, Gorlice County, Austro-Hungarian Empire [present-day Poland] and immigrated in 1892. In 1900 he was listed as a carpet spinner at the Alexander Smith and Sons Carpet Company in Yonkers, N.Y. In 1910 he was a carder in a cotton mill in Middlesex County, Mass., and in 1920 he worked as a weaver in a woolen mill in Providence, R.I. However, the next year he was back in Yonkers, where he operated a grocery store at 441 Nepperhan Ave. In 1928 he was listed as a meat cutter. He was first married to Paraska (née Lazor, 1880–1934) with whom he had Mary, Anna Harrilchak, and Helen. In 1936 he married Paraska (née Dzubak/Holowiak, 1874–1953). Furtak died on June 27, 1938, and was buried in the Oakland Cemetery, Yonkers, N.Y.

---

**Jacob Gambal** was born in 1868 in the Lemko village of Bogusza, Grybów County, Austro-Hungarian Empire [present-day Poland] into the family of Iakov and immigrated in 1890. By 1900 he had a grocery store on Race Street in Olyphant, Pa. His business was later located at 120 Lincoln St. and he was described as "a well-known merchant." He was in business at the time of his death. He played a vital role in local religious development among Rusyns and in 1913 was a charter member of the St. Vladimir Russian

78. Jacob Gambal, 1909

# Michael N. Halkowicz

## Карти Корабельні
### ТОЧНА ПЕРЕСИЛКА ГРОШИЙ ДО ВСІХ ЧАСТИЙ СВІТА.

## Atlas, Penna.

92. Michael N. Halkowicz, 1925

## МИАХИЛЪ ГАЛЬКОВИЧЪ
Продае **шифскарты и посылае гроши** до всѣхъ частей свѣта

M. HALKOWICH,                                      ATLAS, PA.

93. Michael N. Halkowicz, 1930

94. The Halkowicz Family

---

**Nicholas Halkowicz** was born on November 29, 1867, in the Lemko village of Binczarowa, Grybów County, Austro-Hungarian Empire [present-day Poland] and immigrated in 1888. He settled in Mt. Carmel, Pa., where he lost a leg working in a

Orthodox Brotherhood. He was married to Melka (née Homiak) and later to Dominka (née Felenchak, 1880–1955) with whom he had seven children: Nellie Glinsky, Olga, Annie, Michael, Julius, Marie, and Lena. Gambal died on March 2, 1926 and was buried in Holy Sepulcher Cemetery, Cheltenham, Pa.

**ЯКОВЪ ГАМБАЛЬ**
Нашъ русскій человѣкъ мае первоклясну гросерню и бучерню.
У него достане, чего лишь душа запрагне.
**ТОВАРЪ СВѢЖІЙ, ЧИСТЫЙ И ЗДОРОВЫЙ.**
Русскіи люди, держитеся девиза: „СВОЙ ДО СВОГО".
**JACOB GAMBAL** 120 LINCOLN STREET, OLYPHANT, PA.

79. Jacob Gambal, 1921

**Mitrofan Gambal** was born on January 14, 1870, in the Lemko village of Jaszkowa, Gorlice County, Austro-Hungarian Empire [present-day Poland] into the family of Matei and Barbara (née Malyjczak). He immigrated in 1890/1893 and settled in Old Forge, Pa. By 1920, and until 1940, he had a grocery store. He served as a councilman of Old Forge for twelve years and was the first policeman of that borough. He was among the founding directors of the Russian Orthodox Catholic Mutual Aid Society and the Russian Orthodox Fraternity Lubov and served as the founding president of the latter (1912–1925). He was also one of the founders of St. Michael Russian Orthodox Church in Old Forge. He had one son, John, with his first wife. He was later married to Catherine (née Swallow, 1883–1930) with whom he had: Sophie, Anna Yakobchak, Alice, Nicholas, Mary Woytowich, Helen Fregman, Michael, Lottie, Lovie Mustorick, and Vera. Gambal died on January 27, 1943, and was buried in St. Michael Orthodox Cemetery (the new one), Old Forge, Pa.

**Wasco Gambal** was born on March 3, 1874, in the Lemko village of Jaszkowa, Gorlice County, Austro-Hungarian Empire [present-day Poland] into the family of Matei and Barbara (née Malyjczak). He settled in Old Forge, Pa., in 1889 (or possibly 1891) and by 1898 operated a hotel at the corner of Albion and Hickory Streets that was also listed as a retail business. It was later listed at 170 Albion St. In 1920 he was listed as a hotel keeper and in 1928 he was described as a "prominent local resident." By 1930 he had sold his business and purchased a farm. He was one of the founders of St. Michael's Greek Catholic (later Russian Orthodox) Church in Old Forge. He was the school director when Old Forge High School was dedicated and was among the founders of the Russian Orthodox Fraternity Lubov. He was married to Mary (née Duffalo, 1883–1952) with whom he had nine children: Annie, Olga, Alice, Walter, Vera, Tatiana, Mary, Stephen, and Daniel. Gambal died on July 22, 1954, and was buried in St. Michael's Orthodox Cemetery, Old Forge, Pa.

**Thomas M. Gamble** was born on March 4, 1884, in the Lemko village of Bogusza, Grybów County, Austro-Hungarian Empire [present-day Poland] into a Gambal family. He immigrated in 1893. By 1914 he was living in Atlas, Pa., but by 1920 he had moved to Lakewood, Ohio, where in 1920 he worked as a carpenter. By 1930 he had opened his own home building business. In 1940 he was listed as a homebuilding carpenter and was still listed as such in 1958 but had retired by 1960. He was married to Mary (née Schipchik, 1894–1976) with whom he had: Isadore and Anna. Gamble died on January 14, 1968.

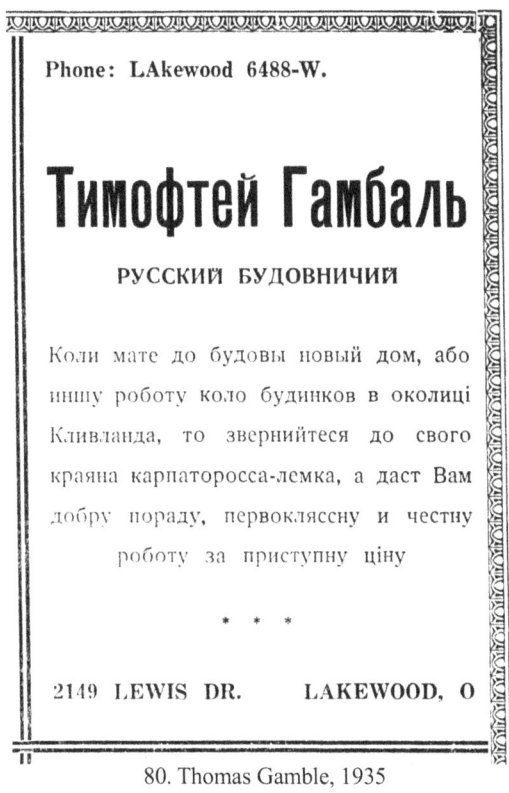

80. Thomas Gamble, 1935

**John Glowa** was born on June 24, 1863, in the Lemko village of Zawadka Rymanowska, Sanok County, Austrian Empire [present-day Poland] and immigrated in 1882. He first settled in Danville, Pa., where he worked at an ironworks company. He later worked building a railroad from Snydertown to Sunbury in Pennsylvania. For seven years he worked at a mine in Excelsior, Pa. In 1889 he settled in Shamokin, Pa., but in 1892 he returned to Excelsior, where he became the postmaster and opened a general store. He operated

81. John Glowa, 1903

the store for 14 years, and in 1906 he moved back to Shamokin, where he had wide business connections. He was the president of the Russian Mercantile Company. He was one of the original directors of the Market Street National Bank (est. 1900 with capital of $100,000) and served in this capacity, probably until his death. He was also a stockholder in the Shamokin and Coal Township Light and Power Company, the Hoven Mercantile Company of New York City, and the Connell Powder Company of Scranton. He was

> ИВАНЪ ГЛОВА
> 
> JOHN GLOVA (POSTMASTER)
> 
> — въ —
> 
> **Excelsior, Pa.**
> 
> ОДИНОКІЙ СТОРЪ НА ЦѢЛЫЙ EXCELSIOR.
> 
> Всякй потребнй рѣчѣ до житя, якъ такожь можна купити убраня майнерскй и звычайнй.
> 
> Посылае такожь грошѣ до всѣхъ частей свѣта, скоро, тано и беспечно.
> 
> ☞ Продае шифкарты. ☜
> 
> Не водъ нынѣ вже знають люде солідного Ивана Глову.

82. John Glowa, 1903

described as "a self-made man, one whose excellent judgment and well-directed executive ability have made him successful in his various undertakings." It was also noted that "he is a very popular citizen of Shamokin, and stands well among his own countrymen there, being president of the Ruthenian Catholic Church, of which he was one of the founders." He served as the first treasurer (1894–1896) and the second president (1896–1898) of the Russian National Union (later Ukrainian National Association). He was first married to Catherine (née Chlebowsky, 1870–1907) with whom he had five children: Mary Kuziw, Michael, Matthew, Walter and Antoinette. His second wife was Ella/Helen (née Emck, 1857/1864–1929). Glowa died on August 11, 1921 and was buried in Transfiguration Ukrainian Catholic Cemetery, Coal Township, Pa. His business undertakings were partially continued by his wife but she died only a few years later.

> ИВАНЪ ГЛОВА
> 
> **JOHN GLOWA**
> 
> EXCELSIOR, PA.
> 
> Предсѣдатель „Союза", почтмайстеръ — менажеръ великого компанічного стору въ Shamokin, Pa. и заряджуе его філіею въ Excelsior, Pa.
> 
> Продае шіфкарты на всѣ лініи корабельнй по найдешевшихъ цѣнахъ, а на добрй корабле. Посылае грошѣ до всѣхъ частей свѣта, таньо и ретельно.
> 
> Впрочемъ Глову кождый знае — вонъ не потребуе нѣчіеи хвальбы. Его хвалить самй честнй его поступки.

83. John Glowa, 1897

**Alexander P. Grega** was born on September 10, 1881, in the Lemko village of Rychwałd, Gorlice County, Austro-Hungarian Empire [present-day Poland]. He immigrated in 1901 and settled in Cohoes, N.Y., where he worked as a carpenter, eventually becoming a foreman before engaging in business. In 1925, in partnership with John H. Guba, he organized the Potato Chip Manufacturing Co., located at 92 Oneida St., moving to 74 Oneida St. in 1929. A year later, it was renamed the G and G Potato Chip Co. By 1931 the business had outgrown the space on Oneida St. and moved to 91 Saratoga St. (on the corner of Ontario), where it remained until 1951. In 1937 Grega replaced Guba as the G and G Company treasurer. The company flourished for a time. In 1943 Anna Grega became vice president/treasurer. In 1951 G and G was sold to Arthur and Roger Hamilton and Grega retired. They ran the business for a year, then sold the site and the building was converted to a private club. Grega was married to Anna (née Lazor, 1881–1960) with whom he had a son, Peter. In 1944 they moved to Boght Corners, N.Y. Grega died on March 12, 1972 in Cohoes, N.Y.

84. Alexander P. Grega

**Charles D. Grucelak** was born on August 15, 1878, in the Lemko village of Leluchów, Nowy Sącz County, Austro-Hungarian Empire [present-day Poland] into the family of Ivan and Anna (née Koznoski). He emigrated in 1894 and first lived in Passaic, N.J. By 1907 he was living in Scranton, Pa., where by 1909 he worked on his own account as a carpenter/home builder. At the time of his death he was still listed as a contractor. He was active in the Ruthenian (later Ukrainain) National Association, including serving as the president of the

Scranton branch, and in 1908 was a founder of St. Vladimir Galician Ruthenian Greek Catholic parish in Scranton. He was married to Tessie "Teckla" (née Lawrick, 1881–1934) with whom he had: Mary Ruschak, Julie Sternowsky, and Anna Wargo. Grucelak died on November 27, 1929, and was buried in Stratford [Avenue] Cemetery, Scranton, Pa.

---

**John H. Guba** was born on February 24, 1900, in the Lemko village of Długie, Gorlice County, Austro-Hungarian Empire [present-day Poland]. He immigrated in 1910 and first worked as a butcher and electric railway conductor. He was among the founders and later trustee and the president of St. Nicholas Russian Orthodox Church in Cohoes, N.Y. In 1925, in partnership with Alexander P. Grega, he organized the Potato Chip Manufacturing Co. located at 92 Oneida St., and moved it to 74 Oneida St. in 1929. A year later it was renamed the G and G Potato Chip Co. By 1931 the business had outgrown the space on Oneida St. and moved to 91 Saratoga St. (on the corner of Ontario), where it remained until 1951. In 1937, Peter Grega replaced John Guba as the G and G Company treasurer. Guba opened a hotel/restaurant in Schenectady, but returned to Cohoes in 1939 to form the Super Crisp Potato Chip Company. The company flourished for a time, was idle between 1945 and 1947, and reopened under the direction of John and Harry Guba. The Super Crisp Company continued its operations at different locations in Cohoes until 1966, when it closed. Guba was married to Anna (née Kopcza, 1902–1982) with whom he had: Tessie Campana, John Joseph, Harry, and Walter. Guba died on June 19, 1973, and was buried in the St. Nicholas Russian Orthodox Cemetery, Boght Corners, N.Y.

---

**Nicefor Habura** was born on November 22, 1872, in the Lemko village of Florynka, Grybów County, Austro-Hungarian Empire [present-day Poland] into the family of Andryi and Paraska (née Maksymchak) and immigrated in 1893 (1889?). He settled in Shamokin, Pa., where he first worked as a clerk in John Glowa's grocery store. In 1903 he was listed as a manager of a store, probably the Russian Mercantile Company. In 1907 he was listed as a saloon owner located at 613 N. Shamokin St. In 1910 he became one of the directors and the manager of the Ruthenian Store Company, which at that time had capital of $5,000. By 1911 he was serving as a postmaster in Excelsior, Pa., where he also opened a store, which was a branch of the Ruthenian Store Company. In 1921 he was one of the founding directors of the People's Trust Co. of Shamokin, Pa., with assets of $250,000. In 1925, the bank's assets were listed at more than $1.3 million. He was still a director of the People's Trust Bank in 1936, when its deposits were a little more than a million dollars. In 1925 he was listed as the president of the People's Home Association. He retired from business in 1944. He was first married to Mary (née Dubec,

> **ДОБРА РАДА!**
>
> Хто хоче шанувати своє здоровлє, нехай не йде до чужих за скислим товаром, коли у нас є сьвіжий. — Хто хоче бути богатий, нехай не просить чужих за свої гроші, коли наша ціна других задивляє. — Хто хоче від 6 до 9 днів переїхати через море, най зголосить ся до нас, понеже ми маємо шифкарти на найліпші лінії як: North German Lloyd, Red Star Line, Hamburg-American Line і Russian-American Line; нетілько ціна низька, але і люде суть дуже приступні. — Хто хоче, аби гроші до пересилки були певні, нехай зголосить ся до нас, а буде вдоволений.
>
> Є то найстарший руський штор в EXCELSIOR, PA.
> і філїя Русьн. Шамокіньського штору
> **Nicefor Habura, Postmaster**
> і співробітник Руського штору

85. Nicefor Habura, 1913

1881–1920) with whom he had: Walter, Anna, Jeannie, Helen, Mary, Eva, and Stella. He was later married to Phoebe (née Murdza). Habura died on September 29, 1945, and was buried in the Transfiguration Ukrainian Catholic Cemetery, Coal Township, Pa. He was remembered as "a well-known retired merchant."

> **RUSSIAN MERCANTILE ASSOCIATION**
>
> Йосиф Пейко, предс.;
> Мих. Лесяк, завід. штору;
> А. Шаршонь, пр.; Кон. Ком.
>
> **PEOPLE'S HOME ASSOCIATION**
>
> Н. Габура, предс.;
> Мирон Козяр, кас.;
> Мих. Пилиняк, секр.
>
> Найстарший український штор в Америці, має завсігди доволі свіжого товару та продає по дуже умеркованих цінах. Посилає також гроші і продає шифкарти до всіх частин світа. Обертає місячно сумою $10.000.
>
> Штор в своїм домі.
>
> NORTH SHAMOKIN STREET,
> **SHAMOKIN, PA.**

86. Nicefor Habura, 1925

**Alex Halaburda** was born on April 23, 1869, in Binczarowa, Grybów County, Austro-Hungarian Empire [present-day Poland]. He immigrated in 1884 and settled in Mt. Carmel, Pa. By 1896 he had a hotel at the Lehigh Valley Depot, which he operated until his death. He was married to Dominika (née Homiak, 1880–1951) and they had three children. Halaburda died on April 23, 1906, and was buried in the Saints Peter and Paul Greek Catholic Cemetery, Mt. Carmel, Pa.

> **Alex Halaburda**
> has occupied the hotel at Vine street and Railroad Avenue, the former location of Enoch Lubesky. Come and see me. I am now ready for business.
> **ALEX HALABURDA.**

87. Alex Halaburda, 1904

> АЛЕКСІЙ ГАЛАБУРДА
>
> ## Alexy Halaburda
>
> MT. CARMEL, PA.
>
> Коло лігайского діпа, єсть въ Mt. Carmel готель Богдана Хмельницкого. Правда, небощикъ Богданъ тамъ вже не заходить, але якъ бы живъ, то певно бы зô своими хоробрыми козаками зайшовъ выпити чарку. За те всѣ Русины, потомки козаковъ выпивають тамъ добре пиво, віску, вино темперъ и всякій другій ласощѣ. Готель чистенькій, услуга чемна, закуска смачна; певно въ цѣлôй Америцѣ нема другого такого порядного, руского готелю.

88. Alex Halaburda, 1897

---

**Michael Halenda** was born on October 5, 1869 in the Lemko village of Wisłok Górny, Sanok County, Austro-Hungarian Empire [present-day Poland] and immigrated in 1893. In 1905 he was listed as a saloon keeper at 338 W Centre St. in Mahanoy City, Pa. He eventually settled in Frackville, Pa., where in 1910 he was listed as working on his own account as a bottler (for the Temperance Beer Company). In 1920 he was listed as an owner of a liquor store in Frackville, and he was one of the directors of the Broad Mountain Building and Loan Association and of People's Trust Co.; total assets of the latter in 1925 were $803,431. At the time of his death he was listed as a hotel keeper. In 1914 a meeting to establish an Orthodox parish in Frackville, Pa. took place in his house and he was among the parish's founders. He was married to Anna (née Uhrin, 1888–1950) with whom he had: John, Olga, and Melvin. Halenda died on May 3, 1935, and was buried in the Holy Ascension Russian Orthodox Cemetery, Frackville, Pa.

**Michael N. Halkowicz** was born on June 2, 1870, in the Lemko village of Bogusza, Grybów County, Austro-Hungarian Empire [present-day Poland] and immigrated in 1887. He first settled in Mt. Carmel, Pa., where in 1900 he was listed as a laborer. He later lived in Diamondtown, Pa., where he had a general store. In 1902 he moved his family to Atlas, Pa., where he opened a hotel and where he also served as the first postmaster (1908–1912, 1923–1936), steamship ticket agent, from 1919, and as a notary public, from 1922. A contemporary account noted, "as the agent for several leading steam ship lines, Mr. Halkowicz had business connections throughout the region." He was active in local politics and served as Mt. Carmel Township's school director. In 1891, the

89. Michael N. Halkowicz, 1908

90. Michael N. Halkowicz, 1915

91. Michael N. Halkowicz, 1919

Brotherhood Society of St. Demetrius was organized under his leadership. In time, this society became the founding organization for the first Greek Catholic parish in Mt. Carmel, of which Halkowicz was a trustee. After a 1907 split he was affiliated with the local St. Michael's Orthodox parish. In 1919 he was among the organizers of a fraternal organization, St. Demeter Russian Society of Mount Carmel. He was married to Lora/Lucy (née Shiposh, 1872–1935) with whom he had: Mary Polanchyck, Alexander, John, Julia Kulmatycki, Elsie, Annie, Thomas, Pearl, and Walter. Halkowicz died on June 28, 1936, and was buried in the St. Michael's Orthodox Cemetery, Mt. Carmel, Pa. It was remembered that "among the people he served so capably, Postmaster Halkowicz was a beloved official and was known well in Mount Carmel and other surrounding towns as he was in his own community."

mine. He then opened a store at 418 Columbia Ave. In 1910 he was listed as a general storekeeper. He was married to Pearl/Paraska (née Wronik, 1874–1952) with whom he had: Mary, Ella, Annie, Michael, George, Victorola, Walter, Catherine, Johanna, and John. Halkowicz died on August 13, 1928, and was buried in Saints Peter and Paul Greek Catholic Cemetery, Mt. Carmel, Pa.

95. Nicholas and Pearl Halkowicz

**Sam Halkovich** was born on March 23, 1891, in Bogusza, Grybów County, Austro Hungarian Empire [present-day Poland] into the family of Hilar and Eva. He immigrated in 1907 and settled in Mt. Carmel, Pa., where he first worked in the mines. He eventually moved to Garfield, N.J., where he opened a grocery/butcher shop in 1919. He remained in business until 1942, when he was forced to close due to illness. For more than twenty years he was a trustee of the Three Saints Russian Orthodox Church in Garfield, N.J., and also served as the president and the secretary of St. John's Society (RBO) in the same city. He helped to establish a branch of the Lemko Association in Passaic, N.J., and in 1948 was the founding editor of the newspaper *Golos Naroda*. In 1958 he moved to Florida, where he also served RBO members. He was married to Julia (née Hatala, 1897–1990) with whom he had: Anna and Peter. Halkowicz died on August 26, 1971, in Miami, Fl.

96. Sam Halkovich

**Peter S. Hardy** was born on January 7, 1897, in the Lemko village of Jurowce, Sanok County, Austro-Hungarian Empire [present-day Poland] as the youngest of seven brothers. He immigrated in 1913 and via New York went to Gary, Indiana. He travelled extensively around the U.S. learning the language, working in foundries, and engaging in various professions, including coal digger, track layer, and cabinet maker. In 1915, during the sinking of the steamer Eastland on the Chicago River, he rescued ten people. The same year, he came to Bridgeport, Conn. He worked at odd jobs, such as machinist and blacksmith, before getting a position with O.K. Platt in 1917, where he worked for seven years. He then started the very successful Health

97. Peter S. Hardy

Developing Apparatus Co. Inc. with its own plant, but new capital maneuvered him out of the picture. He made several attempts to start over again but he had little success. He was, however, able to receive a number of patents for a fastening device (1928, no. 1,696,424), combination shower/bath spray, bath sponge, and massage device (1932, no. 1,840,812), exercising apparatus (1932, no. 1,866,868), exercise machine (1933, no. 1,905,092) as well as a design for a front frame member for rowing machines (1932, Des. 87,059). The first two were done with John Malcolm Thomson. In 1933, he was listed as the president of Parcit Manufacturing Co., located at 170 Cherry St. in Bridgeport, and which specialized in aluminum sand castings. From 1934 to 1935 he was listed as a patternmaker at 50 Remer St. in Bridgeport. A patternmaker makes wooden patterns that are used in the sand-casting molds to create the void into which the molten metal will be poured. It is a very rigorous skill set as the patterns need to consider the shrinkage of the metal. Hardy was a pattern maker by trade and a foundryman by experience. In 1938 he founded Peerless Foundry Co. with Frank J. Karandisevski. Their work initially focused on the manufacture of small bronze castings in a rented barn on Mountain Grove St. in Bridgeport. In 1941, after not being able to secure a bank loan, Hardy borrowed money from a friend and the company moved to a new plant located at 55 Andover St. Peter Petrofsky, a graduate of Yale University, designed the new plant. By 1944 it shifted its primary focus from the production of purely utilitarian aluminum castings to that of airplane bodies. Karandisevski appears to have left the firm around 1947, the same time that the business was reorganized as the Peerless Aluminum Foundry Co. At its height, it employed up to 300 people, who were among the first in the area to receive insurance, pension, hospitalization and death benefits. Hardy, of whom it was said that his "imagination in the treatment of aluminum was uncanny," held the role of the new entity's president and treasurer, while his daughter, Nadine Hardy Penkoff, served as the company's secretary. During his work for the Peerless Aluminum Foundry Co, he received the following patents: method and means for making castings (1948, no. 2,445,141), automobile traction device (1951, no. 2,577,890), elevating travelling conveyer (1951, no. 2,577,891), molders' sand treating and conveying apparatus (1943, no. 2,646,602), lathe (1955, no. 2,700,912), adjustable table mounting (1957, no. 2,932,480), sand molders' workbench

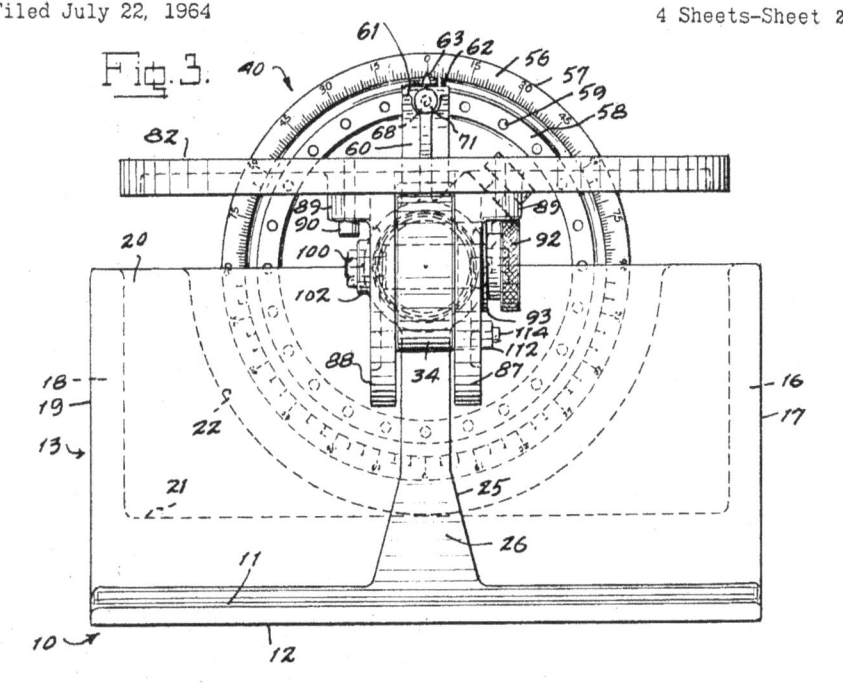
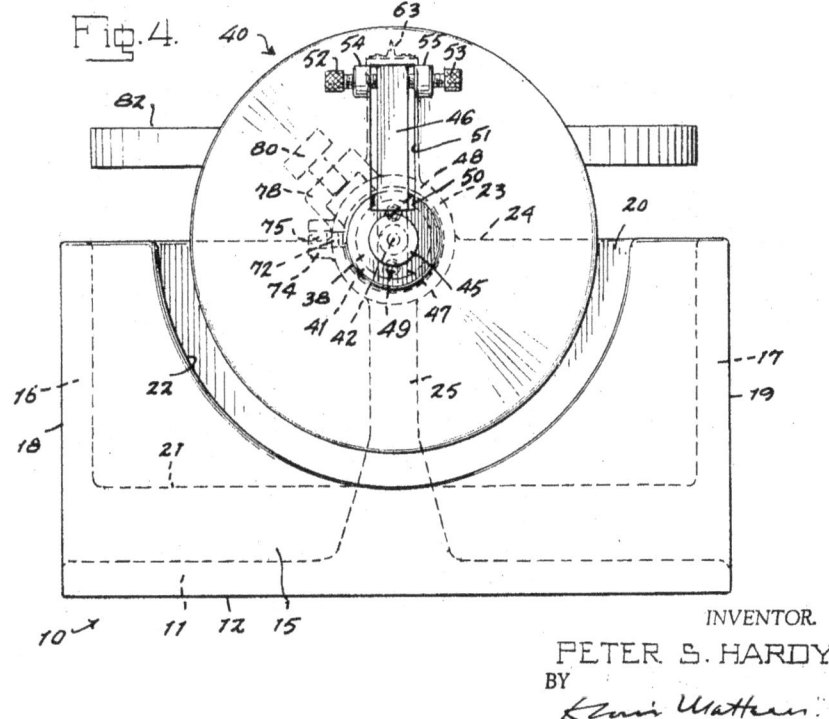

98. Peter S. Hardy's patent for layout fixture, 1967

(1957, design patent no. 180,714), core draw apparatus (1958, no. 2,851,749), portable cook stove (1962, no.3,051,159), abrasive finishing desk (1963, no. 3,086,277), spatula (1963, no. 3,092,411), and layout fixture (1967, no. 3,352,019). Hardy also served as president and chairman of the Board of Trustees of the Park City Hospital, to which in 1957 he donated $25,000 for expansion. In 1972, upon his retirement from the board, he was named an honorary trustee. In Trumbull, Conn., where he lived, he was a member of the Industrial Development Commission (1956–1966?). In 1955, he donated his land so that a new Town Hall could be built and in 1966 was named "Citizen of the Year." After Hardy's retirement, his son, Myron, led the company, eventually turning it into one of the largest producers of aluminum on the East Coast. Hardy continued to be active in the company during his retirement, training new patternmakers. The company was acquired in 2001 by Advanced Aluminum, LLC of Birmingham, Alabama, and shut down in 2010. Hardy was active in Russophile circles and after World War II he created and led the Lemko Relief Committee which was to aid resettled Lemkos in Europe. In the 1960s he created the Carpatho-Russian Literary Association, which reprinted several books. He was married to Anastasia (1893–1987) with whom he had: Myron and Nadine. Hardy died on April 24, 1989, and was buried in the St. John the Baptist Greek Catholic Cemetery, Stratford, Conn.

---

**George Hassick** was born in 1865 in the Lemko village of Florynka, Grybów County, Austrian Empire [present-day Poland] into a Hasych family. He immigrated in 1890 and settled in Shamokin, Pa. In 1900 he was listed as a hotel keeper. In 1901 he was listed as a laborer, but by 1903 he again operated a hotel/saloon. He also worked as a miner. He was married to Dora (née Tatus'ko, 1870–1945) with whom he had Pearl Jadick and Anna Petsock. Hassick died on December 3, 1913, and was buried in the Transfiguration Ukrainian Catholic Cemetery, Coal Township, Pa.

**Григорій М. Гасичь,**
ГОТЕЛЬНИКЪ
Lyndhurst Block — — SHAMOKIN, PA.

Всѣ его напитки дуже добрі. На выборы галицкій до сойму доставъ ордеръ на пиво водъ польско-жидôвского центрального комитету, але хрунямъ не продавъ.
**Чей его знаете!?**

99. George Hassick, 1903

**Thomas Hatala** was born on July 30, 1874, in the Lemko village of Wysowa, Gorlice County, Austro-Hungarian Empire [present-day Poland] into the family of Mykhal and Katrena (née Petryshyn] and immigrated in 1886. He lived in Shenandoah, Pa., Jersey City, N.J., and Yonkers, N.Y. before settling down in Garfield, N.J., in 1899. He worked at New York Belting and Packing Company for eleven years before starting in a meat and provision business on his own account "in which undertaking he met with immediate and marked success." His store was located at 115 Lincoln Pl. He was also "identified with the social and moral interests of the neighborhood." He was among the founders and a trustee of the Russian Orthodox Church of Three Saints. He was married to Paraska (née Demczko, 1875–after 1940) with whom he had 10 children (6 surviving): Julia, Mary, Olga, Stephen, Joseph, and Anna. Hatala died on January 8, 1940, and was buried in the St. Peter's Greek Catholic Cemetery, Garfield, N.J.

---

**Stephen Havrilak** was born in 1876 in the Lemko village of Słotwiny, Nowy Sącz County, Austro-Hungarian Empire [present-day Poland] and immigrated in 1890. By 1909 he had a hotel in Simpson, Pa., on Froebel Sreet, opposite the public school. In 1910 and 1920 he was listed as a hotel owner. He was married to Annie (1880–1918) with whom he

100. Stephen Havrilak, 1909

had: Maria, Ina, Anastasia, Joseph, John, and Michael. Havrilak died on November 5, 1925, and was buried in St. Basil's Russian Orthodox Cemetery, Simpson.

---

**Akim Hawran** was born on April 8, 1868, in the Lemko village of Mochnaczka Niżna, Nowy Sącz County, Austro-Hungarian Empire [present-day Poland] and immigrated in 1886. He settled in Fell Township (Simpson), Pa., where by 1894 he conducted retail business. By 1897 he had a hotel on Rittenhouse Place. In 1906 he received a wholesale license. In 1910 he was listed as a retail merchant (groceries) on Railroad Street near

101. Akim Hawran, 1897

Main Street in Carbondale, Pa. Hawran was among the founders of the Saints Peter and Paul Greek Catholic parish in Simpson, Pa., and was in charge of the local branch of the Ruthenian National Association. He was married to Maria (1864–1913) with whom he had 10 (?) children, Alex, Julia, Eva, Evdokia, Simeon, Michael, John, Harry, Metro and Annie. Hawran died on August 27, 1911, and was buried in Saints Peter and Paul Greek Catholic Cemetery in Simpson. He was remembered as "one of the most prominent residents of Simpson." His retail business was continued by his son, Harry, and his hotel was continued by his son, Metro.

---

**Thomas Hawran** was born in 1867 in the Lemko village of Mochnaczka Niżna, Nowy Sącz County, Austrian Empire [present-day Poland] and immigrated in 1883. He settled in Simpson, Pa., where by 1897 he had a hall. By 1904, he had a hotel/saloon on Morse St. and later on Main St. At the time of his death, he had a farm in Steens, Pa. He was active in local politics and ran for city offices. He was married to Anna (née Dudra) with whom he had: Christine and Mary Pawlik. Hawran died on January 13, 1928, and was buried in the Saints Peter and Paul's Greek Catholic Cemetery in Simpson. He was remembered as "one of the most prominent residents of Simpson who was well-known throughout the upper valley."

---

**Victor P. Hladick** was born on March 6, 1874, in the Lemko village of Kunkowa, Gorlice County, Austro-Hungarian Empire [present-day Poland] and immigrated in 1890. He first worked in the mines of Pennsylvania. From the very outset he became active within the Galician Russophile community and by the beginning of the 20th century he was working as a typesetter for the newspaper *Svît*. In 1902 he was the founding publisher and the editor of a new newspaper, *Pravda* (New York, N.Y.), which a year later he sold to the Russian Brotherhood Organization for $400. For at least two years, 1908–1909, he was listed as a steamship and insurance agent at 59 Morris St., Jersey City, N.J. In 1913 he moved to Canada, where he founded another newspaper, *Russkii narod*, in Winnipeg, Manitoba, serving as editor and publisher until 1918. After a trip to Europe, which included a stopover at the Paris Peace Conference to testify on behalf of the Lemkos, he was back in New York City, where he worked as an insurance agent and journalist. He remained very active in the Lemko community, both as an editor and an organizer. He initiated the organization of Lemkos' Committees of the U.S.A. in various places where Lemkos lived. In the late 1920s he organized and managed several recordings of Lemko folk and Orthodox religious music for mainstream American companies, including Columbia, which met commercial success. He was also involved in their mail distribution from his apartment at 418 E. 69th St., New

102. Victor P. Hiadick

York, N.Y. He was married to Johanna H. (née Wyslocky, 1890–19??). They had no children. Hladick died on April 21, 1947, and was buried in St. Vladimir Russian Orthodox Cemetery, Jackson, N.J.

103. Victor P. Hiadick, 1908

(Form No. 177.—Consular.)
(Corrected October 7, 1913.)

Fee for Passport ................ $1.00
Fee for administering oath and preparing passport application. 1.00

No. 86212

DEPARTMENT PASSPORT APPLICATION.

NATURALIZED.

*Stamp*

MAY 15 1914 — BUREAU OF CITIZENSHIP, DEPT. OF STATE

Issued, ..............

I, *Victor Hladyk*, a NATURALIZED AND LOYAL CITIZEN OF THE UNITED STATES, hereby apply to the Department of State at Washington for a passport for myself, accompanied by my wife, ................................, and minor children, as follows: .................., born at ................ on the .... day of ........., 1...; and ...............

I solemnly swear that I was born at *Kunkowa, Galicia, Austria* on or about the *6* day of *March*, *1874*; that I emigrated to the United States, sailing on board the *Switzerland* from *Antwerpen* on or about the .... day of *March*, 1890; that I resided *23* years, uninterruptedly, in the United States, from *1890* to *1913*, at *Mayfield, Pa. & New York City*; that I was naturalized as a citizen of the United States before the *Commonwealth* Court of *Penna*, at *Scranton, Pa*, on the *23* day of *April*, 1895, as shown by the accompanying Certificate of Naturalization; that I am the bearer of Passport No. ........ issued by ................ on the .... day of ........., 1...., which is returned herewith; that I am the identical person referred to in said certificate and passport; that I am domiciled in the United States, my permanent residence therein being at *New York City*, in the State of *New York*, where I follow the occupation of *Publisher & editor*; that I have been residing abroad temporarily since *March 26, 1913* in the following countries:* *in Canada*; that I last left the United States on the *21* day of *March*, 1913, arriving in *Gol montane Alta* the *26* day of *March*, 1913; that I am now temporarily residing at *Edmonton*; and that I intend to return to the United States within *two* ~~years~~ months with the purpose of residing and performing the duties of citizenship therein.

I have not applied elsewhere for a United States passport or for consular registration and been refused.

I desire the passport for the purpose of *Traveling*

OATH OF ALLEGIANCE.

Further, I do solemnly swear that I will support and defend the Constitution of the United States against all enemies, foreign and domestic; that I will bear true faith and allegiance to the same; and that I take this obligation freely, without any mental reservation or purpose of evasion: So help me God.

*Victor Hladyk*

American *Consulate* at *Edmonton, Canada*

Sworn to before me, this *7* day of *May*, 1914.

*Geo. S. Montgomery*
Consular Agent of the United States of America.

*See ... concerning the Expatriation Act of March 2, 1907.

*Russo-American Line
27 Broadway N.Y.C*

104. Victor P. Hiadick, 1914

**Elias Hylwa** was born on August 13, 1873, in the Lemko village of Pętna, Gorlice County, Austro-Hungarian Empire [present-day Poland] into a Hlywa family and immigrated in 1892. By 1906 he had a saloon at 109 Jersey St. in Ansonia, Conn. However, he soon moved to New Britain, Conn., where by 1908 he had a saloon with a fellow Lemko, John *Parylak, first listed at 11 Spring St. and later at 18 Spring St.

ІЛЬКО ГЛИВА
Знаменито уладжений сальон у власнім домі. Там можна забавить ся, як в дома і голова не буде болїти. Ану, Русини, лиш до свого!
86 Jersey St., ANSONIA, Conn.

105. Elias Hylwa, 1908

By 1912 Parylak had moved to Jamaica, Queens, and Hylwa went back to Ansonia, where in 1913 he was listed as the owner of a saloon at 66 Jersey St. The next year he moved his business to 86 Jersey St., where it remained until at least 1940, being at times described as a billiard room (1920s) or a tavern (1930s). In 1946 it was listed as a vacant store. He was married to Theckla (née Ciok, 1881–1962) with whom he had: Ann, Andrew, Esther, Mary, John, Antinette, Stephanie, and Helen. Hylwa died on November 13, 1948, and was buried in Saints Peter and Paul Greek Catholic Cemetery in Ansonia.

---

**Michael Hoblak** was born on October 27, 1866, in the Lemko village of Balnica, Lisko County, Austrian Empire [present-day Poland] and immigrated in 1886. In 1894 he was listed as a saloon owner in Kingston, Pa., but soon moved to Edwardsville, Pa., where he worked as a butcher. By 1910 he had a butcher shop, which he operated until the late 1940s at 480 Main St. He also had a farm at Harvey's Lake. He was a charter member of St. John's Russian Orthodox Church in Edwardsville. He was married to Anna (née Vrabel, 1878–1963) with whom he had: Helen, Ashton, George, Catherine, Elizabeth, Olga, Anna, Michael, and Joseph. Hoblak died on July 5, 1948, and was buried in Fern Knoll Burial Park, Dallas, Pa.

---

**Stephen Hodio** was born on August 10, 1888, in Budapest, Austro-Hungarian Empire [now Hungary] to a Lemko father and a Rusyn mother. He immigrated in 1902 and settled in Yonkers, N.Y., where by 1908, he worked on his own account as a carpet weaver at 10 Seymour St. In 1910 he was listed as a weaver working in a carpet mill in Yonkers, N.Y. Later on he moved his family to Seymour, Conn. In 1940 he was listed a weaver at a carpet mill. He was married three times: Anna Katrinics, an unknown second wife, and Mary (née Dupay, 1898–1982) and had the following children: Olga, Alexander, Faust, Timothy, and Dorothy. Hodio died on December 1, 1953, and was buried in the Lakeview Cemetery, Bridgeport, Conn.

106. Stephen Hodio, 1908

**John Holda** was born on October 17, 1875, in the Lemko village of Świerżowa Ruska, Jasło County, Austrian Empire [present-day Poland]. He immigrated in 1896 and worked in mining. In 1900 he became the manager of the Little Russian Store Co. at 139 N. Oak St. in Mt. Carmel, Pa., which carried a select line of groceries, dry goods, notions, furnishing goods, and work clothing. However, in 1907, he was forced to file for bankruptcy, at which time he owed $1,000, $500 of which was unsecured. The bankruptcy sale was held later that year. In 1910, 1920, and at the time of his death, he was listed as a miner. In 1917 be became a charter member of the Ruthenian Greek Catholic Saint Demetri Benevolent Society of Mt. Carmel, and he was a Republican committeeman from the Diamondtown district. He was married to Barbara (1878–1932) with whom he had: Paul, Myron, Anna, Mary Simchok, Walter, and Olga. Holda died on March 3, 1930, and was buried in Saints Peter and Paul Greek Catholic Cemetery, Mount Carmel, Pa. He was remembered as "one of the most prominent political leaders of Mt. Carmel."

---

**Dionizi Holod** was born on October 8, 1870, in the Lemko village of Ług, Gorlice County, Austro-Hungarian Empire [present-day Poland] into the family of Ivan and Matrona (née Pavlikovska). He immigrated in 1888 and settled in Jersey City, N.J., where for ten years he worked in a sugar refinery. In 1899 he bought a four-story house and opened a hotel. During the first decade of the 20th century he was listed as the owner of a saloon/café at 38 Green St. By 1917, however, he had moved to Orange, N.Y., where he was listed as a machinist's helper. By 1920 he had moved to Port Jervis, N.Y., where he engaged in business once again as a merchant (grocery), but by 1930 he was once again listed as a machinist's helper. He was married to Olena (née Spiak, 1869–1947) with who he had: Mary Lysiak and Olga Borowski. Holod died on August 11, 1937, and was buried in Saint Mary's Cemetery, Port Jervis, N.Y.

107. Dionizi Holod, 1903

**Paul Holowczak** was born on May 15, 1892, in the Lemko village of Tylicz, Nowy Sącz County, Austro-Hungarian Empire [present-day Poland] and immigrated in 1904. He settled in Cleveland, Ohio, where he was first listed as a laborer. By 1927 he owned Holowczak Funeral Home at 2387 Professor Ave. In 1955 he moved his residence and business to 1208 Kenilworth Ave., a property that he had purchased for $15,000. He was married to Anna (née Pelechaty, 1906–1985) with whom he had: Paul, Peter, and Joseph. Holowczak died on November 26, 1961, and was buried in Saints Peter and Paul Ukrainian Catholic Cemetery, Parma, Ohio. His wife continued to operate his business, which was moved to 5548 State Road, Parma, Ohio. It remains there to this day and continues to be family operated.

108. Paul Holowczak, 1930

109. Paul Holowczak, 1937

110. Paul Holowczak, 1940

**Justin Homiak** was born in 1870 in the Lemko village of Wawrzka, Grybów County, Austro-Hungarian Empire [present-day Poland], immigrated in 1888 and settled in Excelsior, Pa. He later moved to Diamondtown, Pa., just north of Mt. Carmel, where he ran a hotel at 401 Maple St. for twenty years. He also worked in real estate and owned a bowling alley. From 1915 to 1927 he lived in Atlas, Pa. During the Great Depression he lost his business and his home. With his five (six?) children from his first marriage to Mary (née Bencroski) and nine children from his second marriage to Eva (née Worhach), the family became homeless. Not able to provide for their children, the Homiaks decided to send them to Catholic orphanages for care, except for the youngest who was given up for adoption. The parents later lived in Catawissa, Pa., Wilkes-Barre, Pa., again in Exchange, Pa, and finally in Weight Scales, Pa. In 1930, Homiak was listed as a miner. He died on April 2, 1940, and was buried out of St. Michael's Russian Orthodox Church in Mt. Carmel, Pa., where he had been the founding president many years earlier.

### НАЙЛУЧШІЙ РУССКІЙ ГОТЕЛЬ
# ЮСТИНА ХОМЯКА
### 401 Maple St., Mt. Carmel, Pa.

 За барою всегда свѣжое пиво, старо-краевая и тутейшая водка, найлучшіи вина, добрыи цигара и папиросы.

Для пріѣзджаючихъ въ якомъ нибудь дѣлѣ до Мт. Кармелъ безплатно всякая точная и докладная информація въ всякихъ справахъ. Кому интересъ вымагае остатись тутъ пару дней, тотъ знайде у г-на Юстина Хомяка выгодное умѣщеніе, а также здоровую и смачную перекуску.

**Русины памятайте о томъ и не забудьте адресса.**

111. Justin Homiak, 1909

---

**Paul Homiak** was born on July 3, 1870, in the Lemko village of Wawrzka, Grybów County, Austro-Hungarian Empire [present-day Poland] and immigrated in 1886 (1888?). He settled in Shamokin, Pa., where he first worked as a miner. By 1913, he had a saloon/hotel and a boarding house at 500 S. Vine St. In 1920, he was still listed as a hotel keeper, but by 1922 he was listed as a laborer and later as a miner again. He was married to Thecla/Tillie (née Nowak, 1875–1918) with whom he had: John, Mary, Kate, Jennie, Eugenia, Olga, Sophie, Celia, Walter, Anna, Isadore, and Eddie. He also had one son from another relationship. Homiak died on June 26, 1947, and was buried in the Transfiguration Ukrainian Catholic Cemetery, Coal Township, Pa.

**Theodore Homiak** was born in 1859 in the Lemko village of Wawrzka, Grybow County, Austrian Empire [present-day Poland] and immigrated in 1884 or 1885. He first settled in Excelsior, Pa., but in 1896 moved to Mt. Carmel, Pa. In 1900 he was listed as a coal miner. In 1905 he was described as "one of our town's best-known hotel men" and also operated the only licensed saloon in the Seventh Ward of Shamokin, Pa. He was also listed as a saloon owner in 1910 and by 1912 owned a hotel at 409 N. Market St. He retired several years before his death. He was married to Anna (née Gardysh, 1862–1905) with whom he had: John, Steve, Sophia Zuk, Helen Spak, Peter, George, and Theodore. Homiak died on August 19, 1936, and was buried in Saints Peter & Paul Greek Catholic Cemetery. Mt. Carmel, Pa. He was remembered as an "industrious man and was held in high regards by everyone. He took active interests in community affairs."

**Anthony W. Homick** was born on December 25, 1883, in the Lemko village of Świątkowa Wielka, Jasło County, Austro-Hungarian Empire [present-day Poland] and immigrated in 1900. He settled in Waterbury, Conn., where he worked as a laborer and from 1918 as a policeman. In 1921, he opened a beverage business at 12 Vine St. and by 1923 he had created a real estate office there, which in 1930 he moved to 759 Cooke St. He was still working there in 1939 and retired by 1946. He was the owner of a number of houses. He was active in various local Russophile and mainstream American organizations. He set up a local branch of the Russian Brotherhood Organization, which he also served at a national level. He was married to Julia (née Sym, 1883–19??) with whom he had: William, Anna, Stephen, Frank, Mary, and John. Homick died on January 15, 1957.

112. Anthony W. Homick, 1930

**Walter Honcharik** was born on October 9, 1898, in the Lemko village of Hańczowa, Gorlice County, Austro-Hungarian Empire [present-day Poland] and immigrated in 1920. He settled in Yonkers, N.Y., where in 1927 he was listed as a butcher and a year later opened his grocery/butcher shop at 359 Nepperhan Ave. In 1933 his business was listed by the U.S.

Department of Commerce on a National Recovery Administration honor roll. The next year he moved his store to 46 Bennett Ave., where he operated it until his death. In 1939 he received a license to sell beer. He was a member of the Little Russian Corporation and the treasurer of the Lemko Association. He was married to Esther (née Mikuliak, 1898–1991) with whom he had: Mary and Olga. Honcharik died on October 5, 1951, and was buried in Mount Hope Cemetery in Hastings-on-Hudson, N.Y.

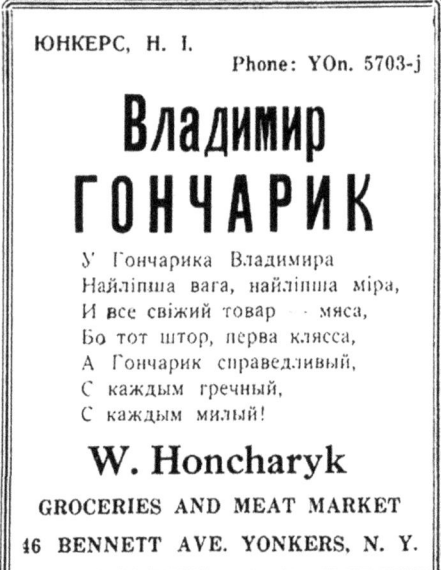

113. Walter Honcharik, 1936    114. Walter Honcharik, 1942

**Alexis Horbal** was born on December 27, 1876, in the Lemko village of Bartne, Gorlice County, Austro-Hungarian Empire [present-day Poland] into the family of Ivan and Maryia (née Dutkanych). He immigrated in 1891 and first lived, probably, in Elmira Heights, N.Y., later for six years somewhere in Pennsylvania, and briefly in Jersey City, N.J., before joining his brother Hieronym in Derby, Conn. In 1900 he was listed as a factory worker, but by 1908 he had a grocery/meat store at 135 Main St. and later also a saloon in partnership with Harry Zuraw. He was also a notary public, sold steamship tickets, arranged travel, and wired money. He was active in the Russian/Little Russian National Union (later Ukrainian National Association) and unsuccessfully ran for its

115. Alexis Horbal, 1913

presidency in 1912. He was married to Theodosia/Tevdozka (née Felenchak, 1881–19??) with whom he had: Olena, Peter, Andrew, Myron, Dorothy, and Louise. On June 20, 1914, his body was found in Lake Housatonic in a canoe; the press reported that he was in financial trouble. The court took control of his twelve properties plus the store, but it was also stated in the press that "at present, the condition of his business is unknown." In 1920 his wife was listed as a grocery owner.

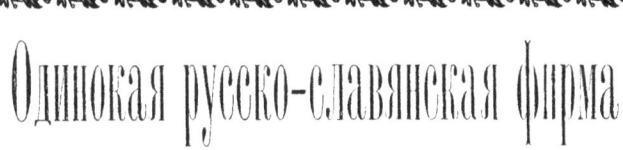

116. Alexis Horbal, 1909

## Алексїй Горбаль
### NOTARY PUBLIC
135 Main Str., ═══════════ Telephone 586-5
### DERBY, CONN.

Має гарно уряджений стор, ґросерню, бучерню і всякого рода инші товари. — Посилає гроші до старого краю дуже скоро, безпечно і тано. — Продає шифкарти на всї корабельні лінії до і з Европи по цїнах установлених головною компанїєю. — Продає драфти котрі суть платнї по цїлім сьвітї. — Вишукує роботу для дївчат і для мужчин. Взагалї помагає всїм, хто до него зголосить ся о пораду.

117. Alexis Horbal, 1910

**Peter Horoschak** was born on July 1, 1868, in the Lemko village of Bogusza, Grybów County, Austro-Hungarian Empire [present-day Poland] to Anastazyia Choroszczak. He immigrated at the age of 16. He settled in Mt. Carmel, Pa., where by 1901, he had a liquor wholesale business at 100 Exchange St. He was married to Sophia (née Shuptar, 1883–1974) with whom he had: Paul, Mary, Theodore, Stella, and Sophia. Horoschak died on November 30, 1915, and was buried in Saints Peter and Paul Greek Catholic Cemetery, Mt. Carmel, Pa. It was remembered that "He was ambitious and energetic and was successful as a businessman. He was a charter member of the St. Demetri Society of the Greek Catholic Church and was well known in this section among men of all nationalities."

ГУРТОВНЫЙ СКЛАДЪ ВСЕЛЯКИХЪ НАПОЕВЪ
## Петра Горощака
100 Exchange, - Mt. Carmel, Pa.

Всякіи замовленія пива, виски или другихъ напоевъ, доставляе сейчасъ власными кôньми на мѣстце; до пива лѣтною порою додае скôлько треба леду, по посудину порожну опять самъ прѣѣзджае, все то безъ ниякои особнои доплаты. За чистоту и доброту напоевъ ручае. На всѣ оказіи, забавы или для домашнього ужитку, повиненъ каждый, потребный напой у Петра Горощака яко честного Русина, ордеровати, а певно каждый якъ изъ напоевъ такъ и обслуги буде вдоволеный.

118. Peter Horoschak, 1901

**Simon Horoshchak** was born on April 4, 1865, in the Lemko village of Bogusza, Grybów County, Austrian Empire [present-day Poland] into the family of Osyf and Fenna (née Chermanski). He immigrated in 1885 and settled in Shamokin, Pa., where in 1909 he was listed as a manager. In 1910 he became one of the directors of the Ruthenian Store Company. He also served as the manager of this company for ten years. For the last nine years of his life he had his own grocery store at 608 East Commerce St., which was continued by his wife. He was married to **Anna** (1885–1953) with whom he had six children: Anna, Mary Howard, Jacob, Walter, August, and Theodore. Horoshchak died on February, 20 1925, and was buried in Transfiguration of Our Lord Greek Catholic Cemetery, Coal Township. He was remembered as "one of Shamokin's best-known merchants and most highly esteemed residents."

---

**John Hotz** was born on September 25, 1889, in the Lemko village of Krempna, Jasło County, Austro-Hungarian Empire [present-day Poland] into the family of Ivan and Anna (née Paryllo). He immigrated in 1905 and settled in Cleveland, Ohio, where he was first listed as a laborer, and later as a fireman. In 1919 he opened Hotz Café, located at 2529 W. 10th St. at the corner of Starkweather Avenue in the Tremont neighborhood where many Rusyns lived. In 1920 he was listed as a saloon keeper. During Prohibition the café served as a speakeasy, an illicit establishment that sold alcoholic beverages, while Hotz was listed as a fireman. During 1939–1940 Hotz was listed as having another bar at 2503 Professor St. After World War II, two of John Hotz's sons, Andrew and Mike, joined the family business, which expanded to a storefront next door, where Andrew's wife operated a beauty salon. John Hotz was first married to Freida (née Rusin, 1893–1920) with whom he had: John, Steve, William, and Mike. He was later married to Barbara (née Zaporach, 1896-1972) with whom he had: Peter and Andrew. Hotz died on February 6, 1974, and was buried at Saint Theodosius Orthodox Cemetery, Brooklyn, Ohio. The current owner of Hotz Café, John Hotz, is the grandson of the founder.

119. John Hotz, 1919

---

**Basil Hrishko** was born on January 6, 1877, in the Lemko village of Szczawne, Sanok County, Austro-Hungarian Empire [present-day Poland] into the family of Antonii and Anastazyia (née Guzy). He immigrated in 1889 and settled in Scranton, Pa., where in 1904 he was first listed as an apprentice at Svoboda newpaper and later as a manager of the First Ruthenian Book Store. In 1910 he was listed as a printer, working on his own account. By 1915 he had his store at 701 Lackawanna Ave. In 1919 he moved to Allentown, Pa. and in 1920 was listed as a bookkeeper working on his own account.

His dry goods store was located at 161 Tilghman St. He was still in business in 1940. From 1908 to 1929 he served the Ruthenian (later Ukrainian) National Association as vice-president and comptroller. He was married to Rose (née Homik, 1884-1938) with whom he had: Gregory, Olga, Myron, Helen Jowyk, Daniel, and Emily Kemmerer. Hrishko died on October 26, 1952, and was buried in St. Mary Ukrainian Orthodox Cemetery, Fullerton, Pa.

> **Василь Гришко**
>
> провадить двадцять шість років одинокий український стор (склеп) на околицю: Алентавн - Бетлегем - Нортгемптон, де можете дістати стемповані річи до вишивання, як: обруси, скарфи, накриття на ліжка, пошивки на подушки і т. п. Нитки до вишивання і геклювання різного кольору і якости.
>
> Великий вибір стінних Календарів з українськими святами і артистичними образками. Українські картки з побажанням Різдвяних і Великодніх Свят.
>
> Великий вибір карток в англійській мові на всі оказії, які трапляються в цілім році і в роднім життю.
>
> **BASIL HRISHKO**
> 161 Tilghman St.        Allentown, Pa.
> Telephone 3-2651

120. Basil Hrishko

---

**Daniel Humecki** was born on January 1, 1893, in the Lemko village of Uście Ruskie, Gorlice County, Austro-Hungarian Empire [present-day Poland] and immigrated in 1909. In 1910 he was listed as a porter in a restaurant in Pittsburgh, Pa. By 1915, and still in 1917, he worked as a waiter. He later had a grocery/meat store in Heidelberg, Pa., but went bankrupt. During the Great Depression he lost his house. In 1930 he was listed as an assessor in Pittsburgh, Pa. From 1926 he held various national posts in the Russian Brotherhood Organization and eventually moved to Philadelphia, Pa., where the organization had its headquarters. By 1942 he had a beer garden/café with a pool room in Philadelphia at 901 N. Fourth Street. He also had a business in Hannover, Pa. He was married to Frances E. (née Mahaven (Muchewicz), 1893–1968) with whom he had: Dorothy, Francis, Irene, and Dolores. Humecki died on April 6, 1970, and was buried in Arlington Cemetery, Drexel Hill, Pa.

---

**Orest Hyra** was born on November 24, 1879, in the Lemko village of Zdynia, Gorlice County, Austro-Hungarian Empire [present-day Poland] into the family of Hryts and Katrena (née Fylak). He immigrated at the age of 18 and at first lived briefly with his brother in West Troy, N.Y., before moving to Yonkers, N.Y. and working for eight years in a foundry in New York City. He then went to a barber school and by 1905 had opened his barber shop, which he sold in 1910 to buy a saloon located at 66 Main St. in Yonkers. In 1918 he sold the saloon and moved to Bridgeport, Conn., where he purchased a grocery/butcher store. After 12 years he sold his store and moved to Brooklyn, N.Y., where he bought a building. There he opened a grocery store and had rooms for rent. He was married to Anna (née Durniak, 1890–1939) with whom he had six children. Hyra died on July 23, 1941, and was buried in the (old) St. Michael Russian Orthodox Cemetery in Old Forge, Pa., from where his wife originated.

## Орестъ Гира

Тримае въ Юнкерсѣ на 66 Мейнъ стритъ

### Добре заряженый русскій ГОТЕЛЬ.

#### Одинъ блокъ отъ дипа.

Перворядный бордъ, добрыи напоѣ, щиро-русска обслуга.

Въ потребѣ каждому добра порада.

**66 Main street.**      **Yonkers, N. Y.**

121. Orest Hyra, 1909

---

**Stephen J. Jewusiak** was born on July 2, 1875, in the Lemko village of Łosie, Gorlice County, Austro-Hungarian Empire [present-day Poland] into the family of Ivan and Maryia (née Voitovych). He immigrated in 1882 and settled in Olyphant, Pa., where he worked at a mine. In 1890 he moved to Bayonne, N.J., where he first worked in various factories. In 1897 he became a director at a funeral home, and in 1900 he opened his funeral home located at 45 Prospect Ave. By 1922 his business was located at 77 Morris St. in Jersey City, N.J., but he still lived in Bayonne. In 1922 his son, Harry, was listed as an embalmer and by 1925, he joined his father as a co-owner. The business was renamed Stephen J. Jewusiak and Son, and limousines to hire were added to its offerings. He was married to Anna (née Mashonski, 1880–1964) with whom he had: Mary, Harry, Joseph, Michael, Walter, and Helen. Jewusiak died on January 24, 1938, and was buried in the Holy Cross Cemetery, North Arlington, N.J. His business was continued by a son.

122. Stephen J. Jewusiak, 1925

123. Stephen J. Jewusiak, 1928

---

**John Kaczmarczyk** was born on February 10, 1879, in the Lemko village of Męcina Wielka, Gorlice County, Austro-Hungarian Empire [present-day Poland] into the family of Mykhal and Iefroska (née Borik). He immigrated in 1898 and a year later he already had a saloon at 213 W. Centre St. in Mahanoy City, Pa. In 1904 he purchased a retail liquor license from Frank E. Mikailek. A year later, he transferred that license to John Cosmarchike. In 1912 he purchased a wholesale license from Ballatine Bottling Company. In 1917 he was listed as the owner of a saloon at 521 W. Pine and a liquor business at 1125 E. Pine St. At the latter address he had a bottling business in the late 1920s. In 1919, he sold a lot in Mahanoy City, Pa., to Metro Humnik for $2,100. He was married to Mary (1889–1927) with whom he had: Julia, Mikhal, Olga, Vladimir, Isabela, and Basil. Kaczmarczyk died on May 8, 1947, and was buried in St. Mary's Greek Catholic (Old) Cemetery, Mahanoy City.

---

**Joseph Kaczmarczyk** was born on January 1, 1870, in the Lemko village of Męcina Wielka, Gorlice County, Austrian Empire [present-day Poland] and immigrated in 1888. By 1897 he had a saloon at 615 W. Pine St., Mahanoy City, Pa., and in the same year filed an application for a retail license. In 1904 he secured transfer of a wholesale license from Jacob *Onuschak for the sale of the products of the Baettle Bottling Co. In 1905 he received a retail license. Since 1909, and at least until 1917, his saloon was located at 511 W. Pine St. In the late 1920s, he was not listed among business owners of Mahanoy City, Pa. He was married to Ethel/Natalka (née Korin, 1877–1946) with whom he had: John, Anna, William, Michael, Stephen, and Theodore. Kaczmarczyk died on March 16, 1931, and was buried in St. Nicholas Ukrainian Catholic Cemetery, Mahanoy City.

---

**Gmitro Kapitula** was born on November 6, 1872, in the Lemko village of Świątkowa Wielka, Jasło County, Austro-Hungarian Empire [present-day Poland]. His parents were Teodor and Mary (née Koban). He immigrated in 1888 and settled in McAdoo, Pa. His first job was picking slate out of coal. He later joined McAdoo's Police Department, from 1897 to 1900, and also worked as a teamster. He opened his hotel in 1901 and ran it at the corner of Grand and Tamaqua Streets until 1926. He served on the directorate of the First National Bank of McAdoo from its establishment in 1907 (with capital of $25,000) until 1918. During later years, he served on the governing body of the McAdoo Property Owners' Association. From 1937 he also worked as an insurance agent and notary public. He served two terms on the City Council (its president 1915–1916), one term as treasurer (1904-1906), several terms as property assessor, Registrar of Vital Statistics (1941–1953), and was the commandant of McAdoo's Police Department (1920–1930). He was one of the founders of St. Mary's Greek Catholic parish. A member of the Russian National Union (later Ukrainian National Association) from 1898, he later served as its national president (1908–1917), and national auditor (1933–1953). He first married, in 1901, Julia (1866–1934) with whom he had Mary Bristow. His second wife was Matrona (née Segletsky/Hladym, 1889–1970) with who he had two step-daughters: Helen Slovik and Stella Stefanisko. Kapitula died on December 25, 1953, and was buried in St. Mary's Ukrainian Catholic Cemetery in McAdoo, Pa.

124. Gmitro Kapitula, 1944

125. Gmitro Kapitula, 1903

126. Gmitro Kapitula, 1913

127. Gmitro Kapitula, 1914

REGISTRATION CARD 3522

SERIAL NUMBER 3499 ORDER NUMBER

1 Gmitro Kapitula
(First name) (Middle name) (Last name)

2 PERMANENT HOME ADDRESS:
103 W Blain str McAdoo Schuylkill Pa
(No.) (Street or R. F. D. No.) (City or town) (County) (State)

Age in Years 3 44 Date of Birth 4 Nov. 3 1873
(Month.) (Day.) (Year.)

RACE

| White | Negro | Oriental | Indian | |
|---|---|---|---|---|
| | | | Citizen | Noncitizen |
| 5 ✓ | 6 | 7 | 8 | 9 |

| U. S. CITIZEN | | | ALIEN | |
|---|---|---|---|---|
| Native Born | Naturalized | Citizen by Father's Naturalization Before Registrant's Majority | Declarant | Non-declarant |
| 10 | 11 ✓ | 12 | 13 | 14 |

15
If not a citizen of the U. S., of what nation are you a citizen or subject?

| PRESENT OCCUPATION | EMPLOYER'S NAME |
|---|---|
| 16 Hotel Keeper and Notary Public | 17 By myself |

18 PLACE OF EMPLOYMENT OR BUSINESS:
103 W. Blain Str McAdoo Schuylkill Pa
(No.) (Street or R. F. D. No.) (City or town) (County) (State)

Wife
NEAREST RELATIVE Name 19 Julia Kapitula
Address 20 103 W. Blain Str McAdoo. Pa
(No.) (Street or R. F. D. No.) (City or town) (County) (State)

I AFFIRM THAT I HAVE VERIFIED ABOVE ANSWERS AND THAT THEY ARE TRUE

P. M. G. O.
Form No. 1 (Red)
Gmitro Kapitula
(Registrant's signature or mark) (OVER)

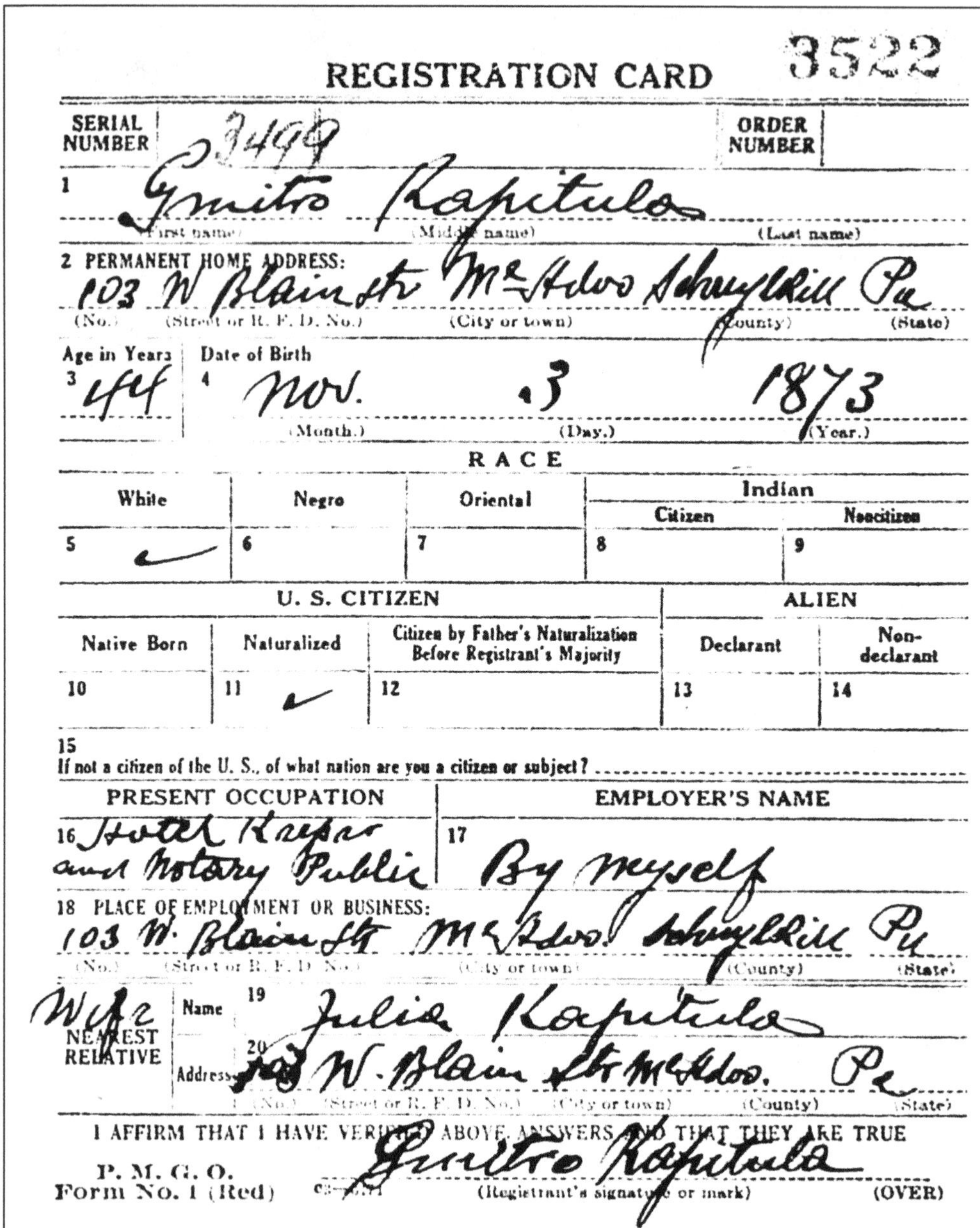

128. Gmitro Kapitula, 1918

---

**Michael Karell** was born on July 17, 1895, in the Lemko village of Łosie, Gorlice County, Austro-Hungarian Empire [present-day Poland] and immigrated in 1913. He settled in Yonkers, N.Y., where he first worked at a carpet factory. In the early 1920s he opened a grocery store at 5 Madison Ave., which he operated for eighteen years. He later worked for Alexander Smith Co. for twenty years. He was married to Eva (née Wojtovich, 1892–1976) with whom he had: Walter, Alexander, and John. Karell died on January 16, 1969.

**Dimitry/Michael W. Karlak** was born on September 7, 1887, in the Lemko village of Nowica, Gorlice County, Austro-Hungarian Empire [present-day Poland] into the family of Wasil and Victoria (née Michniak). He immigrated in 1904 and began working on the railroad, but found the labor to be too rigorous for a small person. He later worked for Seymour Manufacturing, the Brixey Co., and finally Anaconda American Brass, in its plant in Ansonia, Conn., as a master mechanic. He retired from the latter but was called back in 1955 to help after the disastrous 1955 flood. He was one of the nine initial stock owners of the Seymour Russian Company (est. 1913) which was a food cooperative that served the Galician community in Seymour, Conn. From this, he learned the grocery business and started his own meat market at 161 West St., on the corner of New St. (also listed as being on 18 New St.) in Seymour. He ran this business as a side operation with his wife and children assisting him as he also worked in manufacturing. He extended credit to many of his fellow Galicians, but sometimes he had to sue for past due monies; many accounts were in arrears for thousands of dollars. In 1937 he sold the store to Timoleo Miliadou for $2,000. In 1939 his wife Maria bought a meat market grocery business from Jennie Czaplicki in Beacon Falls, Conn. It was located in the Gordon Building. Due to the pressures on manufacturing during World War II, there was no time to properly operate the business, so it was sold. Karlak was very active in the Galician Russophile community and was known as "Mr. Galician Rus'." He held various leadership positions in Galician Russophile organizations. He was an incorporator of the Holy Saint Archangel Michael Society, RBO Lodge 122 (1910) and an incorporator and the president of the St. Vladimir's Russian Orthodox Brotherhood Benevolent. He was also an incorporator and the president of the Galician-Russian American Club, which became the Russian American Club (1932), as well as a founder and Vice-President of the State Russian American Political Club (1938). He was married to Mary (née Michniak, 1886–1961) with whom he had: Ignaty/Otto, Ustina/Eunice, Helen/Olena, John, Peter, Michael, and William. Karlak died on January 23, 1981, and was buried in Pine Grove Cemetery in Ansonia.

129. Dimitry Karlak with family, 1928

130. Dimitry Karlak in Beacon Falls

**Ignatius/Hnat Selvestroff Karlak** was born on July 10, 1885, in the Lemko village of Przysłup, Gorlice County, Austro-Hungarian Empire [present-day Poland] and immigrated in 1904. He first lived in Brooklyn, N.Y., and later at 412 E. 70th St. and 411 E. 88th St. in Mahnattan. From 1925 to 1930 he was listed as a sawyer (?). In 1942 he was listed as the owner of a bar/grill at 1446 Madison Ave. in Manhattan. He was married to Julia (1889–1982) with who he had Nicholas. Karlak died on March 14, 1966.

```
Telephone: ATwater 9-9629

RESTAURANT, BAR & GRILL

ПЕРВОКЛАССНАЯ КУХНЯ
ВСЕВОЗМОЖНЫЕ НАПИТКИ
МѢСТНЫЕ И ИМПОРТИРОВАННЫЕ

Кто прiѣзжаетъ до Нью Іорку на Всемiрную
Выставку, пусть не забудетъ загостити до

ИГНАТІЯ КАРЛЯКА
ЧЛЕНЪ О. Р. Б.

1446 MADISON AVENUE
(Между 99 и 100 ул.)
NEW YORK, N. Y.
```

131. Ignatius Selvestroff Karlak, 1940

**Wasil Karlak** was born on March 31, 1883, in the Lemko village of Nowica, Gorlice County, Austro-Hungarian Empire [present-day Poland] and immigrated in 1901. He settled in New York City, where by 1917 he had a grocery store at 419 E. 70th St. By 1925 his store was located at 535 E. 17th St., where he was still in business in the 1930s. He was married to Mildred/Melania (née Mikulak, 1888–1973) with whom he had: Mary, Paul, Stephen, Joseph, and Annie. Karlak died on October 25, 1970, and was buried in Mt. Olivet Cemetery, Maspeth, N.Y.

```
┌┈┈┈┈┈┈┈┈┈┈┈┈┈┈┈┈┈┈┈┈┈┈┈┈┈┈┈┈┈┈┈┈┈┐
┊        ГРОССЕРНЯ И ДЕЛИКАТЕССЫ        ┊
┊             ВАСИЛІЯ КАРЛЯКА            ┊
┊  Каждый день свѣжи товары: Масло, сыры, ужинины, ┊
┊         консервы. Сендвичи наша спеціяльность!     ┊
┊       Старокраева перворядна брындзя и грибы.      ┊
┊  Высыламе и по почтѣ ордеры C. O. D. можна тоже.   ┊
┊       Брындзѣ въ одной дѣжечкѣ 11 фунтовъ.         ┊
┊                 W. KARLAK                          ┊
┊  535 East 17th Street        Neew York, N. Y.     ┊
└┈┈┈┈┈┈┈┈┈┈┈┈┈┈┈┈┈┈┈┈┈┈┈┈┈┈┈┈┈┈┈┈┈┘
```

132. Wasil Karlak, 1929

**Andrew Kasych** was born on April 26 (May 15?), 1894, in the Lemko village of Świerżowa Ruska, Jasło County, Austro-Hungarian Empire [present-day Poland] and immigrated in 1912. He settled in Cleveland, Ohio, where by 1917, he had a grocery store at 725 Starkweather Ave., which later evolved into a grocery/meat store and by 1925 was moved to 4716 W. 35th St. In 1940 he was listed as the owner of a café and after the early 1940s was listed as the owner of a beer garden at 4716 W. 35th St. He was still in business there in 1958. He was married to Mary (née Nestor, 1898–1945) with whom he had: Daniel and Raymond. Kasych died on April 28, 1959, and was buried in St. Theodosius Orthodox Cemetery, Brooklyn, Ohio.

```
┌─────────────────────────────┐
│   CLEVELAND, OHIO           │
│        Tel. FLorida 2205    │
│                             │
│     Andy Kasych             │
│     Fine Beer & Wine        │
│       and Luncheons         │
│                             │
│  У краяна Андрея Касича     │
│  достанете найлучшу обслугу.│
│    Заходте до свого.        │
│                             │
│ 4716 W. 35 St.  Cleveland 9, Ohio │
└─────────────────────────────┘
```

133. Andrew Kasych, 1949

```
┌─────────────────────────────┐
│   CLEVELAND, OHIO           │
│                             │
│      Tel. FLorida 1-2854    │
│                             │
│      Andy Kasych            │
│      Fine Beer & Wine       │
│        and Luncheons        │
│                             │
│  Андрей Касич краян близкий,│
│  Родом зо Свіржовы Русской, │
│  Добрый лемко, добрый бизнесиста. │
│  У него все полна хижа,     │
│  Свіжы пива — стары вина,   │
│  Из Нью Йорку и с Парижа,   │
│  А и такы вам шампаны,      │
│  Што лем пили давно паны.   │
│  У него сой прекусите       │
│  И здоровля подкріпите.     │
│  У кого здравля найсильнійше,│
│  Тому житья найвеселіьше.   │
│                             │
│     ЗАХОДТЕ ДО НЕГО         │
│ 4716 W. 35 St.  Cleveland 9, Ohio │
└─────────────────────────────┘
```

134. Andrew Kasych, 1958

**Charles Kasych** was born on March 12, 1887, in the Lemko village of Kotań, Jasło County, Austro-Hungarian Empire [present-day Poland] and immigrated in 1904. He first settled in Whitehall, Pa., where in 1910 he was listed as a repairman. By 1917 he had moved to Allentown, Pa., where he was listed as a machinist at Inter Motor Car Co. In 1930 he was listed as a salesman and in 1938 a a trucker. By 1940 he worked for himself. First, he operated a gas station, Kasych Service Station, on MacArthur Road and Schadt Avenue, and later he and his son operated the Highway Army and Navy Store, also on MacArthur Road. He was married to Eva (née Popowchak, 1889–1976)

```
FORM 115.—CERTIFIED COPY OF DECLARATION                TRIPLICATE
No. 16890          U. S. DEPARTMENT OF LABOR      To be given to the person making
                      NATURALIZATION SERVICE            the declaration
```

# UNITED STATES OF AMERICA

## DECLARATION OF INTENTION

☞ Invalid for all purposes seven years after the date hereof.

United States of America } ss:   In the  U. S. District  Court
Northern District of Ohio          of  Cleveland, Ohio

I, Andrew Kasych, aged 24 years, occupation merchant, do declare on oath that my personal description is: Color white, complexion fair, height 5 feet 7 inches, weight 160 pounds, color of hair blond, color of eyes gray, other visible distinctive marks none. I was born in Swierzowa, Jaslo Galicia Austria on the 15 day of May, anno Domini 1894; I now reside at 725 Starkwather Ave., Cleveland, Ohio. I emigrated to the United States of America from Bremen Germany, on the vessel George Washington; my last foreign residence was Swierzowa, Galicia; I am married; the name of my wife is Mary; she was born at Munsen, Pa. and now resides at Cleveland with me. It is my bona fide intention to renounce forever all allegiance and fidelity to any foreign prince, potentate, state, or sovereignty, and particularly to Charles, emperor of Austria and Apostolic king of Hungary, of whom I am now a subject; I arrived at the port of New York, in the State of New York, on or about the 19 day of June, anno Domini 1909; I am not an anarchist; I am not a polygamist nor a believer in the practice of polygamy; and it is my intention in good faith to become a citizen of the United States of America and to permanently reside therein: SO HELP ME GOD.

*Andrew Kasych*
(Original signature of declarant)

Subscribed and sworn to before me in the office of the Clerk of said Court this 11 day of March, anno Domini 1918.

[SEAL]            B. C. Miller,
                Clerk of the U. S. District Court.
            By  M C. Petrich, Deputy Clerk

135. Andrew Kasych, 1918

with whom he had: Charles Jr., Mary Markowicz, Anna, Vera, Julia Olaynick, Helen Buchanan, and Mildred Calkins. Kasych died on November 28, 1975, and was buried in St. Mary's Ukrainian Orthodox Cemetery, Fullerton, Pa.

ORIGINAL
(To be retained by clerk)

No. 7110

# UNITED STATES OF AMERICA

## DECLARATION OF INTENTION
(Invalid for all purposes seven years after the date hereof)

STATE OF PENNSYLVANIA  
COUNTY OF LEHIGH  
ss:

In the COMMON PLEAS Court of LEHIGH COUNTY at ALLENTOWN PA.

I, Charles Kasych now residing at 109 Ridge Ave. Allentown, Lehigh County, Penna. occupation trucker, aged 50 years, do declare on oath that my personal description is: Sex male, color white, complexion fair, color of eyes brown, color of hair brown, height 5 feet 9 inches, weight 176 pounds; visible distinctive marks none, race Polish; nationality Poland. I was born in Kotau Galicia Poland, on Mar. 12, 1887. I am married. The name of my wife or husband is Eva we were married on May 10, 1909, at Brooklyn N.Y.; she or he was born at Krempna Poland, on Apr. 16, 1892, entered the United States at New York N.Y., on Sept. 15, 1906, for permanent residence therein, and now resides at with me. I have 7 children, and the name, date and place of birth, and place of residence of each of said children are as follows: Mary born 2/17/12, Anna 1/11/14, Charles 3/11/16, Julia 11/27/18, Helen 2/4/23, Mildred 5/6/25 & Vera 9/18/27. First 2 born in W. Coplay Pa. Others in Allentown, Pa. where all live with me.

I have no theretofore made a declaration of intention: Number _____, on _____, at _____; my last foreign residence was Kotau Galicia Poland. I emigrated to the United States of America from Bremen, Germany. my lawful entry for permanent residence in the United States was at New York, under the name of Wasyl Kasycz, on Nov. 2-30, 1904 on the vessel SS (unknown).

I will, before being admitted to citizenship, renounce forever all allegiance and fidelity to any foreign prince, potentate, state, or sovereignty, and particularly, by name, to the prince, potentate, state, or sovereignty of which I may be at the time of admission a citizen or subject; I am not an anarchist; I am not a polygamist nor a believer in the practice of polygamy; and it is my intention in good faith to become a citizen of the United States of America and to reside permanently therein; and I certify that the photograph affixed to the duplicate and triplicate hereof is a likeness of me: So HELP ME GOD.

Charles Kasych

Subscribed and sworn to before me in the office of the Clerk of said Court, at Allentown, Pa., this 5th day of Feb. anno Domini 19 38. "By Authority" Certification No. 2x 17110 from the Commissioner of Immigration and Naturalization showing the lawful entry of the declarant for permanent residence on the date stated above, has been received by me. The photograph affixed to the duplicate and triplicate hereof is a likeness of the declarant.

D. E. Serfass

[SEAL] Clerk of the Common Pleas Court.

By _____ , Deputy Clerk.

Form 2202-L-A  
U. S. DEPARTMENT OF LABOR  
IMMIGRATION AND NATURALIZATION SERVICE

[DO NOT ATTACH PHOTOGRAPH TO THIS COPY OF DECLARATION]

No. 42873

136. Charles Kasych, 1938

---

**Василь Касич**

Esso Gas Station

N. 7th St. Pike     Phone 3-9708

Route 1, ALLENTOWN, PA.

QUICK-COURTEOUS-SERVICE

**We also carry a large stock of Army and Navy Surplus Supplies**

137. Charles Kasych, 1949

**Peter Klymash** was born on October 15, 1893, in the Lemko village of Kłopotnica, Jasło County, Austro-Hungarian Empire [present-day Poland], immigrated in 1909 (1912?) and settled in Bridgeport, Conn. In 1917 he was listed as a clerk working in a store owned by fellow Lemkos Awksenty *Telep and Andrew *Dragan. In 1919 he rented a commercial place at 578 Lafayette St. and opened a grocery/meat market there with William Dragon. They were still partnering in 1921. After 1921 he had a meat market at 180 Ogden St. In 1925 he was listed as a butcher in Bridgeport, Conn., but later moved his business to Yonkers, N.Y., where by 1930 he had a meat market and grocery store at 35 Washington St. He was married to Tillie/Tekla (née Pupchyk, 1895–1974) with whom he had: Alice Skrulsky and Mary Sekelsky. Klymash died on July 6, 1963, and was buried in St. John the Baptist Greek Catholic Cemetery, Stratford, Conn.

```
ПЕТРЪ КЛИМАШЪ
ГРОССЕРЪ И БУЧЕРЪ ВЪ ЮНКЕРСЪ
Бо у Петра у Климаша
Всѣ товары перша кляса:
Масло, сыры, солонина,
Яйця, кава, уженина,
Каждый день все свѣжи мяса.
MEAT MARKET AND GROCERY
35 Washington St.          Yonkers, N. Y.
```

138. Peter Klymash, 1930

**Cost Koban** was born on July 8, 1866, in the Lemko village of Stawisza, Grybów County, Austrian Empire [present-day Poland] into the family of Ivan and Anastasia Kieselowska. After immigrating he settled in Olyphant, Pa., where by 1906 he had a liquor retail license and opened a hotel on Race Street. He was a signatory to the charter (1892) and one of the original trustees of St. Cyril's Greek (now Ukrainian) Catholic Church in Olyphant, Pa., and also served as national trustee of the Ruthenian (Ukrainian) National Association. He was married to **Fotina** (née Czar, 1872–1913) with whom he had: William, Vera, Nellie, Peter, Lena, and John. Koban died on July 8, 1908 and was buried in Saints Cyril and Methodius Greek Catholic Cemetery, Peckville, Pa. His wife continued his business, but she died at a young age as well.

**Aftanazy Koblosh** was born on July 17, 1890, in the Lemko village of Wysowa, Gorlice County, Austro-Hungarian Empire [present-day Poland] into the family of Mytro and Eva (née Hatala). He immigrated in 1905 and settled in Yonkers, N.Y., where he first worked in a carpet shop. In 1920 he was listed as a saloon owner, but the same year he opened a grocery/butcher shop at 348 Ashburn Ave. and operated it until his death. The business was continued by his son. He was married to Anna (née Durkot, 1895–1939) with whom he had: Michael and Helen. Koblosh died on May 26, 1938, and was buried in the Oakland Cemetery, Yonkers, N.Y.

**АФТАНАЗІЙ КОБЛОШЪ**

НАШЪ РУССКІЙ ЧЕЛОВѢКЪ

ПРОВАДИТЪ ПЕРВОКЛАСНУЮ

**ГРОСЕРНЮ и БУЧЕРНЮ**

У него получите все, что только захочете: Найлучшого сорта колбасы, солонину, старокраевыи грибы и проч. Кто разъ его товаръ попробуетъ, то не побануетъ, а потому то всегда у него купуетъ. Его адресъ:

**AFTANAZY KOBLOSH,**
348 Ashburton Avenue,
YONKERS, N Y.

139. Aftanazy Koblosh, 1926

**ПЕРВОРЯДНА ГРОССЕРНЯ И БУЧЕРНЯ**

АФТАНАСІЯ КОБЛОША

У Коблоша Афтанаса
Всѣ товары перша кляса:
Масло, сыры, солонина;
Яйця, кава, уженина;
Каждый день все свѣжи мяса,
А найлѣпша ужъ колбаса,
Что хочете, тамъ найдете,
Купите, не жалуете...
Кто разъ въ него попробуе
Ужъ въ другого не купуе...

**AFTANASY KOBLOSH**
GROCEER & BUCHER

348 Ashburton Ave.        Yonkers, N. Y.

140. Aftanazy Koblosh, 1929

Tel. Yonkers 3,2244

Compliments of

**KOBLOSH MARKET**

MEATS — GROCERIES — VEGETABLES

ICE CREAM — CANDY

BEER AND SODA

Въ сторѣ г-на Коблоша можно достати все свѣжи продукты, пиво и соду по найлучшихъ цѣнахъ. Услуга первоклассна.

348 ASHBURTON AVENUE        YONKERS, N. Y.

141. Aftanazy Koblosh, 1942

**Lewis Kochansky** was born in 1864 in the Lemko village of Muszynka, Nowy Sącz County, Austrian Empire [present-day Poland]. For 40 years he had a bottling business in Beaver Meadows, Pa. At the time of death, he was listed as an owner of a beer garden. He was married to Susanna (née Larzo) with whom he had: Joseph, John, Louis, William, Susan Klimkosky, and two other daughters. Kocansky died on September 28, 1938, and was buried in Saints Peter and Paul Byzantine Catholic Cemetery, Beaver Meadows, Pa. He was remembered as a "prominent businessman."

---

**Julian Kopyscianski** was born in 1863 in the Lemko village of Czertyżne, Grybów County, Austrian Empire [present-day Poland] into the family of Ivan and Ioanna. He immigrated in 1884 and settled in Shamokin, Pa. At first, he engaged in business together with Gabriel *Maliniak. They had a beer and liquor wholesale company located at 20 North Market St. By 1894 Kopyscianski had a saloon (described as a hotel in 1901) located at 424 N. Shamokin Street. By 1907 the hotel was located at 418 West Pine St. and was located there at least until 1915. He retired by 1918. Kopyscianski was married to Anna (née Chlebowsky, 1865–1914) with whom he had: John, Michael, Henry, Anthony, Theodore, Helen and Jeannine. Kopyscianski died on October 15, 1918, and was buried in Transfiguration of Our Lord Greek Catholic Cemetery, Coal Township, Pa.

142. Julian Kopyscianski, 1897

143. Julian Kopyscianski, 1897

144. Julian Kopyscianski, 1895

### Юлій Копистяньскій
#### готельникъ
ВЪ SHAMOKIN, PA. — 424 SHAMOKIN STR.

Русины, не минайте свого брата, Юлька, въ него дôстанете якъ найлѣпшій напитки.

145. Julian Kopyscianski

**John Korbelak** was born on October 3, 1866 in the Lemko village of Hańczowa, Gorlice County, Austrian Empire [present-day Poland] and immigrated in 1885/1887. He settled in Bayonne, N.J. In 1910 and 1915 he was listed as a wage-earning painter. In 1920 and still in 1930 he was listed as a painter/contractor working on his own account and employing people. He was also active in politics and was among the organizers and the first president of St. John's Greek Catholic Church, Bayonne, N.J. He was married to Anna (née Janiga, 1867–1938) with whom he had: Stephen, Annie, Julia Pabis, Mary Brady, John, George, and Margaret Cook. Korbelak died on March 31, 1940, and was buried in the Holy Cross Cemetery, North Arlington, N.J. He was remembered as a "well-known painting contractor."

JOHN KORBELAK
146

**Michael Korbelak** was born on March 27, 1889, in the Lemko village of Hańczowa, Gorlice County, Austro-Hungarian Empire [present-day Poland] and immigrated in 1906. In 1910 he was listed as a miner in Shamokin, Pa., but after 1911 he was working as a clerk in Ansonia, Conn. In 1915 he opened his meat market at 26 Clifton St. In 1917 he moved his grocery/meat market to 2 Lester St., where he operated it at least until 1955. In 1965 he was still listed as working in retail. He was married to Julia (née Rotko, 1895–1954) with whom he had: Alexander, William, Lida, Helen, and Louise. Korbelak died on October 20, 1972, and was buried in the Pine Grove Cemetery, Ansonia, Conn.

**Roman Korbicz** was born in December 1862 in the Lemko village of Śnietnica, Grybów County, Austrian Empire [present-day Poland] and immigrated in 1883. He settled in Shamokin, Pa., where in 1900 he was listed as a miner. In 1903 he applied for a retail liquor license and a year later advertised his hotel in Johnson City, outside Shamokin. In 1908 he applied for a general retail license. In 1910 he was listed as a saloon owner. He was in the retail business in 1920, but in 1930 he was listed as a farmer in Ralpho, Pa. He was married to Helen (née Fedko, 1868–1952) with whom he had: Levi, Michael, Susan Wislowskie, Anna Ferants, Anthony, Joseph, Mary Snyder, Stephen, Paul, and John. Korbicz died on October 8, 1932, and was buried in the Transfiguration Ukrainian Catholic Cemetery, Coal Township, Pa.

**Metro Koralko** was born on November 17, 1891, in the Lemko village of Radocyna, Gorlice County, Austro-Hungarian Empire [present-day Poland] into the family of Fetsko Kurylko and Maryia (née Syjczak). He immigrated in 1909 and settled in New York City, where in 1920 he was listed as a carpenter. By 1930 he had a grocery store in Brooklyn at 14 Bedford Ave. He was still in business in 1940. He was first married to Annie (née Wencl/Wenzel, 1894–1919) with whom he had Mary Meder. He was later married to Eva (née Stehnach, 1892–1970) with whom he had: Alexander, Olga Hrobuchak and John Carroll. Koralko died on April 18, 1963, and was buried in the Mount Olivet Cemetery, Maspeth, N.Y.

---

**ДИМИТРІЙ КУРИЛКО**
лемко изъ Радоцины, мае Рроссерню и Деликатессы въ Бруклинѣ. Краева брындзя. Купуйте у свого
GROECERIES & DELICATESSEN, 14 BEDFORD AVE., BROOKLYN

---

147. Metro Koralko, 1930

**Alex Kotys** was born on July 15, 1882, in the Lemko village of Daliowa, Sanok County, Austro-Hungarian Empire [present-day Poland] into the family of Ivan and Mary (née Gabla). He immigrated in 1901 and settled in Monessen, Pa., where in 1920, he was listed as a laborer. By 1924 he had a grocery store at 107 E Schoonmaker Ave. He was still in business in 1942 and at the time of his death was listed as a retired grocery store owner. He was married to Mary (1889–1932) with whom he had: Eva, Nick, Miroslav, Mary, Rose, and Olga. Kotys died on January 4, 1951, and was buried in Grandview Cemetery, Monessen, Pa.

**Alex Kowalchik** was born on March 17, 1871, in the Lemko village of Uście Ruskie, Gorlice County, Austro-Hungarian Empire [present-day Uście Gorlickie, Poland] and immigrated in 1892. By 1909 he was working on his own account as a plumber and tinsmith in Olyphant, Pa. By 1920 and to the time of his death he owned a hardware/furniture store at 116 (later 112-116) Grant St., which was later run by his wife. In the 1920s he was advertised as a dealer of Pratt and Lumber Varnish Products. At least from 1924 to 1931 he was one of the directors of the Miner's Savings Bank, which in 1930 had undivided profits of $160,000. He was also a member of the city council and served in the national leadership of the Russian Brotherhood Organization. He was married to **Kathryn** (née Chowanski, 1872–1952) with whom he had: Theofan, Amelia, Stephen, Olga and John. Kowalchik died on March 9, 1939, and was buried in Saints Cyril and Methodius Greek Catholic Cemetery, Peckville, Pa.

---

**Алексій Ковальчикъ,**
одинокій русскій пльомберъ и бляхаръ!
Race St, Olyphant, Pa.

Принимае всякіи роботы своего фаху. Мае великую роботню. Цѣны найнисшіи, робота совѣстная, артистичное выконанье.
———Русины! Памятайте на него.———

---

148. Alex Kowalchik, 1909

149. Alex Kowalchik, 1915

151. Alex Kowalchik, 1920

152. Alex Kowalchik, 1929

150. Alex Kowalchik, 1929

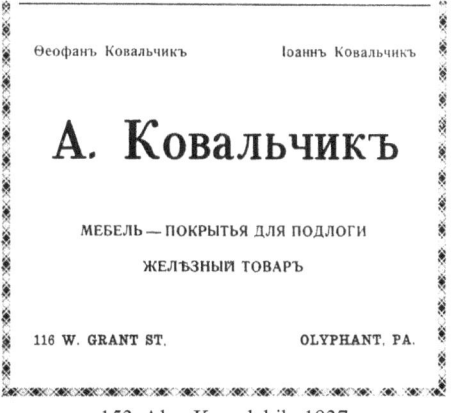

153. Alex Kowalchik, 1937

**Jacob Kowalczyk** was born on October 15, 1875, in the Lemko village of Gładyszów, Gorlice County, Austro-Hungarian Empire [present-day Poland] and immigrated in 1901. He settled in Yonkers, N.Y., where by 1909 he had a grocery store with his brother, Leon, at 449 Nepperhan Ave. By 1912 he had his own grocery at 342 Nepperhan Ave. and a year later moved his business for good to 12 Lockwood Ave. In the 1920s he partnered with John Borowits, whom Kowalczyk bought out in 1926. In 1935 he got a license to sell beer. He was married to Theresa (née Doshna, 1887–1987) with whom he had: Rose, Stephen, and Theodore. Kowalczyk died on

June 20, 1935, and was buried in Mount Hope Cemetery, Hastings-on-Hudson, N.Y.

**ЛАКВУДЪ МАРКЕТЪ**
ПЕРВОКЛАССНАЯ БУЧЕРНЯ И ГРОСЕРНЯ.
ТАМЪ ПОЛУЧИТЕ,
ЩО САМИ ЛИШЕНЬ ЗАХОЧЕТЕ:
СВѢЖОЕ МЯСО,
КОЛБАСУ,
ШИНКУ,
и проч.

Гей, Братья, чему жъ бы своего не поддержати,
а по жидахъ волочитися и
и свого оминати?

**JACOB KOWALCZIK**
12 Lockwood Ave.,     YONKERS, N. Y.

154. Jacob Kowalczyk, 1925

**Kyrylo "Kerey" Kowalczyk** was born on February 26, 1883, in the Lemko village of Łosie, Gorlice County, Austro-Hungarian Empire [present-day Poland] and immigrated in 1900. He settled in Yonkers, N.Y., where in 1903 he opened a grocery/butcher shop at 455 Nepperhan Ave. which he operated until his death. He was married to Johanna (née Skripak, 1884–1952) with whom he had: Stephen, Julia Kelley, Helen Alberts, Michael, Walter, Anne Tayblyn, Lillian, and Alexander. Kowalczyk died on September 2, 1939, and was buried in Mount Hope Cemetery, Hastings-on-Hudson, N.Y.

**Leon Kowalczyk** was born March 5, 1883, in the Lemko village of Gładyszów, Gorlice County, Austro-Hungarian Empire [present-day Poland] and immigrated in 1898. He settled in Yonkers, N.Y., where by 1909 he had a grocery store with his brother, Jacob, at 449 Nepperhan Ave. In 1912 he left that business to establish his own grocery/meat store at 46 Washington St. In the early 1920s his store was located at 61 Riverdale Ave. He also engaged in the insurance and real estate business and served as the president of the Little Russian Cooperative Association and was on the Executive Committee of the Taxpayers' Association of the City of Yonkers. By 1927 he had opened Kowalczyk Funeral Home at 340 Nepperhan Ave., later moved to 364 Nepperhan Ave., and finally to 107 Yonkers Ave. which he led until his retirement in 1951. The business

ЮНКЕРС, Н. Й.
Phone: NEp. 4897.

**L. Kowalchyk & Son**
UNDERTAKERS
COMPLETE AUTO SERVICE

**Л. КОВАЛЬЧИК И СЫН**

Лайснесованый погребник и ембалмер
на Юнкерс Сити, Н. Й.

Винанимат автомобилы на всякы випадкы по уміренной ціні.

Вразі потребы удавайтеся до свого краяна лемка, где достанете добру и честну обслугу.

●

364 NEPPERHAN AVE.,
YONKERS, N. Y.

155. Leon Kowalczyk, 1937

was continued by his son, William, as Community Funeral Home. His other sons, John and Walter, operated a funeral home in Jersey City, N.J., and the fourth son, Harry, operated a funeral home in Auburn, N.Y. All of them originally operated as Kowalczyk/Kowalchyk Funeral Home. He was married to Emelia/Mildred (née Kurylak,

1886–1973) with whom he also had: Mae Schnell and Margaret Zuraw. Kowalczyk died on April 3, 1952, and was buried in Mount Hope Cemetery, Hastings-on-Hudson, N.Y.

**Matthew Kowalczyk** was born on September 15, 1890, in the Lemko village of Łosie, Gorlice County, Austro-Hungarian Empire [present-day Poland] and immigrated in 1907. He settled in Yonkers, N.Y., where he worked at his brother's meat store before opening his own grocery store at 30 Clinton St. He operated it for more than 20 years. He was married to Stella (née Spewak, 1901–1984) with whom he had: John, Paul, Marion, and Lavonia. Kowalczyk died on October 28, 1953, and was buried in the Oakland Cemetery, Yonkers, N.Y.

**Onufer Kowtko** was born in 1872 in the Lemko village of Przegonina, Gorlice County, Austro-Hungarian Empire [present-day Poland] and immigrated in 1890. In 1902 he acquired a hotel license from Stephen Muranko who was not able to continue his business. With that license and a liquor license (issued in 1908) Kowtko operated a hotel at 216 River St. in Olyphant, Pa., until his death. The bar was later operated by his wife, who received help from her son-in-law, Samuel Smakula. The business closed in 1935 but was kept intact per Kowtko's request and was reopened in 1977 for Olyphant's centennial celebration. In 1910 Kowtko was elected Olyphant's councilman. He also held various positions in the St. John the Baptist Beneficial Society in Olyphant, which belonged to the Ukrainian National Association. He was married to Julia (1888–1967) with whom he had: Mary Smakula and Stephanie. Kowtko died on April 7, 1921, and was buried in Saints Cyril and Methodius Greek Catholic Cemetery, Peckville, Pa.

156. Onufer Kowtko, 1908

157. Onufer Kowtko, 1921

**Hilary Krenitsky** was born on March 28, 1886, in the Lemko village of Śnietnica, Grybów County, Austro-Hungarian Empire [present-day Poland] and immigrated in 1904. He first settled in Mayfield, Pa., but later moved to Simpson, Pa. He was listed as a machinist in 1930 and as a watchman in 1940 but also operated a beer garden and a grocery store. He served as a secretary of the local branch of the Russian Brotherhood Organization. He was married to Mary (née Kuzmich, 1894–1950) with whom he had Peter, Secelia, Anna, Al, Olga, Rose, and Harry. Krenitsky died on June 16, 1943, and was buried in the St. Basil's Russian Orthodox Cemetery, Simpson, Pa.

158. Hilary Krenitsky

159. Hilary Krenitsky, 1943

---

**Ilko Kudlik** was born on August 2, 1881, in the Lemko village of Czaszyn, Sanok County, Austro-Hungarian Empire [present-day Poland]. He immigrated in 1899 and in 1910 was listed as a slate picker in Gilberton, Pa. A year later, he moved to Monessen, Pa., where he was listed as a tanner (1911), janitor (1918), and a steward (1920). By 1924 he had opened a butcher shop 143 East Schoonmaker Ave. In 1940 his business was described as a grocery store. At the time of his death he was listed as a merchant. He was married to Justyna (1882–1964) with whom he had: John, Olga, and Walter. Kudlik died on July 16, 1955, and was buried in Grandview Cemetery, Monessen, Pa.

---

**Dennis A. Kulanda** was born in 1877 in the Lemko village of Łabowa, Nowy Sącz County, Austro-Hungarian Empire [present-day Poland] into the family of Afton and Eva (née Murdza). He immigrated in 1897 and settled in Shamokin, Pa., where he first worked as a miner and later as a driver. In 1910 he became one of the directors of Ruthenian Store Company. In 1924 he was listed as a manager at 605 N. Shamokin St. and a grocer at 906 E. Mt. Carmel St. In 1927, after purchasing the Ukrainian Store, he established with his brother, Phillip, the Kulanda Bros. and Co. grocery store at 906 Mt. Carmel St. In 1931 he received $20,500 as an award for damages for his two lots of land which were to be taken over to build an outlet of a state highway. As a result, the store was moved to 515 (later occupied 511-519) E. Independence St. In 1941 he was listed as a grocer at 906 Mt. Carmel St. He was married to Anna Krupa (1883–1965) with whom he had at least: Julia, Alfred? and Anna. Kulanda's date of death is unknown.

160. Dennis A. Kulanda

**Nicholas Kulanda** was born in 1875 in the Lemko village of Łabowa, Nowy Sącz County, Austro-Hungarian Empire [present-day Poland] into the family of Afton and Eva (née Murdza). After immigrating he settled in Shamokin, Pa. In 1901 he was listed as a driver but by 1905 he had a hotel, Washington House at 131 N Franklin St. Kulanda died in 1911 and was buried in Transfiguration of Our Lord Greek Catholic Cemetery in Coal Township, Pa.

> **Никита Кулянда,**
> Руский Готельник
> —мае—
> дуже добре пиво, знамениті вина і лікери
> і смачні циґара.
> 131 COR. FRANKLIN & WEBSTER ST.
> SHAMOKIN, PA.

161. Nicholas Kulanda, 1907

**Phillip Kulanda** was born on November 21, 1885, in the Lemko village of Łabowa, Nowy Sącz County, Austro-Hungarian Empire [present-day Poland] into the family of Afton and Eva (née Murdza). He immigrated in 1901 and settled in Shamokin, Pa., where he was a laborer and later a driver working for a grocery store. In 1927, after purchasing the Ukrainian Store, he established with his brother, Dennis, the Kulanda Bros. and Co.

grocery store at 906 Mt. Carmel St., which by 1937 was located at 515 and later 511-519 E. Independence St. Kulanda assisted in erecting Transfiguration Ukrainian Catholic Church and held various posts in local organizations, including the secretary of the Ukrainian Brotherhood and the treasurer of St. Andrew's Insurance Association. He was married to Catherine (née Moskaluk, 1888–1979) with whom he had seven (four surviving) children: Amelia, Joseph, Catherine Kolody, and Phillip Jr. Kulanda died on May 13, 1960, and was buried in the Transfiguration Ukrainian Catholic Cemetery, Coal Township, Pa.

**Daniel Kurey** was born on September 13, 1880 (1885?) in the Lemko village of Bogusza, Grybów County, Austro-Hungarian Empire [present-day Poland] and immigrated in 1894. He settled in Northampton, Pa., where in 1917 he was listed as a merchant at 1430 Newport Ave. and in 1920 as an owner of a store. He was married to Ahafia (née Salei/Peiko Fedko, 1881–1966) with whom he had: Waldemar, John, Joseph, Mary, and Julia. Kurey died on September 20, 1927, and was buried in Assumption of Virgin Mary Ukrainian Orthodox Cemetery, Northampton, Pa.

**Peter C. Kuzmicz** was born on March 12 (10?), 1874, in the Lemko village of Śnietnica, Grybów County, Austro-Hungarian Empire [present-day Poland] into the family of Shtefan and Varvara. He immigrated in 1895 and settled in Shamokin, Pa., where he started working as a tailor. In 1901 he opened up his own tailoring business at 427 North Shamokin St. A few years later, it was noted that he was "making a substantial position for himself as a high-class tailor and has prospered by hard work and satisfactory service. (…) His customers include some of the best people in Shamokin. He has a high reputation for satisfactory work and is conscientious in filling orders of all kinds, his skill and neatness winning and holding custom and being his best recommendation. He is good citizen of his adopted home, industrious and thrifty, and has a good standing among his fellow countrymen in Shamokin." In 1911 he employed approximately ten to fifteen people, who not only produced new clothes but also offered laundry services. By 1930 he had moved his business to 707 North Liberty St. He was married to Katie (née Anderson, 1883–1979) with whom he had Rosie and Stephen. Kuzmicz died on January 12, 1935.

162. Peter C. Kuzmicz, 1904

163. Peter C. Kuzmicz, 1912

**Samuel Paul Labowsky** was born on February 11, 1897, in the Lemko village of Roztoka Wielka, Nowy Sącz County, Austro-Hungarian Empire [present-day Poland] and immigrated in 1913. By 1930 he had a grocery/meat store at 106 Centre St. in Clifton N.J., which in 1930 was advertised as belonging to his wife under her maiden name. They operated the store for more than twenty years. He was married to Anna (née Sladechak Pelak/Pellack, 1897–1991) with whom he had Mildred and Olga Thorpe and stepsons George and John. Labowsky died on June 12, 1967, and was buried in Cedar Lawn Cemetery, Paterson, N.J.

---

**Thomas Lahutsky** was born on March 16, 1897 (1895?) in the Lemko village of Czeremcha, Sanok County, Austro-Hungarian Empire [present-day Poland] and immigrated in 1904. In 1918 he was listed as a laborer in Gilberton, Pa. In 1930 he was a miner in Frackville, Pa. After 1932 he had a café in Mahanoy City, Pa. In 1940 he was listed as a bartender working for himself. In 1958 his business was located at 500 West Centre St. At the time of his death he was listed as a café owner. He was married to Paraska / Margaret (née Baran) with whom he had: Peter, John, and Russell. Lahutsky died on December 29, 1967, and was buried in Holy Ascension Russian Orthodox Cemetery, Frackville, Pa. He was remembered as a "well-known tavern proprietor."

> **T. Lahutsky Cafe**
> *Cigars - Cigarettes - Candy*
> *Sandwiches*
> *Wine - Liquor - Beer*
> ☆
> 500 West Centre Street
> MAHANOY CITY, PA.

164. Thomas Lahutsky, 1958

---

**Peter Legosh** was born on July 22, 1883, in the Lemko village of Grab, Jasło County, Austro-Hungarian Empire [present-day Poland] and immigrated in 1900. By 1909 he had a meat market at 769 Main St. in Edwardsville, Pa., which by 1911 was located at 767 Main St. and after 1917 at 755 Main St. He was also one of the directors of the People's National Bank of Edwardsville (est. 1910) which in 1928 had assets of more than $2 million. In 1918 it was announced that "the new wholesale house of the Diamond City Beef Company at 54 South Pennsylvania Avenue, Wilkes-Barre. Pa., has been opened. The officers of the company are: Michael Czajkowski, president and manager: Peter Legosh, vice-president, and Joseph Moritz, secretary and treasurer. A building at 54 South Pennsylvania Avenue has been purchased by this company and will be remodeled." In 1921 the company purchased a 12-ton refrigeration machine and high-pressure side from York Manufacturing Co. In 1925 Legosh was listed as the treasurer of this company and at the time of his death, as its president and manager. At that time, he had 520 shares of the common stock and 1280 shares of the preferred stock

> **Peter Legosh's**
> MODEL FOOD MARKET
> **Will Open for**
> **Business**
> **Saturday**
> **Morning**
> Prices Less Than Wholesale
> **SOUVENIRS GIVEN**
> **755 MAIN STREET**
> Edwardsville
> Special Prices for Saturday Only

165. Peter Legosh, 1919

166. Peter Legosh, 1925

of the Diamond City Beef Co., as well as 128 shares of common stock of the People's National Bank of Edwardsville, Pa., 45 shares of common stock of the Kingston Bank and Trust Co., and 20 shares of common stock of the Miner's National Bank, Wilkes-Barre, Pa. He was the president of the Board of Trustees of St. Nicholas Russian Orthodox Church in Edwardsville, Pa. He was first married to Mary (née Kanik/Konic, 1889–1927) with whom he had: Anna Balut, Mathew, and Helen. He was later married to a different Mary with whom he had Olga. Legosh died on January 24, 1933, and was buried in St. Nicholas Russian Orthodox Cemetery, Pringle, Pa. He was remembered as "widely known throughout the valley and for many years (…) a prominent Edwardsville business man."

---

**Efrem Luczkowec** was born on February 6, 1864, in the Lemko village of Kamianna, Grybów County, Austrian Empire [present-day Poland] and immigrated in 1884. He first worked as a miner and by 1897 operated a hotel in Shamokin, Pa., at 717 E. Independence St. He was married to **Maria** (née Steranka) with whom he had five children: Annie Nowak, Sally/Salomea Berezynski, Ella Arsenych, Michael, and one more child. Luczkowec died on August 27, 1902, but his wife continued to operate the hotel until at least 1905.

167. Efrem Luczkowec, 1903

168. Efrem Luczkowec, 1897

169. Maria Luczkowec, 1904

**Ivan Madzelan** was born on June 30, 1862, in the Lemko village of Czertyżne, Grybów County, Austrian Empire [present-day Poland] into the family of Tymko and Iefrozka. He immigrated in 1880 and settled in Shamokin, Pa., as one of the first Lemkos there. In 1904 he advertised his hotel. He was married to Anna (née Dutko, 1870–19??) with whom he had at least one child: Evheniia. Madzelan died in 1910.

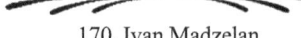

170. Ivan Madzelan

171. Gabriel Maliniak, 1903

**Gabriel Maliniak** was born on April 5, 1868, in the Lemko village of Śnietnica, Grybów County, Austro-Hungarian Empire [present-day Poland] and immigrated in 1886. By 1895 he had an alcohol wholesale business with Julian Kopystianski in Shamokin, Pa. but three years later he was in business by himself. In 1901 his Wines and Liquors wholesale business with bottling works was listed at 20 N. Market St. In 1903 his business and house burned down, and his wife was found guilty of arson. However, she was not convicted and died in 1905 before retrial. Meanwhile, Maliniak rebuilt his house and business in 1904 but now at 10 Market St. He operated his liquor store at least until 1920 (most likely until his death), but during later years it was at yet another location on the southwest corner of Franklin and Spurzheim Streets. After his death his wife and son, Walter, managed Pennsylvania Hotel at Commerce and Liberty Streets. With his first wife he had Walter. In 1909, he married Anna (née Moskaluk, 1876–1960) with whom he had: Stephanie Zieniewicz, Eugene, Henry, and Michael. Maliniak died on May 3, 1922, and was buried in the the Transfiguration Ukrainian Catholic Cemetery, Coal Township, Pa.

172. Gabriel Maliniak, 1914

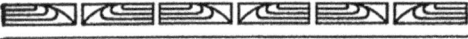

173. Gabriel Maliniak, 1909

**John Malutich** was born on March 17, 1894 in the Lemko village of Ropki, Gorlice County, Austro-Hungarian Empire [present-day Poland] into the family of Havryl and Iuliia (née Dankovska). He immigrated in August 1911 and first settled in Shenandoah, Pa. In 1912 he moved to Minersville, Pa., and worked at a mine. In 1920 he moved to Newark, N.J., and in 1921 to Yonkers, N.Y., where he worked as a painter. In 1928 he opened a grocery at 131 Yonkers Ave. By 1933 he had a license to sell beer and wine. He was still in business at the time of his death. He served as the president of the Carpatho-Russian American Center (Lemko Hall) and as a treasurer of the Lemko Park in Monroe, N.Y. He was married to Barbara (née Mikuliak, 1896–1984) with whom he had a son, Simon, and adopted a daughter, Martha Slivka. Malutich died on May 19, 1964 and was buried in Oakland Cemetery, Yonkers.

174. John Malutich, 1932

175. John Malutich, 1936

176. Michale A. Masley, 1942

**Michael A. Masley** was born in 1895 in the Lemko village of Uhryń (?), Nowy Sącz County, Austro-Hungarian Empire [present-day Poland]. He immigrated in 1903 and first lived in Passaic, N.J. where in 1925 he was listed as a weaver. Since 1926, he had a grocery/butcher shop at 328 Hope Ave. in Clifton, N.J. By 1952 the business was called M. Masley and Son. He was still working at the time of his death. He was married to Antoinette (née Wujcicka, 1899–1985) with whom he had: Peter, William, and Jerry. Masley died on January 16, 1954 and was buried at East Ridgelawn Cemetery, Clifton, N.J.

**Damian Merena** was born on November 14, 1872, in the Lemko village of Florynka, Grybów County, Austro-Hungarian Empire [present-day Poland]. He immigrated in 1893 and first lived near Shamokin, Pa., where he worked in a mine. He later moved to Yonkers, N.Y., where by 1898 he had a saloon at 328 Nepperhan Ave. with a fellow Lemko, Andrew *Dragan. In 1900 he was listed as a liquor dealer. By 1907 he had moved to Cohoes, N.Y., where he also operated a saloon and a grocery/meat market. In 1911 Merena moved to Herkimer, N.Y., where he operated a grocery/butcher store at 317 King St. until his death. He was also a court interpreter for Herkimer County as he spoke four languages and was respected as a friend of the foreign born. He helped many immigrants prepare for citizenship examinations and had served as a witness for them. He was a Republican District Committeeman for a number of years. He was instrumental in building Saints Peter and Paul Greek Catholic Church, Cohoes, N.Y. and was the founding treasurer of the Saints Peter and Paul Greek Catholic Church, Herkimer, N.Y. He was married to Eva (née Haszczyc, 1880-1957) with whom he had five sons: Michael, Peter, Moxy, Metro, Stephen, and three daughters: Anna Wood, Helen Clark, and Pauline. Merena died on July 1, 1951, and was buried in St. Mary's Ukrainian Orthodox Cemetery, Herkimer, N.Y.

ДАМЯНЪ МЕРЕНА
—и—
АНДРЕЙ ДРАГАНЪ

отворили новый, красненькій рускій салюнъ, одинокій на цѣлый Йонкерсъ. Пиво, виска и другѣ рожнородни напитки смачни. єсть газъ „Pool table", де можь забавитись въ кождомъ часѣ. Салюнъ знаходитъ ся подъ № 328 Nepperhan Ave., Yonkers, N. Y.

177. Damian Merena, 1899

Демко Мерена
секретарь Р. Н. Союза въ Cohoes, N. Y. родомъ зъ Флюринки, повѣта Грибовъ въ Галичинѣ. Приѣхавъ до Америки 1888 р. Має лѣтъ 31; єсть готельникомъ.

178. Damian Merena, 1903

---

**Denni Merena** was born in 1875 in the Lemko village of Polany, Grybów County, Austro-Hungarian Empire [present-day Poland] and immigrated in 1892. He settled in Yonkers, N.Y., where he worked as a railway conductor. He was one of the founding directors and later (1911-1912) the secretary of the Little Russian Cooperative Association. In 1914 he was listed as a co-owner of Merena and *Wandzilak grocery at 429 Walnut St. From 1915 to 1917 he had a saloon/hotel at 351 Nepperhan Ave. In 1918 he moved to Ansonia, Conn., where he first worked at the Ansonia Osborne and Cheeseman Company and by 1930 he had a grocery at 119 Westfield Ave. He was still in business in 1950, although he also worked for Ansonia Osborne and Cheeseman Co. He was married to Eva (1878–1952) with whom he had: Anna, Fannie, Mary, and Elsie. Merena died on November 20, 1953.

**John L. Merena** was born on January 7, 1893, in the Lemko village of Florynka, Grybów County, Austro-Hungarian Empire [present-day Poland] into the family of Aleksander and Maryna (née Murawski). He immigrated in 1910 and lived in Cohoes, N.Y., Ranshaw, Pa., and Shamokin, Pa. He first worked as a miner. By 1931 he was a co-owner and a manager of a grocery store in Excelsior, Pa., where he lived and was described as a "well-known postmaster and merchant." In 1936 he was a director and a bookkeeper of the People's Trust Bank in Shamokin, Pa., which had deposits of a little over a million dollars. He resigned as the postmaster in 1957 after serving in this capacity for thirty-two years. The same year he disposed of his grocery story and retired. He was married to Anna (née Dubetz, 1896–1981) with whom he had: John, Mary, Eva, Helen, Olga, Walter, Jean, Stella, and Michael. Merena died on December 23, 1972, and was buried in Transfiguration of Our Lord Greek Catholic Cemetery in Coal Township, Pa.

**ГРОСЕРНЯ И БУЧЕРНЯ**

**ИВАНА МЕРЕНЫ И КОМП.**

ИВАНЪ МЕРЕНА, Менаджеръ

Хочешь брате здоровъ быти?
Мусишь собѣ добри жити—
Ѣсти таке чого любишь
И здоровлю не пошкодишь.
Свѣже масло, телятину,
Колбасу и студенину.
Порцяпъ, мясо, всяке сало,
Чтобы добри смакувало.
У Мерены товаръ свѣжій,
О томъ знаетъ навѣтъ чужій.
Тожъ всѣ идѣтъ, не минайте,
Заробити свому дайте,
А кто въ него заордеруе,
То онъ за привозъ не рахуе.

**JOHN L. MERENA**
Excelsior, Pa.

179. John L. Merena, 1931

**Zachary Merena** was born on September 17, 1887, in the Lemko village of Florynka, Grybów County, Austro-Hungarian Empire [present-day Poland] and immigrated in 1906. He served in the U.S. Army during World War I and then worked as a butcher. By 1920 he had a butcher shop at 86 Centre St. in Clifton, N.J. By 1925 his grocery/butcher shop was located at 127 Ackerman St. It was still there in 1942. He later worked as a meat cutter, including in Hackensack, N.J. He was married to Pearl (1903–1962) with whom he had: Basil, Victoria Windish, and Gregory. Merena died on July 15, 1972, and was buried in Cedar Lawn Cemetery, Paterson, N.J.

Telephone: Passaic 8782

**ПЕРВОРЯДНА БУЧЕРНЯ И ГРОССЕРНЯ**

З. В. МЕРЕНЫ

Вшитки наши русски жены
Берутъ товаръ отъ Мерены,
Бо Мерена «бизнессъ знае
И старого не продае,
Лемъ все свѣже для каждого
Молодого, ци старого.

Z. W. MERENA
127 Ackerman Ave.     Clifton, N. J.

180. Zachary Merena, 1930

**Seman / Simon Metrinko / Mitrenko** was born on September 6, 1867, in the Lemko village of Zawadka Rymanowska, Sanok County, Austro-Hungarian Empire [present-day Poland] into the family of Mykhal Mytrenko and Anastazyia (née Swiatko). He immigrated in the late 1880s and settled in Olyphant, Pa. In 1899, he filed to have a restaurant permit transferred to him from George Chichura. In 1904 he purchased a two-story building at 536 Delaware St. from Peter Grabania. It included a hall, a bar, and

| | |
|---|---|
| ПАССАЙК, Н. ДЖ.  Phone: PAs. 2-8782<br><br>БУЧЕРНЯ И ГРОСЕРНЯ<br><br>**Захария Мерены**<br><br>У Мерены Лемка и краяна,<br>Ци в полудне, в вечер, з рана<br>Все товары перша клясса,<br>Гросерия и колбаса!<br>Свіжы мяса и ярины,<br>Привозят все каждой днины,<br>Бо Мерена бизнес знає<br>И старого не продає.<br><br>**Z. MERENA**<br>BEST MEATS and GROCERIES<br>127 ACKERMAN AVE., CLIFTON, N. J. | TEL. PAssaic 2—8782<br><br>ПЕРВОРЯДНА<br>БУЧЕРНЯ И ГРОСЕРНЯ<br><br>**Захария Мерены**<br><br>В шторі Мерены, краяна,<br>Як в полудне, в вечер, рано,<br>Товар мате першу кляссу,<br>Гросерию и колбасы.<br>Свіжы мяса и ярины<br>Привозят там каждой днины,<br>Бо Мерена бизнес знає,<br>И старого не продає.<br><br>**ZACHARY MERENA**<br>GROCERY & BUTCHER STORE<br>127 ACKERMAN AVE., CLIFTON, N. J. |
| 181. Zachary Merrena, 1937 | 182. Zachary Merrena |

apartments. He operated this business until his death. It was a place for weddings, dances, political rallies, and sporting events like basketball games and boxing matches. In 1920 and 1930 he was also listed as an owner of a grocery store. Metrinko served as a borough councilman in Olyphant for several terms. He was married to Pelagia (née Mudryk, 18??–1962) with whom he had: Mary Thissell, Michael, John, Peter, Olga, Anna, Harry, Lubor, Eva, and Sam. Metrinko died on March 5, 1939, and was buried in Saints Cyril and Methodius Greek Catholic Cemetery, Peckville, Pa. His sons, Peter and Harry, operated Metriko's Café. The last social function in the hall was held in 1941. The hall eventually fell into disuse and disrepair and had to be demolished in 1981.

183. Seman Metrinko

**Lucas Mihalak** was born on September 15, 1876, in the Lemko village of Gładyszów, Gorlice County, Austro-Hungarian Empire [present-day Poland] and immigrated in 1901. He settled in Yonkers, N.Y., where for 37 years he had a grocery store at 452 Saw Mill River Rd. By 1937 he had a license to sell beer. He was married to Rose/Eufrozina (née Schmyda, 1884–1972) with whom he had: Harold, Olga Slota, and Martha Driscoll. Mihalak died in 1948 and was buried in the Oakland Cemetery, Yonkers, N.Y.

```
ЮНКЕРС, Н. І.          Phone: NEp. 273
         БУЧЕРНЯ И ГРОСЕРНЯ
            Лукача Михаляка
         Мае добрый товар с мяса,
         Вшытко в него перша клясса,
         То наш краян с Гладышова
         И продає всьо дешево!
              LUKACH MIHALAK
         452 SAW MILL RIVER RD.
              YONKERS, N. Y.
```

184. Lucas Mihalak, 1936

```
Nepeprhan 273
              Л. Г. МИХАЛЯКЪ
      ГРОССЕРЪ И БУЧЕРЪ ВЪ ЮНКЕРСЪ, Н. І.
            До краяна Михаляка
            Идутъ люде изъ далека
            За товаромъ до гроссерни
            И за мясомъ до бучерни,
            Въ Михаляка все достане
            Ци въ полудне въ вечеръ рано
            Все наважатъ Вамъ свѣжого
            Порахуютъ недорого.
                L. H. MIHALAK
            Meat Market and Grocery
      452 Saw Mill River Road     Yonkers, N. Y.
```

185. Lucas Mihalak, 1930

**Peter Mihalak** was born in 1884 in the Lemko village of Gładyszów, Gorlice County, Austro-Hungarian Empire [present-day Poland] and immigrated in 1904 (?). He settled in Yonkers N.Y., where he worked as a butcher, and later as an insurance agent. By 1923 he had a tavern/saloon at 49 Clinton St. In 1926 he was listed as a cigar seller at the same address. In 1930 he was listed as a saloon keeper. He was married to Anastasia (née Woytowik, 1888–1965) with whom he had: Simeon, Anastasia/Nancy Chamberlain, Antoinette McCurdy, Pauline Olson, and Peter. Mihalak died on October 30, 1930, and was buried in the Oakland Cemetery, Yonkers, N.Y. At the time of his death his estate was valued at $22,334.

РУССКІЙ ЗАѢЗДНЫЙ ДОМЪ

Кто до Юнкерсъ пріѣзжаетъ,
Най отъ Петра Мигаляка адресъ
маетъ
Онъ краянъ добре знаный,
До него повинны всѣ заѣзжати.

Тамъ получатъ перекуски,
Выпьютъ собѣ славной соды,
И всякой минеральной воды,
Кто якои потребуетъ,
У Мигаляка покоштуетъ.

Его адресъ:

PETER MIHALAK, 49 CLINTON ST., YONKERS, N. Y.

186. Peter Mihalak, 1923

**Joseph Monchak** was born on April 6, 1893, in the Lemko village of Łabowa, Nowy Sącz County, Austro-Hungarian Empire [present-day Poland] and immigrated in 1912. In 1919 he was listed as a mill hand and in 1920 as a weaver at the Silk Mill in Clifton N.J. By 1924 he had a meat market at 62 E. Clifton Ave. in Clifton, N.J. By 1929 his business was listed as a grocery/butcher shop and was located at 112 Van Ripper Ave. in Clifton. He was still in business in 1960. He was married to Helen (née Grusha, 1894–1976) with whom he had: Samuel, Peter, and Olga Krenicki. Monchak died on September 7, 1975, and was buried in George Washington Memorial Park, Paramus, N.J.

ПЕРВОРЯДНА ГРОССЕРНЯ И БУЧЕРНЯ
ІОСИФА МОНЧАКА

До Іосифа, до Мончака
Идутъ люде изъ далека,
Не лемъ русски, а и чужи,
Бо всѣ знаютъ, же обслужитъ
Ци то свого, ци чужого
Ци малого, великого
Однаково справедливо,
Честно, скоро, что ажъ мило...
Есть у него свѣже мясо,
И то все, не лемъ такъ «часомъ»...
Ци Вамъ треба изъ «бучерни»,
Ци дачого изъ «Гроссерни»,
Вшиткого тамъ достанете
И такъ, что не пожалуете!

JOSEPH MONCHAK
112 Van Riper Avenue    Clifton, N. J.

187. Joseph Monchak, 1929

**John Muchnacky** was born on June 18, 1895, in the Lemko village of Kamianna, Grybów County, Austro-Hungarian Empire [present-day Poland] and immigrated before World War I. In 1917 he lived in Dutchess, N.Y. and was listed as a laborer. By 1936 he ran an embroidery business in Rutherford, N.J., and was still listed as self-employed during World War II. He was married to Victoria (1886–1974). Muchnacky died on January 14, 1969 in Carlstadt, N.J. and was buried in the Crest Haven Memorial Park, Clifton, N.J.

```
РУТЕРФОРД, Н. ДЖ.

Русскы и всякого рода

"ВЫШЫВКЫ"

Иван Мухнацкий

Лемко из села Камяна повіта
Новый Санч.

Краяне Лемкы-Карпасороссы в потребі
удавайтеся до свого

John Muchnacky
EMBROIDER
195 HACKENSAK STREET
RUTERFORD, N. J.
```

188. John Muchnacky, 1936

---

**Onufry Joseph Murdza** was born on June 6, 1866, in the Lemko village of Łabowa, Nowy Sącz County, Austrian Empire [present-day Poland] into the family of Osyf and Maryia (née Bobak). He immigrated in 1884 and settled in Shamokin, Pa. where his first job was as a clerk in the Excelsior Company store. In 1892 he moved to Mt. Carmel, Pa. where he eventually opened a grocery store with John *Talpash. Later he became associated in business with his brothers, Stephen and Phillip. In 1910 he was listed as working on his own account (grocery store at 42 W. 2nd St.) but later on that year he disposed of his business interests and took up mining. He was among the organizers of Greek Catholic churches both in Shamokin, Pa., and Mt. Carmel, Pa., and served the latter parish in many capacities, including as the president of its board of trustees. In 1894 he was among the founders of the Russian National Union (later Ukrainian National Association).

```
ОНУФРІЙ МУРДЗА И БРАТЪ
{ O. Murdza and Bro's }
Mt. CARMEL, PA.

Сторъ великій, запотребує бôлшу по-
ловину Русинôвъ такъ въ Mt. Carmel,
якъ и на околици — особливо на
Paterson. Кождый вдоволеный,
бо достає добрй товары,
таньо и въ часъ. —
Нѣкого не
зôдре, бо свôй чоло-
вѣкъ, Русинъ, христіянинъ.
Посылає такожь грошѣ до Ев-
ропы по низькихъ цѣнахъ, а скоро
и безпечно. — Вже то Мурдзôвъ всѣ
знають и безъ хвальбы.
```

189. Onufry Joseph Murdza, 1897

He was also a charter member of the Ruthenian Greek Catholic Saint Demetri Benevolent Society of Mt. Carmel (1917). He was married to Maria (née Halaburda, 1873–1959) with whom he had: Nicholas, Benedict (Benjamin), Magdalena, Vladimir, and Olga. Murdza died on December 8, 1940 and was buried in Saints Peter and Paul Greek Catholic Cemetery, Mt. Carmel, Pa. He was remembered as an "esteemed resident and churchman."

> **Najlepsza i najtańsza Grocernia!**
> Jeśli chcecie otrzymywać dobrą wagę i uczciwą cenę, udajcie się do nas. Towar zawsze świeży, obsługa szybka.
> **MURDZA & BRO.**
> 42 West 2nd st., Mt. Carmel, Pa.

190. Onufry Joseph Murdza, 1902

**Phillip Murdza** was born in 1865, in the Lemko village of Łabowa, Nowy Sącz County, Austrian Empire [present-day Poland] into the family of Osyf and Maryia (née Bobak). He immigrated in 1890 and settled in Shamokin with his brother Stephen. He later moved to Mt. Carmel, Pa. where he run a grocery business with his other brother Onufry. He was married to Catherine (née Fetko, 1871-1933) with whom he had Joseph and Anna Ladika. Murdza died on February 2, 1950 and was buried in Saints Peter and Paul Greek Catholic Cemetery, Mt. Carmel, Pa.

**Stephen Murdza** was born on April 9, 1855, in the Lemko village of Łabowa, Nowy Sącz County, Austrian Empire [present-day Poland] into the family of Osyf and Maryia (née Bobak). He immigrated in 1881 and settled in Shamokin, Pa. By 1897 he was a co-manager of the Russian Mercantile Company. In 1900 he was listed as a miner and in 1910 as a laborer, working odd jobs. He was married to Theodora (née Moszczar, 1859–1931) with whom he had: Mary, Anna, Natalie, and Lena. Murdza died on November 9, 1920, and was buried in Transfiguration of Our Lord Greek Catholic Cemetery in Coal Township, Pa.

**Paul Nescott/Nyskot [Nyshchot]** was born on July 16, 1889 (1887?) in the Lemko village of Pętna, Gorlice County, Austro-Hungarian Empire [present-day Poland] into the family of Aksenty and Maria (née Stashchak). He immigrated in 1904 and settled in Jeannette, Pa., where by 1920 he had a grocery and butcher store. He was still in business at the time of his death. He was married to Mary Elizabeth (née Zawada, 1899–1935) with whom he had: Catherine, George, Nicholas, Pearl, Ellen, and William. Nescott died on January 29, 1946, and was buried in the Sacred Heart Cemetery, Jeannette, Pa.

**Paul W. Olenich** was born on October 25, 1894, in the Lemko village of Pielgrzymka, Jasło County, Austro-Hungarian Empire [present-day Poland] into the family of Wasil and Justyna (née Jankoski). He immigrated in 1912 and settled in Little Falls, N.J. By 1928 he worked on his own account as a painter. In the late 1930s and into the 1940s, he

```
ВЕЛИКІЙ КОМПАНІЧНЫЙ СТОРЪ
```
# Russian Mercantile Co. Ld.
— въ —
# Shamokin, Pa.
**327 Shamokin, str.**

Найбольшій рускій компанічный сторъ въ Америцѣ. Заложеный ще въ роцѣ 1889 а теперь побольшеный, украшеный и на ново уряджений. Новый домъ великій, красный, котрый компанія купила 1896 року за $18.000 показуе, що може компанічна робота. — Всѣ розумни Русины належать до тои компаніи, купують зо своего власного стору значить, спомагають самыхъ себе. — Мѣсячно обертае сторъ сумою $2000. Заряджають нимъ

Стефанъ Мурдза
— и —
Теодоръ Федько

191. Stephen Murdza, 1897

---

advertised himself as a painter and decorator at 26 Woodhull Ave. He later worked as a painter for Friedman Brothers Co., Clifton, N.J., retiring in 1960. From its beginning in 1930 he was involved with the First Russian National Home, Inc. on Woodhull Ave. including as its secretary in the 1930s, when it received a plenary retail consumption license and liquor license, and in the early 1940s he served as the treasurer. He was married to Helen (née Smarsh, 1900–1961) with whom he had: Betty Dutko, Olga Vander Pyle, and Walter. Olenich died on June 25, 1981, and was buried in East Ridgelawn Cemetery, Clifton, N.J.

---

**Harry Onuschak** was born on July 26, 1871, in the Lemko village of Hańczowa, Gorlice County, Austro-Hungarian Empire [present-day Poland] to Aleksander and Aquilina (née Pyrcz). He immigrated in 1882. By 1910 he had a store in North Catasauqua, Pa., at 1054 3rd St. In 1916 he was described as "the prominent merchant of Catasauqua." He operated his meat market and grocery at least until 1940 but during later years, due to marital problems, his wife Anna (née Warren/Wawryn, 1877–1960) was formally the owner of the store and its manager. Onuschak died on May 22, 1947, and was buried in the Saints Cyril and Methodius (now Holy Trinity) Russian Orthodox Cemetery, North Catasauqua.

## ГАВРІИЛЪ ОНУЩАКЪ

Утримуе шторъ съ полотномъ, обувьемъ и всѣ кухонны снаряды, якъ тоже генеральну гросерію. Всякіи мясны продукты, такъ свѣжое якъ и вуженина. Краева бриндза. Кто желалъ бы получити най посылае гроши на адресу:

**HARRY ONUSCHAK,**
1054 — 3rd St., — Catasauqua, Pa.

192. Harry Onushchak, 1920

## ГАВРІИЛЪ ОНУЩАКЪ КАРПАТОРОССЪ-ЛЕМКО

:—: УТРИМУЕТЪ ГЕНЕРАЛЬНЫЙ ШТОРЪ :—:

мае 65 лотовъ на продажь на той самой улицѣ, що мае и шторъ; дуже дешево. Кто купитъ теперь, тотъ не пожалуе, бо заробитъ три раза столько. Лоты суть величины — 30 x 180. — Его адресъ:

**H. ONUSCHAK,**
1054-56 3rd STREET, CATASAUQUA, PA.
Telephone: 572-J

193. Harry Onushchak, 1929

## ГАВРІИЛЪ ОНУЩАКЪ

Лемко изъ Ганчовы.
Мае шторъ въ Катасаква, Па.
уже 33 роки.
**HARRY ONUSCHAK**
1054-1056 Third Street
Catasaqua, Pa.

194. Harry Onuschak, 1934

**Jacob Onuschak** was born on April 19, 1876, in the Lemko village of Hańczowa, Gorlice County, Austro-Hungarian Empire [present-day Poland] into the family of Aleksander and Maria (née Durniak). He immigrated in 1891. By 1905 he had a saloon at 615 W. Pine St. in Mahanoy City, Pa. In 1910 he was listed as an owner of a liquor wholesale business in Whitehall, Pa. Possibly the same year, he moved to Northampton, Pa., where he ran a "flourishing" soft and carbonated drinks bottling business at 1618 Newport Ave. until his death. The business was taken over by his son, John, and later his grandson, Jerome, who retired in 1991. Onuschak was remembered as a "prominent businessman and fraternal man who took quite an interest in his fellow men." He was married to Anna (née Hadik, 1878–1966) with whom he had: John, Mary Verbicky, Anna Wagiel, Helen, Elizabeth, Michael, and Margaret Zarayko. Onuschak died on January 26, 1927, and was buried in Assumption of Virgin Mary Ukrainian Orthodox Cemetery, Northampton, Pa.

195. Jacob Onuschak, Jacob on right, Northampton, Pa.

---

**Joseph Oseniak** was born in 1866 (1872?) in Uście Ruskie, Gorlice County, Austria [present-day Uście Gorlickie, Poland] and immigrated in 1883. He settled in Olyphant, Pa., where in 1898 he filed an application for a liquor license for his hotel at 128 River St. By 1900 he had a grocery store and was still in business in 1920 but at 203 River Avenue. In 1930 he was listed as a laborer at a coal mine but at the time of his death he was listed as a retired merchant. He was married to Theodosia (née Hopiak, 1875–1956) with whom he had: Genevieve, Olga, Martha, and Mary. Oseniak died on November 2, 1937, and was buried in All Saints Russian Orthodox Cemetery, Peckville, Pa.

```
Русскій Шторъ
Іосифа Осеняка
203 River Ave., Olyphant, Pa.

Хочешь брате здоровъ быти,
Мусишь собѣ добре жити,
Ѣсти таке, що не смердитъ
И здоровью не вредитъ.
Въ Осеняка товаръ свѣжій,
О томъ знае навѣть чужій,
Тожъ всѣ идѣтъ, не минайте,
Вторговати свому дайте.
```

196. Joseph Oseniak, 1920

**John Pancio** was born on March 15, 1895, in the Lemko village of Tylawa, Krosno County, Austrian Empire [present-day Poland] in the family of Petro and Rozalyia (née Pushkar). He immigrated in 1914 and came to Betula, Pa., where he worked at a chemical plant. In 1920 he moved to Olean, N.Y., where he first worked for Vacuum Oil Company. When his brother Paul moved there in 1922 they opened a grocery/meat store in which the third brother, Theodore, had a stake as well. The store was located at 1826 Johnson St. In 1926 he opened his own grocery/butcher store next to his house at 1009 Homer St. On Wednesdays and Saturdays, he filled his truck with sides of beef and meat loins and went house to house cutting meat for his customers. He later moved his business to a rented place at 1217 North Union St. in North Olean, which he eventually bought and remodeled. He ran his store for thirty years and his son, Peter, continued the business for twenty-five more years. He was married to Anastasia/Nellie (née Pushkar, 1890–1979) with whom he had: Paul, Eva Plano, Mary Piechota, Frank, Anna Bush, Peter, Andrew, Rose Kwiatkowski, Teresa Moszak, Catherine, Paul, and Helena Scott. Pancio died on July 17, 1961, and was buried in Saint Bonaventure Cemetery, Allegany, N.Y.

**Paul Pancio** was born on February 6, 1890, in the Lemko village of Tylawa, Krosno County, Austrian Empire [present-day Poland] into the family of Petro and Rozalyia (née Pushkar). He immigrated in 1905 and first lived in Cross Fork, Pa., Pittsburgh, Pa., and Betula, Pa. In 1922 he moved to Olean, N.Y., where he opened a grocery/meat store in which the third brother, Theodore, had a stake as well. The store was located at 1826 Johnson St. He retired from business in 1960. Pancio was an organizer of local branches of Russian Brotherhood Organization in places where he lived. He was also the secretary of Branch No. 402 of the Greek Catholic Union for more than forty years. He was instrumental in building and for many years serving as the president of St. Mary Byzantine Catholic Church in Olean. He was married to Anastasia (née Lega, 1893–1970) with whom he had: Mary Maksymik, John, Michael, Eva Smolnycki, Daniel, Rose Bungo, Anna Padlo, Helen Scott, Stephen, Paul, and George. Pancio died on August 13, 1967, and was buried in Saint Bonaventure Cemetery, Allegany, N.Y.

197. Paul, Teodor and John Pancio

198. Paul Pancio in the Paul Pancio Grocery Store
circa 1928

**Theodore / Frank Pancio** was born on February 22, 1880, in the Lemko village of Tylawa, Krosno County, Austrian Empire [present-day Poland] into the family of Petro and Rozalyia (née Pushkar). He immigrated in 1909 and went to Jersey City, N.J. He later lived in Betula, Pa., where he worked at a stave mill (1913–1925). After moving to Olean, N.Y., he joined his brothers in operating a grocery/meat store at 1826 Johnson St. He later moved to Auburn, N.Y., where he opened a grocery store. In 1942 he was listed as self-employed. He also worked for International Harvester. He was married to Pelagia (née Shwahla, 1885–1954) with whom he had: Daniel, Mary Theodora Hoxie, Anna Bunga, Anastasia (Nellie) Panko, Peter, Wasyl (Charles), Rosalie Greve, and Platt. Pancio died on March 22, 1955, and was buried in Saint Nicholas Half Acre Cemetery, Half Acre, N.Y.

---

**John Parylak** was born on April 17, 1866, in the Lemko village of Mszana, Krosno County, Austrian Empire [present-day Poland] into the family of Il'ko and Tekla. He immigrated in 1888. That year he was already in the cigar manufacturing business and the next year he filed naturalization papers. His shop was first located in New York City, possibly at 413 E. 70th St., where he was living in 1903, and by 1906 was located in Terryville, Conn. By 1908 he had a saloon with a fellow Lemko, Elias *Hylwa, first listed at 11 Spring St. and later at 18 Spring St. in New Britain, Conn. By 1912, he moved to Jamaica, Queens where in 1920 he was listed as an ex-saloon keeper working on his own account. He was active in Ukrainian circles and served as vice-president of the Ruthenian National Association (1906–1908). He was first married to Justina (née Broda, 1870–1908) with whom he had: Michael, William, and Alex. His second wife was Eva (née Hasko, 1877–1961) with whom he had: Annie, Nicholas and Olga. Parylak died on April 16, 1926 in Queens, N.Y., and was buried in Calvary Cemetery, Maspeth/Woodside, N.Y. He was remembered as "a retired cigar maker."

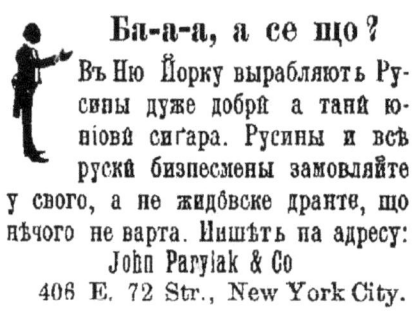

199. John Parylak, 1901

200. John Parylak, 1906

# District Court of the United States
## FOR THE EASTERN DISTRICT OF NEW YORK.

IN THE MATTER OF THE APPLICATION OF

John Parylak

By occupation Cigar maker

TO BE ADMITTED A CITIZEN OF THE UNITED STATES OF AMERICA.

PETITION.

Filed Jan'y 3rd 1899

The above-named applicant, being over twenty-one years of age, hereby petitions to be admitted to become a Citizen of the United States of America, and avers that two years or more have elapsed since he declared his intention to become such Citizen, and that a certified copy of said declaration is hereunto annexed.

Subscribed and sworn to before me this 3rd day of Jan'y 1899

John Parylak, Applicant.

Richard ?. Dale, Commissioner.

---

**United States District Court,** Eastern District of New York.

IN THE MATTER of the application of the above named applicant to be admitted a Citizen of the United States.

REPORT. Filed Jan'y 3rd 1899

To the Honorable the Judge of the District Court of the United States for the Eastern District of N. Y.:

IN PURSUANCE of a rule of this Court adopted March 1st, 1898, I, the undersigned special Commissioner, do respectfully report:

That I have been attended on such reference by the applicant and his witness, who have been by me orally examined, and have taken the proofs offered by him which are hereto annexed.

And I find and report thereon that the said applicant has complied with the requirements of Statute in regard to admission to become a Citizen. I further find that said applicant can speak, but not read write the English language intelligibly.

Dated Jan'y 3rd 1899

Richard ?. Dale, Commissioner.

---

IN THE MATTER of the application of the above named applicant to be admitted a Citizen of the United States.

TESTIMONY ON REFERENCE.

Anton Kotyza, 149 Driggs Ave, being duly sworn, deposes and says, that he resides at _____ Borough of Brooklyn, _____ City of New York, and is by occupation a Cigar maker, that he is a citizen of the United States of America, and personally acquainted with the above named applicant for admission to citizenship of the said United States and has known him for the past 6 years; that his occupation is that of Cigar maker and that he resides at No. 319 E 73rd Street, Borough of Manhattan, City of New York, that he personally knows that the applicant has resided continuously within the limits and under the jurisdiction of the United States of America since July 1892, and continuously within the State of New York, since July 1892, and that during the said time of his residence within the United States and within the State he has behaved as a man of good moral character, attached to the principles of the Constitution of the United States, and well disposed to the good order and happiness of the same.

Sworn to before me, this 3rd day of Jan'y 1899

Anton Kotyza, Witness.

Richard ?. Dale, Commissioner.

---

John Parylak being duly sworn, deposes and says, that he is the above named applicant for admission as a Citizen of the United States of America, that he was born in Austria on the 17th day of April in the year one thousand eight hundred and sixty six and emigrated to the United States, landing at the Port of New York in the State of New York on or about the 23rd day of August A. D. 1888 and that he now resides at No. 319 East 73rd Street, Borough of Manhattan in the City of New York; that he has arrived at the age of twenty-one years; that he has resided continuously within the United States since August 1888, in Manhattan N.Y. City and continuously within the State of New York since August 1888.

Sworn to before me, this 3rd day of Jan'y 189_

John Parylak, Applicant.

Richard ?. Dale, Commissioner.

---

201. John Parylak, Application for Citizenship, 1899

> 370    NEW BRITAIN [P] DIRECTORY
>
> Particki Michael lab h 40 Booth
> Parylak George groceries and meats 35 Lafayette bds do
> Parylak John (Parylak & Hlywa) 11 Spring, h 101 Hartford av
> **PARYLAK & HLYWA** (John Parylak and Ylko Hlywa), saloon 11 Spring—See p 91.
> Parzych Ignatz emp U Mfg Co h 222 Broad

202. John Parylak, 1909

---

**Emil J. Paulishak** was born on August 10, 1890, in the Lemko village of Tylicz, Nowy Sącz County, Austro-Hungarian Empire [present-day Poland] into a Pavlishak family and immigrated in 1902. He settled in Olyphant, Pa., where he was later listed as a milk dealer (1920), merchant/milk dairy owner (1930), and the owner of the Olyphant Dairy at 130 River St. (1937), also known as Hemlock Farm Dairy. He was married to Julia (née Lashenik, 1897–1975) with whom he had: Joseph, Olga, Theofan, Anna, Stephen, William, Vera, Eugene, and Paulina Lalka. Paulishak died on February 23, 1972, and was buried in All Saints Russian Orthodox Cemetery, Peckville, Pa. Thereafter, his children were involved in running his business.

---

> РУССКА МОЛОЧАРНЯ
> **ЭМЛІАНА ПАВЛИШАКА**
>
> Въ той молочарни всегда получите свѣже масло, сыръ сметану и молоко.
> Попробуйте и потому также другимъ скажить, что нашъ русскій призывъ есть: „Свой до свого".
>
> **EMILIAN PAWLYSHAK**
> **130 RIVER AVE.**, New Phone 255-W. **OLYPHANT, PA.**

203. Emil Paulishak, 1920

---

> **OLYPHANT DAIRY**
> E. J. PAULISHAK
> МОЛОКО, СМЕТАНА, ДОМАШНЕЕ
> МАСЛО, СЫРЪ, МАСЛЯНКА
> ПІЙТЕ МОЛОКО ДЛЯ ЗДОРОВЬЯ
> Молоко всегда найлучше пити.
> СВОЙ ДО СВОГО
> За скорую услугу телефонуйте:
> **OLYPHANT DAIRY**
> Phone 9113
> **130 RIVER STREET, OLYPHANT, PA.**

204. Emil Paulishak, 1940

**Andrew Pedbereznak** was born in 1866 in the Lemko village of Bartne, Gorlice Country, Austrian Empire [present-day Poland] and after immigrating he settled in Ansonia, Conn. By 1897 he had a saloon at 30 Liberty St., which was later located at 2 Railroad Ave. (1899–1906). He also had a confectionary store at 16 Maple St. (1908), and again a saloon at 252 Main St. (1909–1913) and at 7 Canal St. (1914–1915). He retired in 1916. He was married to Helena (1869–1942) with whom he had: Mary, Joseph, Michael, Theresa, and John. Pedbereznak died on June 28, 1944, and was buried in Saints Peter and Paul Ukrainian Greek Catholic Cemetery, Derby, Conn.

---

**Joseph Pelak** was born on January 10, 1887, in the Lemko village of Wola Cieklińska, Jasło County, Austro-Hungarian Empire [present-day Poland] into the family of Andryi and Maryia (née Olenich). He immigrated in 1904 and settled in Hudson, Pa,. where he first worked as a miner. In 1930 and 1940 he was listed as a proprietor. In 1943, he was listed as the owner of Pelak Café and in 1947 of Pelak's Tavern. He was a charter member of the Holy Resurrection Russian Orthodox Cathedral in Wilkes-Barre, Pa. He was married to Anna (née Ference, 1888–1968) with whom he had: Mary, Olga Regula, Anastasia, Stephen, Timothy, John, Peter, Anna, Joseph, and Nathalie. Pelak died on August 22, 1956, and was buried in the Holy Resurrection Russian Orthodox Cemetery, Plains, Pa.

---

**Max Pelak** was born in 1866/1870 in the Lemko village of Kotów, Nowy Sącz County, Austro-Hungarian Empire [present-day Poland] and immigrated in 1888. He settled in Shamokin, Pa., where he was first employed as a clerk in a store. By 1905 and until 1913 he was listed as a manager. By 1915 he had a grocery store at 201 N. Franklin St. (corner of Webster Street) which he operated until he got sick in 1931. He was a treasurer of the local St. Cyril and Methody Society. He was married to Tekla (née Kopysczianski, 1879–1933) with whom he had: Mary, Michael, and Theodore. Pelak died on February 12, 1936, and was buried in the Transfiguration Ukrainian Catholic Cemetery, Coal Township, Pa. He was remembered as "a well-known resident." After his death his children moved into what was the store and rented the other half. The family sold the house in 1994.

205. Max and Tekla Pelak

**Andrew Pelechacz** was born on October 1, 1874, in the Lemko village of Wirchne, Gorlice County, Austro-Hungarian Empire [present-day Poland] and immigrated in 1890. He settled in Hazleton, Pa., where in 1900 he was listed as a grocer at 209 Pine St. His business was later located at 198 S. Pine St. and was listed as a tavern (1910), grocery (1914–1929), liquor store (1935) and restaurant (1935). In 1935 he received a liquor license and a year later he expanded to 196-198 S. Pine St., where his business was listed as a saloon (1937) and a café (1942). At the time of his death he was listed as a hotel keeper. He was the founder of the local lodge of the Ruthenian National Association (1903) and of St. Michael Greek Catholic Church (1910). He was married to Susan (née Gutter/Goodard, 1878–1946) with whom he had: Mary, Anna Solowich, Michael, Rose Mantone, Helen Klimkosky, and Peter. Pelechacz died on March 29, 1949, and was buried in St. Michael Ukrainian Greek Catholic Cemetery, Hazleton, Pa.

> **A. PELECHACZ**
> TONIGHT'S SPECIAL
> Meat Balls & Spaghetti
> Entertainment
> 196-198 S. Pine St., City.

206. Andrew Pelechacz, 1935

> **PELECHACZ**
> 198 S. Pine St.
> Stuffed Mangoes
> and Holupki, 10c
> Tonite Special
> Whiskeys 5c and 10c
> Beers . . . 5c and 10c

207. Andrew Pelechacz, 1936

---

**Dimitro Pelesh** was born on September 1, 1876, in the Lemko village of Grab, Jasło County, Austro-Hungarian Empire [present-day Poland] and immigrated in 1896 (1897?). He worked as a wire roller at the American Brass Co. in Ansonia, Conn., before opening a grocery store at 26 Clifton Ave. in Ansonia (1918). By 1920 he was also selling meat there and continued this business until his death. He was married to Eva (née Koval, 1881–1957) with whom he had: William/Basil, John, Mary Merancy, and Louis. Pelesh died on January 14, 1952, and was buried in the Pine Grove Cemetery, Ansonia, Conn.

---

**Peter T. Pelesh** was born on January 15, 1880, in the Lemko village of Bartne, Gorlice County, Austro-Hungarian Empire [present-day Poland] into the family of Teofil'. He immigrated in 1900 and worked as a clerk in Gabriel *Dziadik's store at 130 Main St. in Ansonia, Conn. (1901–1902). He later formed a short-lived grocery partnership with Alex *Horbal at 127 Main St. (1904). After a visit home to Bartne (1905), he formed another short-lived partnership with Gabriel *Dziadik at 127 Main St. (1907). In 1908 he opened a grocery and meat store at 20 Star St., which was later listed at various locations: 12 Bridge St. (1911), 24 Clifton Ave. (1910,1912), 26 Clifton Ave. (1913–1914), 123 N. State St. (1916–1917), 26 Clifton Ave. (1918), before committing in 1919 to 53 Bridge St., where he worked throughout most of the 1920s. In 1929 he was listed as a clerk and in the early 1930s as a salaried butcher working in Seymour, Conn. He was the founding president of the Russian National Home, Inc. at 28 Lester St. (1918). He was married to Helen (née Felenchak, 1882–1951) with whom he had: Harry, Annie, Julian, Sophia, and Lillian. Pelesh died on April 25, 1935 and was buried in Three Saints Russian Orthodox Church Cemetery in Derby, Conn.

---

**Theodozy / Teodozii P. Perich** was born on June 9, 1881, in the Lemko village of Wysowa, Gorlice County, Austro-Hungarian Empire [present-day Poland] into the family of Petro and Maryia (née Cimbalak). He immigrated in 1903. By 1925 and until 1929 he had a butcher/grocery store at 263 Saw Mill Rd., Yonkers, N.Y. From 1930 until his retirement he worked as a loom fixer at the Alexander Smith and Sons Carpet Company. He was married to Katherine (née Taciga, 1888–1961) with whom he had: Andrew, John, Theodore, Martha Pearce, Olga Liptak, and Vera Golubowski. Perich died on April 8, 1965, and was buried in Oakland Cemetery in Yonkers.

> **ѲЕОДОРЪ ПЕРОГЪ**
> Свѣжее и хорошее мясо, овощи и ярины
> всегда найдете у
> THEO. P. PERICH,
> 263 Saw Mill River Road,        Yonkers, N. Y.

208. Theo Perich, 1925

---

**John Perun** was born on October 13, 1859, in the Lemko village of Bartne, Gorlice County, Austrian Empire [present-day Poland] into the family of Toma and Teresa (née Chomik) and immigrated in 1889 (1890?). By 1900 he had returned to Bartne, where his son, Stephen, was born. He was back in Ansonia by 1903 and was running a saloon and a hall at 109 Jersey St. by 1907. In 1930 he was still listed as a bartender working on his own account. He had four sons and four daughters with Anna (née Tezbir, 1872–1937). Perun died on June 25, 1931, and was buried in Saints Peter and Paul Greek Catholic Ukrainian Cemetery in Derby, Conn.

> **ІВАН ПЕРУН**
> Сальон, галя на балї, весїля і забави, найсмачнїйші напитки, знамениті циґара. Русини, памятайте, що і свій хоче жити!
> 109 Jersey St., ANSONIA, Conn.

209. John Perun, 1909

---

**Nicholas Popiwchak** was born on December 17, 1891, in the Lemko village of Polany, Krosno County, Austro-Hungarian Empire [present-day Poland]. By 1927 he had a grocery/butcher store at 104 Chestnut St., Garfield, N.J. He was still in business in 1942. He was married to Anastasia/Nellie (née Glaskow, 1897–1982) with whom he had: John,

Mary, Olga, Anna, and Helen. Popiwchak died on May 18, 1948, and was buried in East Ridgelawn Cemetery in Clifton, N.J.

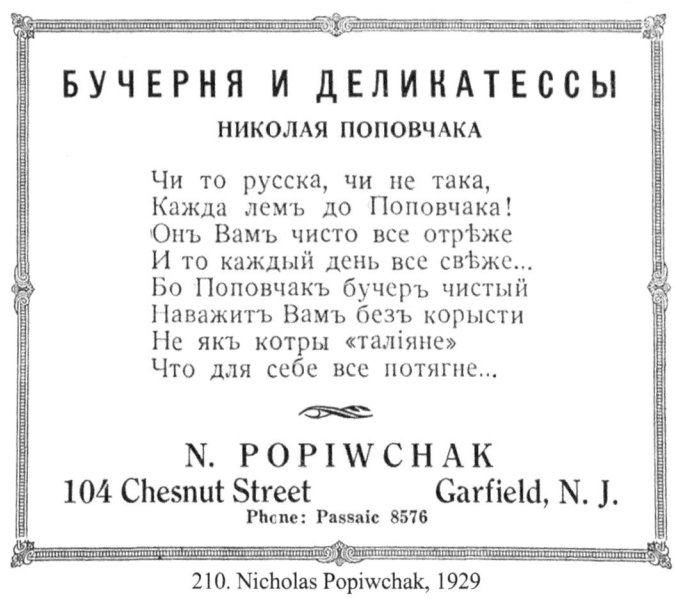

210. Nicholas Popiwchak, 1929

**Michael / Mytro / Metro Porada** was born on May 16, 1881, in the Lemko village of Daliowa, Sanok County, Austro-Hungarian Empire [present-day Poland] and immigrated in 1898. He settled in McKees Rocks, Pa., where he had his business at 330 Helen St. by 1910 and still in 1922. At different points in time it was listed as a saloon, a tavern, and a hotel. In 1920–1921 he was the president of the small State Banking Co. in McKees Rocks, which received a private bankers' license in 1919. In 1930 he was listed as a contractor. He was one of the founders of Ruthenian National Society of McKees Rocks (1914) and was instrumental in founding Ruthenian (today Ukrainian) National Home, which was built in 1914 at the cost of $28,000 with 1,000 stock holders, many of whom were convinced by him to join. He was also the president of Narodna Pomich, a Ukrainian fraternal organization. He was married to Cecilia (née Redmerska) with whom he had Mary and John. Porada died in 1951 and was buried in St. Mary Cemetery, Kennedy Township, Pa.

**Charles Powanda** was born on January 10, 1879 (1881?) in the Lemko village of Gładyszów, Gorlice County, Austro-Hungarian Empire [present-day Poland] and immigrated in 1896. By 1908 he had a grocery store at 11 3rd St. in Seymour, Conn. In 1909 his meat/grocery store was listed at the corner of Bank and Franklin Streets. In 1911 Powanda was listed as a business partner with Julius Adamovich running a meat/grocery store at 78 Bank St., but a year later he was the sole owner of that store. By 1914 he moved to Ansonia, Conn., where he opened a grocery/meat store first at 137 N. Main St. and by 1927 the shop had moved to 483 Main St. In 1937 he opened Old Town Tavern. By 1945 he turned the business over to his son, John. He was married to Anna (née Kowtko, 1885–1973) with whom he had: Milia, Elsie, John, Emma, William, Helen, Joseph, and Daniel. Powanda died on March 25, 1949, and was buried in Saints Peter and Paul Ukrainian Greek Catholic Cemetery, Derby, Conn.

**CHARLES POWANDA,**
DEALER IN
**Meats, Vegetables and Groceries,**
Flour, Tea, Coffee and Spices.
FRESH BUTTER, CHEESE AND EGGS
A SPECIALTY.
**11 THIRD ST., SEYMOUR, CONN.**

211. Charles Powanda, 1908

**Aftan Pupchyk** was born on January 19, 1886, in the Lemko village of Smerekowiec, Gorlice County, Austro-Hungarian Empire [present-day Poland] and immigrated in 1903. He settled in Yonkers, N.Y., where for 28 years he ran a business at 361 Nepperhan Ave., first a saloon and after 1927 a soft drinks store (with beer by 1933). For ten years before his retirement he operated Yonkers Avenue Grill at 89 Yonkers Ave. Upon his retirement in 1947 he became the president of the Little Russian Cooperative Association and held this position until his death. He was married to Paraska/Tessie (née Yacewycz, 1891–1979) with whom he had: Peter and Anna. Pupchyk died on December 3, 1951, and was buried in the Oakland Cemetery, Yonkers, N.Y.

**John Puschak** was born on April 27, 1889, in the Lemko village of Surowica (?), Sanok County, Austro-Hungarian Empire [present-day Poland] into the family of Nicholas and Mary (née Hernaga). He immigrated in 1909 and settled in Coaldale, Pa. From at least 1930 and through at least 1940 he had a grocery/butcher shop. At the time of his death he was described as a retired businessman. He served as a councilman in Coaldale, Pa., for 12 years. He was married to Mary (née Hudock, 1892–1982) with whom he had: Mary, Anna, Theodore, and John. Puschak died on May 7, 1947, and was buried in St. Mary Russian Orthodox Cemetery, Summit Hill, Pa.

**Michael Radio** was born on May 15, 1896, in the Lemko village of Rzepedź, Sanok County, Austro-Hungarian Empire [present day Poland]. He immigrated in 1912 and went to Minersville, Pa. He later settled in Allentown, Pa., where he operated Radio's Confectionary Store at 167 Tilghman St. (1921–1961). He also worked as a painter for the City of Allentown Parks Department (1957–1967). He was a founding member, vice-president, and treasurer of St. Mary's Ukrainian Orthodox Church in Allentown. He was married to Catherine (née Evanik, 1898–1989) with whom he had John, Peter, William, Dolores Bochnak, and Nicholas Rad. Radio died on March 12, 1989, and was buried in St. Mary's Ukrainian Orthodox Church Cemetery, Fullerton, Pa.

212. Michael and Catherine Radio

**John Renchkovsky/Renchkowsky** was born on January 24, 1885, in the Lemko village of Kunkowa (?), Gorlice County, Austro-Hungarian Empire [present-day Poland] into the family of Mykhal and Maryia (née Andrash). After immigrating, he lived in Follansbee, W.V., and New York, N.Y. From 1907 he operated a grocery/butcher shop in Charleroi, Pa. He retired in 1952. He was married to Mary (née Trembach, 1887–1962) with whom he had: Michael, Nicholas, and Olga. Renchkovsky died on August 24, 1968, and was buried in Charleroi Cemetery, Charleroi, Pa.

---

**John Repa** was born on April 4, 1867, in the Lemko village of Grab, Jasło County, Austrian Empire [present-day Poland] into the family of Osyf and Maryia (née Hoshko). He immigrated in 1883 and for a time worked as a slate picker in Jeddo, Pa., continuing working in and around the mines until 1890, when he opened his hotel in Hudson, Pa. After five years there he went to Wilkes-Barre, Pa., where for twenty-five years he operated Exchange Hotel and Restaurant on the corner of Grand and Coal Streets. He was one of the founding directors and later vice-president of the Heights Deposit Bank of Wilkes-Barre, which in 1909 had a capital and surplus of more than $200,000. In 1920 he moved to Kingston, Pa., and entered into realty and fire insurance operations under his own name. In 1931 he was described as a "prominent citizen, for many years active in the business life of Wilkes-Barre." Repa was an early supporter of Father Alexis Toth. He was one of the founders of the Holy Resurrection Russian Orthodox parish in Wilkes-Barre, Pa. (1892) and of the Russian Orthodox Catholic Mutual Aid Society of the United States of America (1895) for which he was later a national treasurer. He was of great help to the immigrant community in Wilkes-Barre by providing preparatory instruction to those wanting to become American citizens, and arranging bus trips to the naturalization offices in Scranton, Pa. He was married to Julianna (née Vanat, 1872–1959) with whom he had: Mary Krashkevich, John, Michael, Anna Williams, Julia, Joseph, and George. Repa died on September 3, 1957, and was buried in Fern Knoll Burial Park, Dallas, Pa.

213. John Repa, 1896

214. John Repa, 1932

```
┌─────────────────────────────────────────────────────┐
│              ИВАНЪ О. РЕПА                          │
│    ПЕРВЫЙ РУССКІЙ АССЕКУРАЦІЙНЫЙ АГЕНТЪ             │
│              ──── отъ огня на ────                  │
│            Вилкесъ-Барской околицѣ.                 │
│   Ассекуруе домы, мебли и прочи домашны вещи отъ огня. │
│          Спродае домы и другіи маетки.              │
│      ПЕРЕСЫЛАЕ ГРОШИ ДО СТАРОГО КРАЮ.               │
│                  J O H N  O.  R E P A               │
│     84 East Market Street,  Room 11,  Wilkes Barre, Pa. │
└─────────────────────────────────────────────────────┘

215. John Repa, 1929

---

**George Retick / Wretic / Vretik** was born as Hryts Hureitiak on April 14, 1860, in the Lemko village of Uście Ruskie, Gorlice County, Austrian Empire [present-day Poland] into a Vretyk family. He immigrated in 1881. In 1890 he purchased the stock of the dissolved Shenandoah Russian Store Company of East Center St. By 1900 he had a salon and a grocery store at 13 Gilbert St. He later moved them to 337 and 339 W. Centre St., where in 1907 he was robbed. In 1919 he was described as a "well-known businessman." By 1930 his business was again located at 13 Gilbert St. He retired before 1940. Retick served as national treasurer of the Russian Broth-

216. George Retick, 1915

erhood Organization and was among the founders of St. Michael's Greek Catholic Church in Shenandoah, Pa. He was married to Mary (née Fecica Dudek, 1861–1919) with whom he had: Joseph, Alfred, Anna Manko, Ella and Helene. Retick died on July 12, 1945, and was buried in St. Michael's Greek Catholic Church Cemetery, Shenandoah Heights, Pa.

┌─────────────────────────────────────────────────────┐
│              РУССКІЙ СТОРЪ И САЛОНЪ                 │
│                                                     │
│              **Георгія Вретяка.**                   │
│                  (George Vretyk,)                   │
│                                    Shenandoah, Pa.  │
│                                                     │
│   Въ красно заряджономъ сторѣ спродае найлучшій     │
│   гросеровый товаръ по дешевыхъ цѣнахъ.             │
│                                                     │
│   Въ красномъ и чистомъ салонѣ за барою мае най-    │
│   лѣпшіи, все свѣжіи пива, всякіи найлучшіи американ. │
│   и старокраевыи вина, палюнки, темперъ и цигары.   │
│                                                     │
│   Продае тожъ старокраеве сало                      │
│   Посылае гроши до всѣхъ частей свѣта скоро, таньо  │
│   и беспечно.                                       │
│                                                     │
│   Имя г. Георгія Вретяка въ Америцѣ всюда знаює     │
│   Онъ есть гол. кассіеромъ „Общества Русскихъ Братствъ". │
│   Братья Русины поддерживуйте своихъ!               │
└─────────────────────────────────────────────────────┘

217. George Retick, 1902
```

**Alex Anthony Rusynk** was born on March 30, 1877, in the Lemko village of Świątkowa Wielka, Jasło County, Austro-Hungarian Empire [present-day Poland] into the family of Antoni and Teresa. He immigrated in 1892. In 1910 he was listed as an agent for an insurance company. In 1917, he opened a funeral home located at 738 Starkweather Ave. in Cleveland, Ohio. In 1920 he was listed as an agent working for a steamship company. By 1926, he was an undertaker again and in 1930 was listed as a director of Alex Rusynyk and Son Funeral Home at 738 Starkweather Ave. The funeral home was renamed Rusynyk-Yurch Funeral Home in 1942, when Michael Yurch joined it. Following the retirement of Alex Rusynyk, the funeral home was renamed Yurch Funeral Home and in 1973 it was relocated to its current location on Broadview Road in Parma, Ohio. Rusynyk was married to Julia (née Greshko, 1880–1968) with whom he had: Anna, Stephan, and Helen. Rusynyk died on July 14, 1964, and was buried in Saint Theodosius Orthodox Cemetery, Brooklyn, Ohio.

```
РУССКІЙ ПОРЕБНИКЪ
АЛЕКСѢЙ РУСИНИКЪ
нашъ русскій лемко изъ Святковой обслужитъ Васъ честно.
ALEX RUSYNYK & SON
Funeral Directors
2824 W. 14th St.          Ph.: Atlantic 1436
ST. RUSYNYK
738 Starkweather Ave.   Phone: Atlantic 0088   Cleveland, Ohio.
```

218. Alex Rusynyk, 1930

**Prokop/Perry Rusynyk** was born on November 23, 1888, in the Lemko village of Świątkowa Wielka, Jasło County, Austro-Hungarian Empire [present-day Poland] into the family of Antonii and Teresa. He immigrated in 1906. In 1913 he was listed as a clerk; in 1915 as a laborer; and in 1920 as a painter working at the railroads. By 1930 he had a grocery/delicatessen and a candy store at 1507 Rowley St., Cleveland, Ohio. He was married to Julia (née Bagan, 1891–1920) with whom he had: Julia, John and George. His second wife was Eva (née Kieleczawa Kovalczyk, 1895–1978), with whom he had a daughter, Olga. Rusynyk died on March 14, 1956, and was buried in St. Theodosius Orthodox Cemetery, Brooklyn, Ohio.

```
Гроссерня, Деликатессы и Кендишторъ
ПРОКОПІЯ РУСИНИКА
Секретаря Лемковского Союза ч. 6. въ Кливландъ

Где можете въ Кливландъ поговорити о нашихъ русскихъ дѣлахъ?
У своего краяна, Прокопа Русиника, нашого краяна лемка изъ Святковой.
Тамъ получите всяки освѣжающи напитки и айскримъ.

PROKOP RUSYNUK
1507 Rowley Avenue,                    Cleveland, Ohio
```

219. Prokop/Perry Rusynyk, 1930

**Wasyl Seedor** was born on June 9, 1893, in the Lemko village of Kulaszne, Sanok County, Austro-Hungarian Empire [present-day Poland] and immigrated in 1907. He lived in Glen Carbon, Pa., and Buck Run, Pa., before settling in Frackville, Pa., where in 1920 he was listed as a miner. By 1930 he had a grocery/butcher shop at 404 S. Lehigh St. At the time of his death he was listed as a merchant. He was first married to Anna (née Hanczar, 1894–1915) and later to Anna (née Socker, 1901–1982) with whom he had: Marie, Catherine Lipscius, Vera, Anabelle, and John. Seedor died on February 6, 1949, and was buried in St. Michael Ukrainian Greek Catholic Cemetery, Frackville, Pa. He was remembered as a "well-known businessman."

```
Phone 283

ВАСИЛІЙ СИДОРЪ
РУССКІЙ БУЧЕРЪ

Кто въ СИДОРА торгуе,
Тотъ николи не журуе.
Бо СИДОРЪ добрый штофъ мае,
И тунько его продае.
Кто хочеся переконати,
Най стане въ него куповати,
Въ СИДОРА всегда свѣжина
Тому здорова будетъ Ваша родина

WASYL SEEDOR
404 S. LEHIGH AVENUE
FRACKVILLE, PA.
```

220. Wasyl Seedor, 1939

---

**Daniel Senkowicz** was born on March 14, 1898, in the Lemko village of Myscowa, Krosno County, Austro-Hungarian Empire [present-day Poland] and immigrated in 1914. He lived in New Britain, Conn., before moving to New Haven, Conn., where by 1947, he operated the Old Spot Restaurant at 110 Fillmore St. He was still in business there in 1955. By 1958, and probably until his death he owned the Pioneer Restaurant at 20 E. Grand Ave., New Haven, Conn. He never married. Senkowicz died on April 14, 1968, and was buried in Pine Grove Cemetery, Ansonia, Conn.

221. Daniel Senkowicz, 1958

**Steve Serafin** was born on October 28, 1895, in the Lemko village of Pielgrzymka, Jasło County, Austro-Hungarian Empire [present-day Poland] into the family of Hnat and Anastazyia (née Myscovski). He immigrated in 1905, went back, and arrived in the U.S. again in 1909. He first lived in Pennsylvania and in 1920 was listed as a laborer at a power house in New York City. In 1926 he was listed as a laborer in Waterbury, Conn., but by 1928 he had a grocery/delicatessen at 409 E. 70th St. in Manhattan. In 1940 he was listed as a bartender at 410 E. 70th St. and two years later worked at the Naval Medical Supply Depot in New York City. He was married to Mary (née Fedak, 1894–1976) with whom he had Michael and William. Serafin died on June 27, 1982 and was buried in St. Vladimir Russian Orthodox Cemetery, Jackson, N.J.

222. Steve Serafin, 1930

**Peter Serniak** was born in 1874 in the Lemko village of Pielgrzymka, Jasło County, Austro-Hungarian Empire [present-day Poland]. He immigrated in 1891 (possibly in 1893) and settled in Mayfield, Pa., where he first worked as a miner. By 1910 he had Serniak's Plumbing and Heating business and was still in business in 1948 at 621 Hill St. He was in business for more than forty years and handed it over to his son John. He was first married to Justina (née Gunia, 1884–1918) with whom he had: Stephen, Nicholas, Justina Merva, John, Paul, and Julia. He was later married to Mary (née Roman / Gunia, 1882–1969). Serniak died on January 30, 1952, and was buried in St. John's Russian Orthodox Cemetery, Mayfield, Pa.

223. Peter Serniak, 1929

**Alexis Sharshon** was born on March 28, 1865, in the Lemko village of Muszynka, Nowy Sącz County, Austrian Empire [present-day Poland] into the family of Ivan and Anna (née Koval'chŷk). He immigrated in 1884 and first worked on a farm. He lived in Shenandoah, Pa., and Greenback, Pa., before settling in Shamokin, Pa. In 1900 he was listed as a miner but soon opened a shoe store on South Franklin St. By 1901 he had a grocery store at 524 E Pine St. He had this business at least until 1919. He was also one of the directors of Ruthenian Building and Real Estate Company, which was established in 1910 with capital of $9,000 with the goal of "purchasing and selling real estate and for holding the same under lease and leasing the same." Sharshon was also involved with the Russian Mercantile Company and was one of the directors of Dime Trust and Safe Deposit Company, from its establishment in 1910 until 1921. In 1916 the bank had almost $1 million in assets and in 1925, $2.3 million. When the bank merged with the National Bank of Shamokin, he became a director of People's Banking Company. By 1929, and still in 1941, he was a director of the People's Trust Company in Shamokin, Pa., which had deposits of little more than $1 million. He served for a long time as the national treasurer (1900–1917), national secretary (1900–1902) and a trustee of the Little Russian National Union (later Ukrainian National Association). He was first married to Anna (née Dzhumbeliak, 1870–1913) with whom he had: George, Walter, Peter, and Anna Skweir. In 1914 he married Anna (née Leszczynska). Sharshon died on March 25, 1944, and was buried in the Transfiguration Ukrainian Catholic Cemetery, Coal Township, Pa. He was remembered as a "prominently-known businessman."

224. Alexis Sharshon, 1903

225. Alexis Sharshon, 1910

226. Alexis Sharshon, 1911

227. Alexis Sharshon, 1925

228. Alexis Sharshon, 1925

**Michael H. Shkimba** was born on December 11, 1889, in the Lemko village of Wołowiec, Gorlice County, Austro-Hungarian Empire [present-day Poland] and immigrated in 1906. He first settled in Brooklyn, N.Y. In 1915 he moved to Waterbury, Conn., where he worked at Scovill Manufacturing Company. By 1928 he had a billiard/pool room place at 84 Hill St., which was also listed as a beverage retail establishment and where he sold Lemko records. By 1937 he had a tavern at 147 Hill St. He was still in business in 1945

229. Michael H. Shkimba, 1930

and retired by 1952. He was first married to Julia (née Wolovich, d. 1947) and later to Julia (née Obuch, 1893–19??) with whom he had: Olga and Joseph. Shkimba died on December 23, 1968.

230. Michael H. and Julia Shkimba with twins, Joe and Olga

**Alex Shlanta** was born on April 7, 1868, in the Lemko village of Łosie, Gorlice County, Austro-Hungarian Empire [present-day Poland]. He immigrated in 1882 and settled in Mayfield, Pa., where he eventually was "widely and favorably known." He operated his own store for four years before teaming up with other Lemkos to set up the Russian Store Company (1900). It was incorporated in 1905 with capital of $9,000 with the goal of "conducting and carrying on a general retail mercantile store for the buying and selling dry goods, groceries, provisions, general household goods, wearing apparel, mining tools and supplies, at retail." The same year it was conducting business that amounted to $4,000 per month. In 1908 he was the manager of the Russian Store Company. He also ran a small store, which was attached to his own dwelling. He was agent for many of the ocean steamship lines and conducted a large banking business. Shlanta also served in the capacity of postmaster from 1898 (at least until 1908) and was credited for the duties of the office being performed in "a highly creditable and efficient manner." He was also a member of the Council of Mayfield Borough for six years, and a member of the school board for a number of years. He served on the Board of the School Directors' Association of Lackawanna County, including as its president. He was among the founders of the St. John the Baptist Greek Catholic (later Russian Orthodox) Church, Mayfield, Pa. He was first involved with the Russian National Union, later known as the Little Russian National Union as its treasurer but switched to the Russian Brotherhood Organization and served as the president of its publishing house. In 1912 he co-founded another fraternal, called the Russian Orthodox Fraternity Lubov. He was married to Martha (née Kossman, 1877-1944) with whom he had: Walter/Vladimir, Myra, Barbara, Olga, Bohdan, and Nestor. Shlanta died on December 6, 1923, in Mayfield, Pa. and was buried in St. John's Russian Orthodox Cemetery, Mayfield, Pa.

231. Alex Shlanta, 1897

ЧИ ЗНАЕТЕ ДОРОГУ ДО
## АЛЕКСІЯ ШЛЯНТЫ
**Русского почтаря въ Мейфильдъ, Па. и кассіера „Р. Н. Союза"?**

Его знаютъ не отъ теперь всѣ Русины.

**Посылае гроши до старого краю** дуже скоро, безпечно и таньо.

**Продае шифкарты** на найпоспѣшнѣйши пароходы (шифы) отъ всѣхъ пар. компаній.

**Мае великій складъ** обувя разного сорта по найумѣреннѣйшой цѣнѣ.

☞ Незабывайте, що у него можете въ горячи дни охолодигися свѣжою минеральною водою и здоровыми овощами. ☜

Удавайтесь до него во всѣхъ справахъ, чи то въ старокраевыхъ чи американскихъ. Онъ яко нашъ щирый Русинъ во всемъ дасть каждому добру раду. ЕГО АДРЕСЪ:

**ALEX SHLANTA,**
Mayfield, Pa. — — — Lackawanna Co.

232. Alex Shlanta, 1902

# Русскій Компаничный Шторъ
**СВОЙ ДО СВОГО!** ВЪ МЕЙФИЛДЪ, ПА. **СВОЙ ДО СВОГО!**

**ПРОДАЕ** всѣ виктуалы споживныи: обувье такъ до роботы якъ и на свято; полотно, перкалѣ, фланелѣ. Также можете тамъ достати для мужчинъ сорочки, кальсохи, колнѣрики, краватки и прч. Кромѣ сего есть и

### БУЧЕРНЯ
съ всякого роди мясами и колбасами, а все свѣжое и дешевее.

Въ томъ шторѣ можете купити для худобы сѣно, отрубы и овесъ.

Управителемъ сего штору есть

**Алексій Шлянта,**
который высылае гроши до всѣхъ частей свѣта. Выготовляе полномочія и полагоджуе всякіи старокраевыи справы и прч.

Если кто мае яку будь справу, чи то домову, чи судову, най удастся до Ал. Шлянты, а съ певностію буде задоволеный. Ал. Шлянту знаютъ не лишь Русины, но и чужіи, яко честного и справедливого человѣка. Есть онъ почтаремъ въ Мейфилдъ, а кромѣ того нашъ щирый русскій патріотъ. Идѣтъ до него!

**Братя Русины! Купуйте тамъ, где поддержите своихъ и самыхъ себе.**

233. Alex Shlanta, 1909

**Daniel Shost** was born on October 17, 1884, in the Lemko village of Mochnaczka, Nowy Sącz County, Austro-Hungarian Empire [present-day Poland] and immigrated in 1902. He settled in Yonkers, N.Y., where he worked as a printer in a carpet factory. From 1915 he was listed as a builder/carpenter and his business was located at various points in time at 99 Harty St., 51 Centre Ave., 49 Center Ave, 54 Coolidge Ave., and in the early 1930s, at 50 Coolidge Ave. He either built or renovated houses. He was on the Executive Committee of the Taxpayers' Association of the City of Yonkers. He was married to Mary (née Duda, 1892–1976) with whom he had: Thomas, Peter, and Paul. Shost died on March 18, 1973, and was buried in Mt. Hope Cemetery, Hastings-on-Hudson, N.Y.

> СВОЙ ДО СВОГО
>
> Строитъ домы, ремонтуетъ и краситъ
>
> РУССКІЙ КОНТРАКТОРЪ
>
> Даетъ раду, якъ начати и якъ грошей на будову дома пожичати.
>
> Гарантируетъ за постройку, и що треба до газдовки.
>
> ДІОНИЗІЙ ШОСТЪ
>
> 50 Coolidge Ave., Yonkers, N. Y.

234. Daniel Shost, 1931

**Michael Shostak** was born on November 20, 1894, in the Lemko village of Pielgrzymka, Jasło County, Austro-Hungarian Empire [present-day Poland] and immigrated in 1912. He settled in West Hazleton, Pa., where he for many years worked at a coal mine. By 1953 he ran a grocery store at his house at 436 W. Green St. He served as West Hazelton's Democratic Committeeman and was the organizer of the Lemko Association's branch in West Hazleton, Pa. He was first married to Pauline/Pajza (née Valko, 1898–1932) with whom he had: Mary Yandrofski, Anna Majchrowicz, Rose Nevick, Eva Tomkiewicz, Andrew, and John. He was later married to Nellie (née Koziel, 1915–1982) with whom he had: Helen Rossi, Michael, Justine Miller, and Terrence. Shostak died on March 10, 1966, and was buried in St. Michael's Ukrainian Catholic Church Cemetery, Hazleton, Pa.

235. Michael Shostak, first marriage

236. Michael Shostak Family

237. Michael Shostak

238. Michael Shostak Family

**Nicholas Shutowich** was born on December 15, 1889, in the Lemko village of Regietów Wyżny, Gorlice County, Austro-Hungarian Empire [present-day Poland] and immigrated in 1901. He lived for two years in Freedom, Pa., before arriving in New York City where he lived in Manhattan and by 1917 was working in the cigar manufacturing business. In 1925 he was listed as working for Acme Cigar Manufacturing Co. In 1926 he opened his cigar manufacturing shop at 444 Saw Mill River Rd. in Yonkers, N.Y. By 1931 his business was listed at 221 Nepperhan Ave. and by 1937 his cigar manufacturing business was located in Passaic, N.J. He was married to Barbara (née Chuchta, 1891–1956) with whom he had Michael. Shutowich died on February 22, 1942, and was buried in Mount Olivet Cemetery, Maspeth, N.Y.

---

**Lazor Sirotiak** was born on November 22, 1865, in the Lemko village of Gładyszów, Gorlice County, Austrian Empire [present-day Poland] into the family of Iustin and Iefroska (née Skripak). He immigrated in 1884 and by 1898 had a grocery/meat store at 42 Washington St., in Yonkers, N.Y. He was later also a steamship agent and in 1907 was listed as a notary public. In 1901 he was one of the founding directors of the Little Russian Cooperative Association. In 1906 he was one of the founding directors of The Nepperhan Valley Realty Company of Yonkers, which was established with capital stock of $60,000 divided into $100 shares. He was also engaged in private banking. He disappeared in early 1908 when it became known that $16,000 given to him to be transferred to Europe went astray. The same year, the Yonkers Savings Bank brought foreclosure proceedings against Sirotiak and others and sold their property listed on Mulberry Street at auction. Sirotiak was apprehended and placed on trial in 1909 and charged with grand larceny in the first degree. He claimed that the missing monies went to Leon Karybski, another banker who, according to Sirotiak, failed to forward it to Europe. The outcome of the trial is not known. In 1913 Sirotiak became a carpenter/building contractor and remained in this profession until 1928. In 1930 he was listed as the owner of a butcher shop. He was married to Marina (Mary) (née Cecewa, 1868–1942) with whom he had: Alexander, Peter, Anastasia Magnitzky, Simeon, Helen Winters, Konrad, Martha Cihi, Amelia Mildred, Anna Hall, George, Marion Hendricks, and Lydia Ramsay. Sirotiak died on February 17, 1949.

239. Lazor Sirotiak, 1899

240. Lazor Sirotiak, 1903

> **LAZOR SIROTIAK**
> Special to THE NEW YORK TIMES.
>
> YONKERS, N. Y., Feb. 18—Lazor Sirotiak of 107 Colin Street, a retired building contractor and a former proprietor of a steamship agency here, died last night in St. John's Riverside Hospital. His age was 83. He is survived by seven daughters, four sons and a sister.

241. Lazor Sirotiak, 1949

**Stephen Skimba / Shkimba** was born on February 3, 1885, in the Lemko village of Wołowiec, Gorlice County, Austro-Hungarian Empire [present-day Poland] into the family of Hnat and Maryia Shkymba. He immigrated in 1912 and lived in several places before settling in Waterbury, Conn. in 1915. He first worked there as a day watchman and later he worked on street cars. In 1926 he moved to New York City, where he became a motorman on streetcars. In 1928 he convinced Okeh Recording Company to release one Lemko record and after it became a commercial success, he signed a three-year contract (later bought out by Columbia) to record more Lemko and Polish music. Skimba also participated in recordings either as a musician or a managing agent and engaged in mail distribution of his records from his home at 69 Bedford Ave., Brooklyn, N.Y. The price was set at $0.75 per record but quantity discount was also available (twelve records for $6.75). With his twenty-two releases he is believed to have sold over 100,000 records. Starting in 1930 he was busy in New York with his radio show, which aired on WLBX and later on WLWL, WMBQ, and WBBS stations. For his radio show he formed and managed yet another orchestra, which also performed at weddings, public dances, and at other events. In the early 1930s he operated a restaurant/saloon, Carpathian Mountains, at 321 E. 71st St. Despite all these commercial undertakings, in 1940 he was still listed as a motorman and was remembered mainly as a tireless cultural activist. He was married to Maria (née Wyslocki, 1897–1985). Skimba died on November 16, 1966, and was buried in the St. Mary's Russian Orthodox Cemetery, Waterbury, N.Y.

242. Stephen Skimba

243. Stephen Skimba

**Andrew Skwier / Skweir** was born on July 29, 1855, in the Lemko village of Krempna, Jasło County, Austrian Empire [present-day Poland] to Tymko Skvir and Anna (née Doliniak). He attended school until he was 15 and then for five years worked on his father's farm. At the age of 23 he immigrated and settled in Jeansville, Pa., where he obtained a position as a hoisting and pump engineer. After eight years he moved to Hazleton, Pa. He started out in business with a horse and wagon, offering taxi service from the train at Hazleton Junction to nearby settlers' farms, or up to the coal mines. The wagon also carried essential items for sale. He later engaged in the wholesale liquor and grocery business. In 1890 he went to McAdoo, Pa., which was then a settlement with only a few inhabitants, where he erected a building and engaged in the grocery and hardware business. In 1900 he was listed as a hotel keeper. In 1905 he was appointed postmaster and the post office was moved to what was known as the Skwier Building on West Blaine Street. It remained there until 1915, managed by his children, Anthony and Anna Postupack. Skweir was twice elected to terms for a period of six years in the Borough Council of McAdoo on the Republican ticket. He was also a prominent member of the Citizens' Club of McAdoo. Skweir was married to Eva (née Yonkovig/Jankowicz, 1870–1941) and they had ten (seven surviving) children: Anna, John, Anthony, Michael, Mary, Julia, and Helen. Skwier died on June 29, 1918, and was buried in St. Mary's Greek Catholic Cemetery, McAdoo.

244. Andrew Skweir, 1908

**John Smerechniak** was born on January 15, 1887, in the Lemko village of Smerekowiec, Gorlice County, Austro-Hungarian Empire [present-day Poland] and immigrated in 1903. He lived in Yonkers, N.Y., where in 1917 he worked at the Federal Sugar Refinery. In 1920 he was listed as a motor repairman working for the railroads in New York City. By 1930 he had a grocery store in Manhattan at 419 E. 70th St. He was still in business in 1940.

НЬЮ ЮРК, Н. І.

ГРОСЕРНЯ И ДЕЛИКАТЕСЫ

**Ивана Смеречняка**

У Ивана Смеречняка
Купуєте на вірняка,
Його товар так хороший,
Што не жаль Вам буде грошей!

JOHN SMERECHNIAK
419 E. 70th ST. — NEW YOK, N. Y.

245. John Smerechniak, 1936

He was married to Mary (née Haytko, 1890–1959) with whom he had Jerry and Walter. Smerechniak died in July of 1962.

---

**Elias Smerek** was born on August 2, 1876, in the Lemko village of Wysowa, Gorlice County, Austro-Hungarian Empire [present-day Poland] and immigrated in 1882. In 1915 he lived in Yonkers, N.Y., and in 1920 in Manhattan, N.Y. and worked as a weaver at Alex Smith & Son Carpet Company, Yonkers, N.Y. In 1921 he was back in Yonkers and continued to work at the carper factory until 1927. From 1928 he operated a grocery store at 886 Old Nepperhan Ave. in Yonkers with his wife. He was married to **Anna** (née Kurylo) who was born on July 30, 1884, in the village of Wysowa and with whom he had four children: Julia Reid, Olga Gould, Anna Little, and one who died at a young age. Smerek died on June 30, 1929, and was buried in the Oakland Cemetery, Yonkers, N.Y. In 1940 the store was still open and run by his wife, who also owned a building. She died on September 19, 1970, and was buried next to her husband.

246. Elias Smerek, wedding, 1902

247. Elias Smerek with family

---

**Marko Smetana** was born on July 1, 1880, in the Lemko village of Kotów, Nowy Sącz County, Austro-Hungarian Empire [present-day Poland] and immigrated in 1902. He settled in Shamokin, Pa. By 1905 he was working at the Russian Mercantile Company, where he later became a manager. In 1925 he purchased a property at 905 W. Arch St. from John Wargo. After renovation, he opened a grocery/meat store there, which he operated until his death. He was married to Alice (née Yadlowsky, 1893–1965) with whom he had: Alexander, Helen, and Sonia Peters. Smetana died on February 6, 1949, and was buried in the Transfiguration Ukrainian Catholic Cemetery, Coal Township, Pa. He was remembered as a "widely known Coal Township businessman."

**Марко Сметана**
— має —
**Гросерню і Бучерню**
У ВЛАСНІМ ДОМІ
905. W. ARCH ST.,
**SHAMOKIN, PENNA.**

248. Marko Smetana, 1925

# M. SMETANA WILL ENGAGE IN BUSINESS

## Well Known Citizen Buys Business Location on West Arch Street

Marko Smetana, one of Shamokin's best known and most highly respected citizens, has purchased the valuable property at 905 West Arch street from John Wargo and is perfecting plans for opening a mercantile establishment at that location within the next week or ten days.

Mr. Smetana plans to make some extensive changes and improvements to the store room with a view of making it one of the most up-to-date business places in West Coal township. He will engage in the sale of groceries, green truck and high grade meats.

Mr. Smetana was formerly manager of the Russian Mercantile company and the experience gained there will stand him in good stead in his new business venture. He has the best wishes of his many friends for success in his new undertaking.

249. Marko Smetana, 1925

**Nikolay Smey** was born on May 24, 1874, in the Lemko village of Banica, Gorlice County, Austro-Hungarian Empire [present-day Poland] and immigrated in 1890. In 1904–1905 he was listed as a clerk in Seymour, Conn. In 1906 he opened a meat market at 11 Third Ave. in that city. By 1910 the store expanded into a grocery/meat market and was moved to 24 Third Ave. In 1916 he opened a saloon/restaurant at 12-16 Housatonic Ave. and operated it until at least 1920. That year he signed a $65,000 contract to have a theatre built in Bridgeport, Conn., in partnership with Samuel *Telep. He also purchased Colonial Theatre at 830 Boston Ave. in Bridgeport, but the theatre was confiscated by IRS for nonpayment of taxes and auctioned in 1923, together with the land it stood on. He moved from Derby, Conn. to Bridgeport in 1924 and was listed there as a butcher. From 1927 he had a grocery at 1273 Pembroke St., which he operated until at least 1944. In 1948 he was listed as the owner of a restaurant at 18 Broad St. in Seymour, Conn. He was married to Sophia (née Telep, 1879–1962) with whom he had: Anna, William, Judith Apster, Peter, Mary Kuzma, Mildred Kopp, Helen Francik, John and Pauline Steele. Smey died on January 23, 1949, and was buried in St. John the Baptist Greek Catholic Cemetery, Stratford, Conn.

```
ANSONIA, DERBY (1917) SHELTON DIRECTORY   45

              Nikolay Smey
              Cafe and Restaurant
                  The Best on Earth
       A Full Line of Choice Ales, Wines, Liquors and Cigars

                  Telephone Connection
   12-16 Housatonic Avenue          Derby, Conn.
```

250. Nikolay Smey, 1917

**Peter Sopchak** was born on July 12, 1889, in the Lemko village of Śnietnica, Grybów County, Austro-Hungarian Empire [present-day Poland] into the family of Aleksander and Jaqueline (née Adamiak). He immigrated in 1906 and settled in Simpson (Fell Township), Pa. In 1913 he was listed as a laborer. By 1926 he had a grocery store at 67 Frobel St. He was still in business in 1948. He was married to Helen (née Patsey/Pecuch, 1894–1973) with whom he had: Michael, Martha, Alex, George, Daniel, Anna, and Wasil. Sopchak died on March 8, 1954, and was buried in St. Basil's Russian Orthodox Cemetery, Simpson, Pa.

251. Peter Sopchak with family

## ГРОССЕРНЯ И БУЧЕРНЯ
### ПЕТРА СОПЧАКА

Изъ Снѣтницѣ у Сопчака
Въ его шторѣ звычка така,
Что каждому добре даютъ
И то все Вамъ преважаютъ
Свѣже масло, сыръ молоко
Грушки, ябка, кава, коко,
Сальцесоны, солонина
«Гемъ» и «Бейкенъ», уженина
Вшитко того перва клясса
А найлѣпша ужъ колбаса...
Его штору не минайте
Вторговати свому дайте!

### PETER SOPCHAK
67 Frobol Street      Simpson, Pa.

252. Peter Sopchak, 1929

---

**John Spiak** was born on April 18, 1876, in the Lemko village of Ług, Gorlice County, Austro-Hungarian Empire [present-day Poland] and immigrated in 1895. He settled in Yonkers, N.Y., where he worked in the hat and sugar industries. From 1905 to 1935 he served as the treasurer of the Little Russian Cooperative Association / Little Russian Corporation. In 1917 he entered into a partnership with Jacob *Wandzilak and they operated a meat market at 441 Walnut St. By 1922 Wandzilak left to open his own store and Spiak managed the grocery/meat market by himself. He still had the store in 1936 and in 1940 was listed as a clerk in a store but was retired as of 1942. He was married to Justina (née Waszczyszak, 1879–1937) with whom he had: Josephine Pastorak, Rose Wasicko, Peter, Mary Broderick, Anne Kinanrd, Andrew, Mildred Acciardi, Stephen, and Tekla/Tillie DiFate. Spiak died on September 5, 1948, and was buried in Oakland Cemetery, Yonkers, N.Y.

---

**Michael Stefansky** was born in 1861 (1859?) in the Lemko village of Brunary, Grybów County, Austrian Empire [present-day Poland] and immigrated in 1882. He first lived in Scranton, Pa., where he got married, but moved many times, doing construction jobs in St. Louis, Mo., Saginaw, Mich., Cleveland, Ohio, and Buffalo, N.Y. In 1899, on advice from a German friend, he moved his family to Detroit, Mich., where he settled among the Germans on the city's East Side. He first worked at a factory manufacturing copper wires but in a few years began building homes on Detroit's West Side, where he also moved his family. He built a house on Gilbert Street, with a general store, beer garden, meat market, and grocery attached. He also had a house with a store on Cicotte Street. In 1910 he was listed as a carpenter. In 1911 he filed articles of association for the American Building Club, where he was the principal stockholder. The organization had capital of $1,000. In 1919 he received a patent for resilient tires. In 1920 he was listed as an inspector and retired by 1930. Stefansky helped to establish two Detroit parishes: St. John's Greek (now Ukrainian) Catholic (1905), where he financed and built a church building with his sons on land donated to him by the Webber Lumber Co., as well as Saints Peter and Paul Russian Orthodox Cathedral (1907). He was married to Mary (née Onuschak, 1877–1946) with whom he had eight children (five survived): George, Peter, Anna Zadosko, Rose Powanda, and John. Stefansky, who "was well known to Slavic groups in Detroit," died on November 30, 1953, and was buried at the Holy Cross Catholic Cemetery, Detroit, Mich.

253. Michael Stefansky patent for resilient tire, 1919

**Fannie Stoppi (née Fenna Kicak)** was born on July 3, 1893, in the Lemko village of Kulaszne, Sanok County, Austro-Hungarian Empire [present-day Poland] and immigrated in 1909. She settled in Frackville, Pa., where she was first married to Metro Ritzko/Hrytsko (1890–1918) with whom she had: Michael, Mary Ploxa, and Anna Bendinsky. She was later married to Joseph Stoppi/Stapai (1888–1933) with whom she had: Margaret Uranko, Susan Spadaro, and Anna Heller as well as step children: John, Frank, Michael, and Peter. Another son was Metreo Keetsock. Both of her husbands were miners. Probably after her second husband died she opened a café (first noted in 1934) at 433 W. Pine St., which was later located at 402 S Lehigh Ave, and again at 433 W. Pine St., where she was still in business in 1953. Stoppi died on August 16, 1987, and was buried in Holy Ascension Russian Orthodox Cemetery, Frackville, Pa.

In Our New Location
**FANNY STOPPI'S CAFE**
402 South Lehigh Avenue, Frackville

SPECIAL PLATTERS
DEVILED CRABS
HAMBURGERS

BEERS — WINES — LIQUORS

254. Fannie Stoppi, 1941

*Compliments of*
**Fannie Stoppi's Cafe**
Beer, Liquors & Wine

Поздравления всім от краянки Фенны Стапей из села Куляшне, повіт Сянок.

ЗАХОДТЕ ДО НАС!

433 W. Pine St.    Frackville, Pa.

255. Fannie Stoppi, 1953

СЛАВЯНСКО-РУССКА
**ПЕРВОРЯДНА ГОСТИНИЦА**

ФЕННА СТАППЕЙ, Власт.

У ней сходятся краяне, русскы и славяне, штобы приятно провести свой час.

*
* *

BEER GARDEN
FANNIE STOPPI, Prop.

202 So. Lehigh Ave.

FRACKVILLE, PA.

256. Fannie Stoppi, 1946

Music-Dancing
and the best of
FOOD!

FREE DANCE TUESDAY NIGHT

**Fanny Stoppi**

433 West Pine Street,    Frackville, Pa.

257. Fannie Stoppi, 1934

**Wasily Sudia** was born on January 17, 1885, in the Lemko village of Daliowa, Krosno County, Austro-Hungarian Empire [present-day Poland] into the family of Ivan and Anna (née Barna). He immigrated in 1903. By 1917 and still in 1922 he had a butcher/grocery store in Grapeville (Hempfield Township), Pa. By 1930 he had moved to Detroit, Pa., where he had a butcher shop at different times listed at 7186, 6400, and 6641 Tireman Ave. He was the organizer of local Russian Brotherhood Organization branches in the city and was active in the organization on the national level. He was also assistant church president of Saints Peter and Paul's Russian Orthodox Church. He was married to Maria (née Hudak, 1885–1945) with whom he had: John, Michael, Annie, James, Walter, and Mary Gurin. Sudia died on November 11, 1961.

258. Wasily Sudia, 1940

**Dimitro Sydoriak** was born on May 16, 1873, in the Lemko village of Wołowiec, Gorlice County, Austro-Hungarian Empire [present-day Poland] and immigrated in 1895. By 1902 he had opened a saloon at 22 State St. in Ansonia, Conn. By 1904 he had turned his attention to the grocery business, purchasing a store from Harry *Zuraw at 19 High St., which he later moved to 37 High St. and finally to 57 High St. It eventually evolved into a grocery/meat market, which he ran until at least 1937. In 1940 he was listed as a laborer. He was married to Mary (née Tanich, 1877–1936) with whom he had seven children: Nasta, Wasil, Mike, Lena, Esther, Anna, and Antoinette. Sydoriak died on March 3, 1946.

> ДИМИТРІЙ СИДОРЯК
> має гарно уладжений стор, гросерню і бучерню. Завсїгди сьвіжий товар. Русини! Час уже зрозуміти клич: „Свій до свого."
> 37 High St., ANSONIA, CONN.

259. Dimitro Sydoriak, 1909

**Teodore Swantko** was born on May 28, 1875, in the Lemko village of Zawadka Rymanowska, Sanok County, Austro-Hungarian Empire [present-day Poland] and immigrated in 1898. He first lived in Freeland, Pa., and by 1912 in Nanticoke, Pa., where he worked as a miner. In 1923 he opened a general store at 230 Pine St. The store's business grew rapidly and by 1930, it was turned over to his sons: John, Russell, Peter, and Steven. The store was thoroughly renovated in 1932 so that it stood out "as the last thing in a modern grocery, fruit, vegetable, and meat market" while its founder was described as a "prominent merchant." Swantko was married to Anna (née Hromchak, 1881–1936) with whom he had: John, Russell, Peter, Steven, Mary, Andrew, Theodore, and Michael. Swantko died on September 15, 1954, and was buried in Holy Transfiguration Ukrainian Greek Catholic Cemetery, Nanticoke, Pa.

## Local Store Holds Grand Opening

Grand opening of the newly renovated store in honor of their tenth anniversary in business is being observed by Swantko's Market, 228 Pine street, Hanover section of this city. The occasion is being celebrated elaborately.

Swantko's market now stands as one of the largest food centers in Hanover after enjoying rapid strides of growth in its ten years of business. Having been remodeled, it stands out as the last thing in a modern grocery, fruit, vegetable and meat market and is a credit to the business life of Hanover.

The market is managed by John Swantko, son of Mr. and Mrs. Theodore Swantko, of 230 Pine street, Hanover, and is a member of the Fairlawn stores, of which the former is vice-president. Its steady growth has placed it foremost in the minds of the people of Hanover as they have learned from experience that it handles only quality goods. Swantko's market is run strictly on a two-weeks' cash basis and has always catered to selective trade, thus affording the best for the least money.

Mr. Swantko's father established the business ten years ago, but its guiding spirit now is John Swantko, one of the city's most promising business men. Born in Freeland the aggressive manager came to Hanover with his parents when a boy and for several years worked in the mines of the Truesdale colliery of the Glen Alden Coal Company. Being determined to make good in business, he took to aiding his father and eventually became the manager. Assisting him in conducting the business are his three brothers, Russell, Peter and Stephen and Andrew Lawrence.

Russell and Stephen are the store solicitors. They are keen business men having been taught by their older brother. Stephen is a graduate of Nanticoke high school and a student at Penn State college. The meat department is under the supervision of Peter, Lawrence's duties are confined to delivering orders and assisting in the store work. He has proven a very capable man in this line.

The work of remodeling the market was done by Fred Schmidt of Hanover, while D. W. Davis did the plumbing work.

The store has been modernly equipped with display cases, an electric coffee mill, meat slicer and other equipment that goes to make up a real market. It has a porcelain cooling system, manufactured by Ottenheimer Brothers of Baltimore, Md., and installed by Kline Brothers, Wilkes-Barre, distributors. The system is one of the finest in the country and can be found in most of the leading market.

The canned goods, fruits, vegetables, meats, fresh and smoked, handled by Swantko's market come from the best houses and markets. It has been a policy of this store to serve only the best at all times and have earned many staunch friends and patrons by so doing.

During the grand opening—tenth anniversary celebration at Swantko's market, special prices will prevail in all departments. The public is cordially invited to this newly renovated market. Souvenirs will be given to all who visit the market during the celebration.

260. Teodore Swantko, 1932

**Marko Symochko** was born on December 13, 1903, in the Lemko village of Blechnarka, Gorlice County, Austro-Hungarian Empire [present-day Poland] into the family of Hilar and Tekla (née Hatala). He immigrated in 1921 and settled in Yonkers, N.Y. He worked in Jersey City, N.J., for Colgate for two years and returned to Yonkers, N.Y., to work at Alexander Smith Carpet Factory for five years. He then worked as a butcher boy with his brother, Nicholas, for thirteen years. With his wife he later operated Marko's Bar and Grill Restaurant at 44 Woodworth Ave. and Marko's Wine and Liquor Package Store at 53 Tuckahoe Rd., both in Yonkers. He retired in 1958. After the death of his wife he lived in Pompano Beach, Fl. He was married to Eva (née Dzula, 1907–1984). They had no children. Symochko died on November 18, 1999, and was buried in Mt. Hope Cemetery, Hastings-on-Hudson, N.Y.

261. Marko Symochko, 1940

262. Marko Symochko, 1956

**Nicholas Symochko** was born on December 15, 1896, in the Lemko village of Blechnarka, Gorlice County, Austro-Hungarian Empire [present-day Poland] into the family of Hilar and Tekla (née Hatala). He immigrated in 1912 and in 1919 settled in Yonkers, N.Y., where he worked as a molder. In 1924 he was listed as a clerk and in 1925, he opened a meat/grocery store at 2 Seymour St., which was later located at 20 Croton Terrace. He was still in business in 1942. From 1949 he worked for Diamond K Market near Manor House Square and retired in 1958. He was first married to Stephanie (née Durkot, 1900?–1938) and later to Anna (née Fedorko, 1908–1986). He had no children. Symochko died on May 14, 1962, and was buried in Mt. Hope Cemetery, Hastings-on-Hudson, N.Y.

```
ПЕРВОРЯДНА ГРОССЕРНЯ И БУЧЕРНЯ
        Н. СИМОЧКА
Всегда свѣже мясо, ярины, уженины, всяки консервы
въ кенахъ, перворядна, свѣжа кава, чай и т. д.
Русски люди поддержуйте своего человѣка.
          N. SYMOCHKO
       GROCERIES & MEAT MARKET
20 Croton Terrace,           Yonkers, N. Y.
```

263. Nicholas Symochko, 1929

---

**John Talpash** was born on November 11, 1866, in the Lemko village of Łabowa, Nowy Sącz County, Austrian Empire [present-day Poland] into the family of Luka and Katrena (née Polianska). He immigrated around 1886 and worked as a miner in Shamokin, Pa. By 1894 he operated a grocery store in partnership with Ia. Zylich then owned a hotel/saloon with his brothers. The brothers apparently had disagreements about the mutually owned business and John left in 1895 to work in a coal mine in Mt. Carmel, Pa., where he also conducted grocery business with Onufry Joseph *Murdza. In 1896 he moved his family to Canmore, Northwest Territories (now Alberta), Canada, where he worked as a miner and moved around a few times.

```
Наши русскіи братья
ТАЛПАШЪ и ЖИЛИЧЪ
(Talpash and Zylich)
въ ШАМОКИНѢ, Па.
Утримуютъ одну изъ найбольшихъ
и найтаньшихъ Гросернь.
Тѣ наши братья стараются о
томъ, щобъ своихъ братьевъ,
выслужити добрымъ, чис-
тымъ и при томъ таньымъ
товаромъ, прото заслужатъ
они того, щобъ всѣ Русины на
той околицѣ, у нихъ куповали!
БРАТЬЯ ДОРОГІИ! Если сами
неподтримуемъ своихъ людей,
кто же буде ихъ подтримовавъ?
```

264. John Talpash and Zylich

In 1901 he moved to Frank, NWT (also now in Alberta) where he worked as a miner, and his wife ran a boarding house for about sixteen laborers. They hired a Chinese cook. In 1904 they moved to a farm near Bawlf, Alberta. In 1909 they bought a half-section (possibly a section?) of uncleared bushland near Colinton, Alberta, for $1,000. They cleared an area for a farmstead and built their home. They had a large herd of cattle and Talpash's wife used to make 40 pounds of butter a week. They engaged in mixed farming. Talpash would often ship a whole rail car of pigs or cattle to market. He sold the family farm for $18,000, and in 1925 purchased the Colinton Hotel. For 25 years his wife cooked meals for guests of their hotel, while Talpash managed the saloon. They probably sold the Colinton Hotel in 1945 and retired in Colinton. Talpash was married to Barbara (née

Molodchak, 18??–1957) with whom he had: Alice, Michael, Sadie, Mary, Samuel, Julia, Anna, Sally, Kate, Twins A and B, Ben, and Millie. Talpash died on June 27, 1948, and was buried in the Colinton Cemetery.

265. John Talpash, 1928

**Theodore Talpash** was born on October 28, 1859, in the Lemko village of Łabowa, Nowy Sącz County, Austrian Empire [present-day Poland] into the family of Luka and Katrena (née Polianska). He worked as a farmer and served in the Army before immigrating in 1884. He settled in Shamokin, Pa., where he worked for five years as a coal miner for Baumgardner and Douty, at the Enterprise Colliery. He then opened a store on North Shamokin Street but closed it after only seven months and, with his wife, started a boarding house at 246 Pearl St. that by 1894 expanded to include a restaurant, saloon, and grocery store. By 1907 he was listed as a saloon owner at 318 Sunbury St. In 1911 it was noted that "his cafe and hotel are well managed, and he has a profitable patronage, built up by excellent business methods and successful catering to the wants of his customers. His reputation as a citizen and businessman has always been above reproach." In 1912 he also took over the management of the Hotel Vanderbilt at 320 Sunbury St. and later bought it. In 1913 he was still listed in Shamokin as a saloon owner but later moved to New Jersey. By 1918 he lived in Newark, N.J., where in 1920 he was listed as a laborer in a factory. He later lived with his daughter in New York. He

266. Theodore Talpash, 1897

was among the organizers of the local Greek Catholic parish in Shamokin, Pa., as well as the Russian National Union (later Ukrainian National Association) and served as its first president (1894–1895), then vice-president (1895), and after 1896 sat on the Board as a Councilor. He promoted unity, education and improvement of material security of members through insurance policies managed by their own organization. He was married to Anastasia (née Maliniak, 1877–1949) with whom he had: Olga Buckley, Jennie Savitsky, Eugene, Helen, Annie Clemens and John. Talpash died on October 27, 1938, during a visit to New York City and was buried in Saint Boniface Cemetery, Elmont, N.Y.

267. Theodore Talpash, 1899

268. Theodore Talpash, 1909

**John Tatusko** was born on August 15, 1886, in the Lemko village of Binczarowa, Grybów County, Austro-Hungarian Empire [present-day Poland] and immigrated in 1905 (1907?). He lived in Yonkers, N.Y., Lansford, Pa., Coaldale, Pa., and in 1915 moved to Frackville, Pa. In 1920 he was listed as a carpenter but by 1930 he opened a barber shop. He was still in business in 1950 when he was appointed Justice of the Peace in Frackville, Pa. He was still holding this post at the time of his death. He was married to Mary (née Dubec, 1886–1973) with whom he had: Michael, Steven, Anna Krill, Russel, Nicholas, Olga Crush, Nita Zarutskie, and Genevieve. Tatusko died on February 27, 1960, and was buried in Holy Ascension Russian Orthodox Cemetery, Frackville, Pa.

**Michael Tehansky** was born on April 15, 1862, in the Lemko village of Muszynka, Nowy Sącz County, Austrian Empire [present-day Poland] and immigrated in 1882. He eventually settled in Shamokin, Pa., where by 1901, he had a grocery/confectionery store at 516 East Pine St. From 1909 until 1922, when he retired, his business was located at 203 S. Shamokin St. He was married to Anna (née Galak, 1867–1928) with whom he had: Andrew, Mary, Pearl, Stephen, Anthony, Julia, John, Nellie, Michael, Joseph, Peter Tehan and Emily. Tehansky died on February 3, 1942, and was buried in Transfiguration Ukrainian Catholic Cemetery, Coal Township, Pa.

```
Никита Тиханьский
має добру ґросерню 516 Pine St.
продає також одіне до роботи,
полотно, буты і черевики.
SHAMOKIN, PA.
```
269. Michael Tehansky, 1901

```
Іван Тиханьский
руський, знаменито уряджений
стор, продає полотно, сорочки і
всьо, що кому потрібно до їдженя. Желїзні і бляшані товари.
203 Cor. Shamokin and Pine St.
SHAMOKIN, PA.
```
270. Michael Tehansky, 1909

---

**Awksenty Telep** was born on March 15, 1878, in the Lemko village of Wirchne, Gorlice County, Austro-Hungarian Empire [present-day Poland]. He immigrated in 1895 and settled in Yonkers, N.Y. In 1901 he was one of the founding directors of the Little Russian Cooperative Association. By 1903, and until 1915 he had a meat market at 46 Washington St. In 1916 he moved to Bridgeport, Conn., where he ran a grocery/meat market with Andrew *Dragan, first at 706 Hallett St. and later at 681 Hallett St. From 1921 and until at least 1949 he had his own grocery/meat market at the latter address. He was married to Eufrosine/Rose (née Gibey) with whom he had: George, Joseph, Catherine, Eugene, and Clement. Telep died on March 8, 1963, and was buried in St. John the Baptist Greek Catholic Cemetery, Stratford, Conn.

---

**Samuel Andrew Telep** was born on April 10, 1889, in the Lemko village of Wirchne, Gorlice County, Austro-Hungarian Empire [present-day Poland] and immigrated in 1909. He first lived in Yonkers, N.Y., where he worked as a machinist in a hat factory and later as a clerk. In 1914 he moved to Bridgeport, Conn., where he partnered with Andrew *Dragan to operate a grocery at 705 Hallett St. The following year Telep ran two groceries by himself, one at 623 Hallett St. and the other at 2066 Seaview Ave. He later moved the latter one to 1078 Ogden St. Ext. During 1918–1919 he partnered with George *Dudycz. In 1920 he signed a $65,000 contract to have a theatre built in Bridgeport, Conn., in partnership with Nikolay Smey. By 1923 he had part-

```
СТАМФОРД, КОНН.
PHONE: STamford 3 — 4705.
Samuel A. Telep
MEAT MARKET & GROCERY
Delicatessen, Fruit & Beers.

Кед хочете здравя мати,
Треба його шанувати.
Свіжый товар треба брати,
А знати где купувати.
Не заходте до ворогов,
А лем своих посіщайте,
Ворог в біді не поможе,
Сами о том добрі знайте!

●

779 ATLANTIC AVE.,
            STAMFORD, CONN.
```
271. Samuel Andrew Telep, 1937

[Edition of 1911.]
[FORM FOR NATURALIZED CITIZEN.]

No..........
Issued ..........

*BUREAU OF CITIZENSHIP — MAY 3 1912 — DEPT. OF STATE*

# UNITED STATES OF AMERICA.

STATE OF New York
COUNTY OF Westchester ss:

I, Awksenty Telep, a NATURALIZED AND LOYAL CITIZEN OF THE UNITED STATES, hereby apply to the Department of State, at Washington, for a passport for myself, ~~accompanied by my wife,~~ ~~and minor children, as follows:~~

1. .........., born at .........., ..........
2. .........., born at .........., ..........
3. .........., born at .........., ..........
4. .........., born at .........., ..........

I solemnly swear that I was born at Wichne, Gladyszow, Austria on or about the 15 day of March, 1878; that I emigrated to the United States, sailing on board of the Bremen Line from Bremen, Germany about March, 1895; that I resided 17 years, uninterruptedly, in the United States, from 1895 to 1912, at Yonkers West Co. N.Y.; that I was naturalized as a citizen of the United States before the Supreme Court of New York at White Plains, N.Y. on June 22, 1900, as shown by the accompanying Certificate of Naturalization; that I am the IDENTICAL PERSON described in said Certificate; that I am domiciled in the United States, my permanent residence being at Yonkers, in the State of New York, where I follow the occupation of Grocer + Butcher; that I am about to go abroad temporarily; and that I intend to return to the United States within four months, with the purpose of residing and performing the duties of citizenship therein.

### OATH OF ALLEGIANCE.

Further, I do solemnly swear that I will support and defend the Constitution of the United States against all enemies, foreign and domestic; that I will bear true faith and allegiance to the same; and that I take this obligation freely, without any mental reservation or purpose of evasion: So help me God.

Awksenty Telep
(Signature of applicant.)

Sworn to before me this 2 day of May, 1912. Kathryn M Powers
Daniel J Cashin   Notary Public

### DESCRIPTION OF APPLICANT.

Age: 34 years.
Stature: 5 feet, 8 inches, Eng.
Forehead: almost straight
Eyes: blue grey
Nose: straight
Mouth: large
Chin: indented chin
Hair: brown
Complexion: strawberry
Face: red-brown mustache

### IDENTIFICATION.

May 2, 1912

I hereby certify that I have known the above-named Awksenty Telep personally for 5 years, and know him to be the identical person referred to in the within-described Certificate of Naturalization, and that the facts stated in his affidavit are true to the best of my knowledge and belief.

Daniel J Cashin
Atty at Law
[Address of witness.] 2 Hudson St Yonkers NY

Applicant desires passport sent to following address
Awksenty Telep
46 Washington St
Yonkers NY

272. Awksenty Telep, 1912

nered with Philip Korin and they operated a grocery/meat market at 721 Atlantic St., Stamford, Conn., through the late 1920s. From 1929 to his death, he independently ran Belltown Meat Market on Belltown Road and a grocery at 779 Atlantic St., both in Stamford, Conn. He was married to Katherine (1892–1992) with whom he had two daughters: Maria and Olga. Telep died on July 29, 1938, and was buried in Woodland Cemetery, Stamford, Conn.

273. Samuel Andrew Telep, 1909

СТАМФОРД, КОНН.

PHONE: STamford 3-1705

## Samuel A. Telep

FANCY FRUIT & VEGETABLES
MEAT, GROCERIES
and
DELICATESSEN

Компанійчыны бизнесс-шторы
Нашы вспольны суг ворогы.
Бизнессмена, роботника
И бідного человіка.
Не купуйте у ворога
И с далека го минайте,
Зато Вы свого шторника
Все в потребі посіщайте!

779 ATLANTIC AVE,
STAMFORD, CONN.

274. Samuel Andrew Telep, 1936

**Stephen F. Telep** was born on December 13, 1881, in the Lemko village of Pielgrzymka, Jasło County, Austro-Hungarian Empire [present-day Poland] into the family of Fetsko and Maryia (née Paiko). He immigrated in 1900. He first worked in a mine (Jermyn, Pa.) and later at the railways. In his free time, he learned printing and gradually increased his printing production. In the 1920s he engaged in this line of business full time, serving both Lemko and American communities. He published Liubov, the flagship publication of the Russian Orthodox Fraternity Lubov, which he also edited (1925–1957), and served as the financial secretary of that organization. He also published, with his son Andrew serving as editor a weekly English language newspaper, *Mayfield News* (1929–1958). His printing business grew so extensively that he purchased additional printing presses, at the cost of $17,000 each. Telep wrote short plays and composed primers for Sunday schools, which were then printed in his print shop.

275. Stephen F. Telep

He had a book store in which he also offered framed paintings. He was very active in the local Lemko community. He was married to Mary (née Senio, 1888–1973), with whom he had: Justina, Andrew, Helen, and Walter. After the sudden death of his son Andrew (1957) he became ill and retired. Telep died on June 19, 1965, and was buried in St. John the Baptist Russian Orthodox Cemetery, Mayfield, Pa.

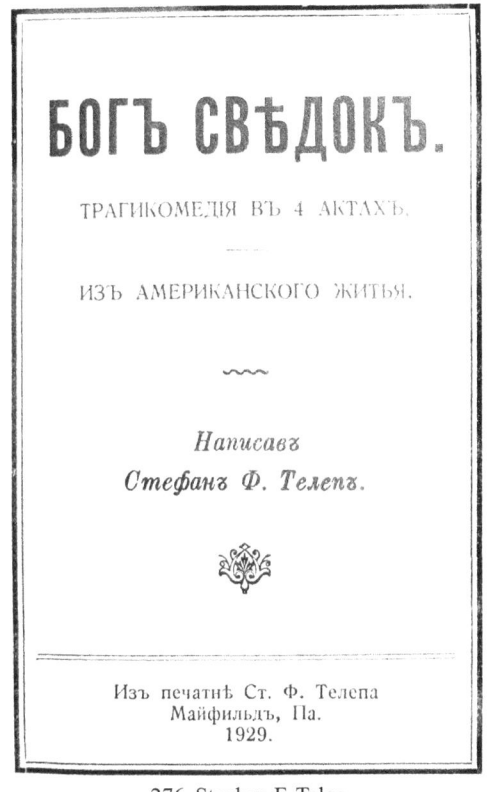

276. Stephen F. Telep

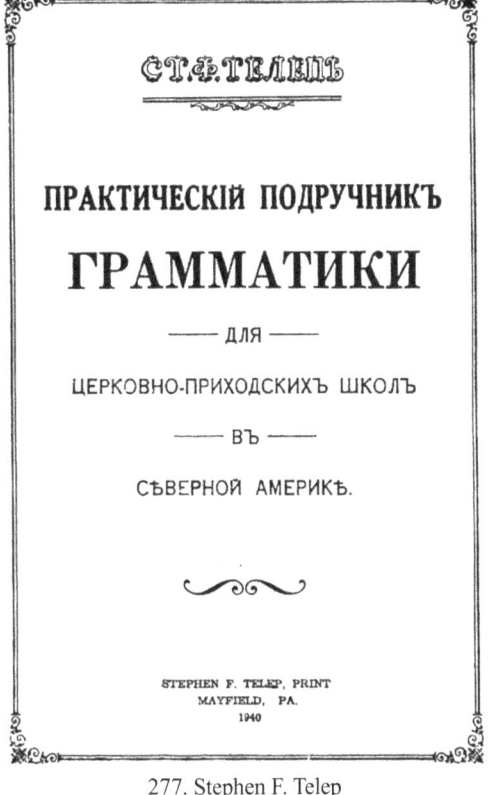

277. Stephen F. Telep

**Nazar Telischak** was born on October 24, 1879, in the Lemko village of Jastrzębik, Nowy Sącz County, Austro-Hungarian Empire [present-day Poland] and immigrated in 1901. He settled in Clifton, N.J., where in 1910 he was listed as a mill hand and in 1920 as a foreman. By 1923 he had a grocery/butcher shop, first at 71 Mahar Ave. and later at

278. Nazar Telischak, 1923

72 Mahar Ave., Clifton. In 1930 he was listed as a butcher working on his own account. He later operated a stationery business on Monroe Street in Passaic, N.J. He was married to Fotia (née Markovich, 1884–1945) with whom he had: Anna, John, and Alexander. Telischak died on October 22, 1933, and was buried in Saints Peter and Paul Orthodox Cemetery, Saddle Brook, N.J.

279. Nazar Telischak, 1926

280. Nazar Telischak, 1929

---

**Arkhip/Archie Trembach** was born on March 2, 1873, in the Lemko village of Łosie, Gorlice County, Austro-Hungarian Empire [present-day Poland] into the family of Theodore and Anastasia (née Pawlak). He immigrated in 1893 and settled in Mayfield, Pa. By 1900 he had a butcher/grocery store at 712 Hill St. He was still in business in 1948. He was married to Solomia (née Telech, 1881–1970) with whom he had: Stefka, Ludmila, Julia, Nikolay, John, Evhenia, Dorothy, Virginia, and Jerome. Trembach died on December 26, 1966, and was buried in St. John Russian Orthodox Cemetery, Mayfield, Pa.

---

**Enoch/Hnat Trochanowski (Enoch Henry Trohan)** was born on October 20, 1874, in the Lemko Region and immigrated in 1894. He settled in Mt. Carmel, Pa., and by 1899 he had a meat market at 24 W. Second Street. In 1907 it was noted that "Enoch Trochanowski will equip his meat market with a 2-ton "Larsen" refrigerating plant, to be installed by the Keystone Engineering Co., Philadelphia, Pa." By 1909 his store evolved into a butcher shop/grocery and had a sausage-making machine; he also sold ship tickets and wired money. He was still in business in 1927 when he employed a fellow Lemko, Joseph Szczypczyk, as a butcher. In 1905, he ran in the Democratic primary for city council but lost. He was one of the original trustees of the Saints Peter and Paul Greek (now Ukrainian) Catholic Church in Mt. Carmel. He was married to Bertha (née Skindzier, 1880–1965) with whom he had: Walter, Irene Small, and Leon/Lee. By 1930 he was living in Chicago, Ill. Trochanowski died on December 2, 1953.

281. Enoch Trochanowski, 1900

282. Enoch Trochanowski, 1903

---

**Samuel A. Trohanowsky** was born on September 2, 1880, in the Lemko village of Binczarowa, Grybów County, Austro-Hungarian Empire [present-day Poland]. Trohanowsky immigrated before 1904. From 1917, Trohanowsky served as a director of the Hungarian Russian Slavonic State Bank based in Johnstown, Pa., which was still open in 1920. At the same time, he was listed as a driver, railroad laborer and carpenter (from 1907 to the time of his death). Trohanowsky was married to Barbara (née Talabovich, 1886–1933) with whom he had: Anna Kalinyak, Mary, Julia, John, Barbara Hazc, and Olga. Trohanowsky died on April 21, 1934, and was buried in Holy Trinity Byzantine Catholic Cemetery, East Taylor Township, Pa.

**Simon T. Turchick** was born on October 15, 1879, in the Lemko village of Żydowskie, Jasło County, Austro-Hungarian Empire [present-day Poland]. He immigrated in 1896 and briefly lived in New Jersey before settling in Yonkers, N.Y., where by 1909 and until the time of his death he had a grocery/butcher shop at 2 Seymour St. In 1925 he successfully petitioned the Common Council of Yonkers to change the zoning of his store's immediate neighborhood from residential to business. He was active in the Russian Brotherhood Organization, serving as its national treasurer (1921–1929). He was among the founders of the Holy Trinity Orthodox parish, St. John the Baptist Society, and Prot. Tovt Society (RBO). He was married to Margaret (1888–1982) with whom he had: Olga Nayduch, Elizabeth Wilchek, and Boris. Turchik died on October 8, 1939, and was buried in Oakland Cemetery, Yonkers, N.Y.

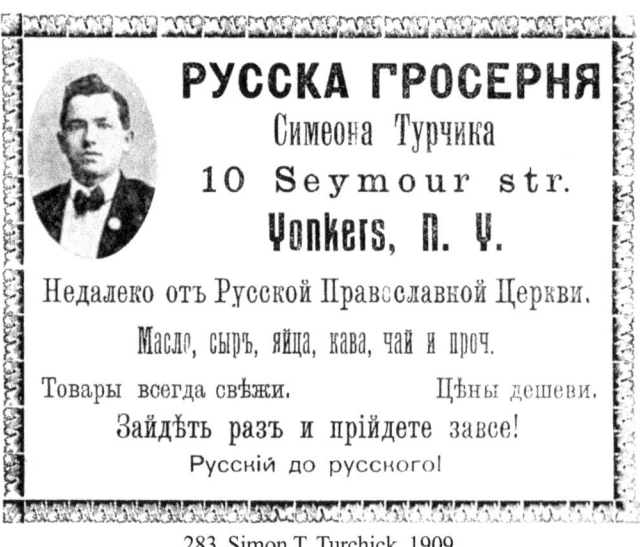

283. Simon T. Turchick, 1909

284. Simon T. Turchick, 1929

> **РУССКАЯ ГРОСЕРНЯ**
> ## Симеона Турчика
> НАЙДЕТЕ ТУТЪ ВСЕ, ЩО ВАМЪ ТРЕБА.
> Никто и нигде не обслужитъ
> Васъ лучше.
> **10 SEYMOUR ST.        YONKERS, N. Y.**
> Telephone 1978.

285. Simon T. Turchick, 1917

**John W. Turko** was born on February 8, 1891, in the Lemko village of Zawadka Rymanowska, Sanok County, Austro-Hungarian Empire [present-day Poland] into the family of Wasyl and Mary (née Pitenko). He immigrated in 1894 and settled in Olyphant, Pa. In 1910 he was listed as a bartender in a saloon. By 1930 he was operating John W. Turko Funeral Home and continued to do so until his death. He was active in business and ethnic/religious organizations, serving as a secretary of the board of trustees of the Scranton State Hospital and third vice-president of the Lackawanna County Funeral Directors' Association. He also served on the board of directors of Volunteers of America, was a director of the Olyphant School District, a trustee of the Fairview State Hospital, and a founder and charter member of the Olyphant Business and Professional Men's Club. He was also a treasurer of the Ukrainian Republican Division of Lackawanna County and served for many years as the president and vice-president of Saints Cyril and Methodius Greek Catholic Church. He was married to Tekla / Tillie (née Sanko, 1901–1961) with whom he had: Mildred Soroka, Johanna Durka, Mary, John and Eugen. Turko died on November 23, 1945, and was buried in Saints Cyril and Methodius Catholic Cemetery, Perckville, Pa. He was rememered as a "well-known midvalley funeral director." The business was continued by his wife and two sons, but Eugen left it in 1980. John J. Turko and Sons Funeral Home is still in business at 404 Susquehanna Ave. in Olyphant.

**Theodor Wachna** was born on June 18, 1867, in the Lemko village of Łosie, Nowy Sącz County, Austro-Hungarian Empire [present-day Poland]. He immigrated in 1886. By 1896 he operated a hotel in Mayfield, Pa., on Hill Street. In 1899 he moved his family from the property near the Hudson and Delaware Depot. In 1900 he was listed as a hotel keeper. In 1910 he was listed as working in retail. In 1916, together with John D. Costeinek and John P. Palko, he chartered the Oak Run Coal Co. of Scranton, Pa., with capital of $5,000. This small company produced some 4,000 tons of coal in 1919 but was offered for sale at public auction in 1924. In 1930 he was listed as a retail merchant operating a grocery store. He retired by 1940, but his store and hotel continued to operate. Wachna was serving on the Mayfield City Council by 1898, and was its chairman (1910-1911). He was among charter members of the Russian Orthodox Greek Catholic Church of St. John the Baptist (1902) and Russian Fire Company of Mayfield, Pa. (1900). He was married to Theodora (née Mieiska, 1870–1947) with whom he had seven children. Wachna died on June 5, 1940, and was buried in St. John the Baptist Russian Orthodox Cemetery in Mayfield.

> ТЕОДОРЪ ВАХНА
> 
> **THEODOR WACHNA**
> 
> УТРиМУЕ ГОТЕЛЬ НЕ ДАЛЕКО РУСКОИ ЦЕРКВИ
> въ Mayfield, Pa.
> 
> За барою мае завсѣгды свѣже пиво и другй здоровй напитки. Мае такожь галю на забавы.
> 
> Хто хоче выпити що доброго, хто хоче забавити ся честно и по люцки, хто хоче вечеромъ здыбати ся зô своими добрыми кумами и пріятелями най просто йде до Вахны, а не пожалуе!

286. Theodor Wachna, 1897

**Theodosy Wachna** was born on January 24, 1874, in the Lemko village of Nowa Wieś, Nowy Sącz County, Austro-Hungarian Empire [present-day Poland]. He completed three years of gymnasium before immigrating in 1894. He first settled in Mayfield, Pa., and worked as a miner. After being injured on the job, he switched to working at a printing shop and later a brewery. In 1897 he moved to Winnipeg, Manitoba, where the Commissioner of Immigration, who also served as the Mayor of Winnipeg, William McCreary, appointed Wachna as his immigration agent, who was to lead Galician immigrants to their appointed territory near the southeastern border of Manitoba known as Stuartburn. Besides farming and minding the store, Wachna helped organize the Municipality of Stuartburn and served as its secretary-treasurer and magistrate, notary public, and secretary of the twelve schools he had organized. In his 50s he operated two large stores and bought, rented, and sold farms, houses, and apartments. He handled leases, loans, and mortgages, completed deeds on properties, translated and wrote letters and documents, surveyed farms, and established roadway rights-of-way. Over 60 years Wachna held various offices and was a counselor and adviser to people of the district. He was married to Ann (née Prygrocky, 1882-1980) with whom he had fifteen children, including Maria, Katherine, Olena, Zofia, Elijah, Johan, Wolodimyr B. "Walter", Antonia, Kozma, Claudia, Olga, and Wyronia; many of whom engaged in business. Wachna died on January 21, 1960 and was buried in St. Alphonsus Cemetery, Windsor, Ontario. He was inducted posthumously in the Manitoba Agricultural Hall of Fame and is listed among Memorable Manitobans by the Manitoba Historical Society.

**Jacob Wandzilak** was born on October 20, 1884, in the Lemko village of Hańczowa, Austro-Hungarian Empire [present-day Poland] into the family of Teodor and Paraska. He immigrated in 1904 and first lived in Brooklyn, N.Y. In 1907 he moved to Yonkers, N.Y. In 1914 he was a co-owner of a grocery store with Dennis Merena at 429 Walnut St., but a year later took over operation himself. From 1917 he was listed working in partnership with John *Spiak operating a meat market at 441 Walnut St. until at least 1919. By 1922 he ran a butcher shop by himself at 156 Yonkers Ave. He also had another butcher shop in Hastings-on-the-Hudson, N.Y. Wandzilak retired in 1936. He served as one of the (original?) directors of the Little Russian Cooperative Association. He was also a secretary and treasurer of St. Michael's Ukrainian Catholic Church, secretary-treasurer of the St. Michael's Society, and an officer of the Providence Association of

Ukrainian Catholics in America. He was married to Melania (née Honcharik, 1885–1944) with whom he had: Theodore, William, Rosalie, Natalie Adamo, and Olga Rudin. Wandzilak died on February 14, 1953, and was buried in Mt. Hope Cemetery, Hastings-on-the-Hudson, N.Y.

**Joseph Waniga** was born on January 1, 1883, in the Lemko village of Ożenna, Jasło County, Austro-Hungarian Empire [present-day Poland]. He immigrated in 1902 and settled in Ansonia, Conn. In 1910 he was listed as a weaver at a velvet factory and in 1920, as a wire drawer working in the brass industry. By 1924 he opened a grocery store at 18 Howard Ave. and operated it until at least 1935. He was also active in real estate. In 1940 he was back working in the brass industry. He was married to Tillie/Tekla (née Zawada, 1883–1963) with whom he had: Ross, Nicholas, Peter, Howard, Fred, and Julia. Waniga died on October 25, 1958, and was buried in the Pine Grove Cemetery, Ansonia, Conn.

287. Joseph Waniga, 1928

**Joseph Warcholic** was born on April 15, 1860, in the Lemko village of Przegonina, Gorlice County, Austrian Empire [present-day Poland] to Daniel and Anastasia (née Zhelem). He immigrated in 1886, and settled in Ansonia, Conn., where he soon became the leader of the local Lemko community. He first worked at Ansonia Brass and Copper Company, but by 1900 he had a saloon at 51 Jersey St., which by 1904 was moved to 53 Jersey St. In 1906 he moved his billiard and pool business to 160 Jersey St., where he soon expanded to two other buildings, at 158 and 162. At the time this was one of the largest buildings on the west side of Ansonia, containing three stores on the ground floor, a large hall with a stage in the rear, and a number of tenants. Warcholic also sold ship tickets and wired money. He was instrumental in the creation of the Orthodox parish today known as Three Saints Russian Orthodox Church, and he served as a member of the

288. Joseph Warcholic, 1915

national Russian Brotherhood Organization leadership. He was married to Julia (née Bilcznianski, 1868–1926) with whom he had: Anna, Mary, and Anton. Warcholic died on July 5, 1927, and was buried in Pine Grove Cemetery, Ansonia, Conn., where his gravestone towers over a small section with parishioners of Three Saints Russian Orthodox Church. His business, referred to as Warcholic Hall, was sold in 1931 by his daughter-in-law to a fellow Lemko, Joseph *Comcowich.

> Ансонѣйцѣ читайте и памятайте, що если хочете напитися здорового пива, токайского вина, краевой сливовицѣ, або закурити смачного цигара, то идѣтъ до
> 
> **Іосифа Вархолика**
> 
> 160 Jersey Street,      Ansonia, Conn.
> 
> Г-нъ ВАРХОЛИКЪ пошле вамъ тоже гроши, где только хочете, спродастъ шифкарту и во всемъ дастъ добру раду, якъ честный русскій патріотъ.
> 
> **Въ готели г-на Вархолика** находится великій автоматичный фортепнъ, котрый для розвеселеня грае мельодіи найславнѣйшихъ композиторовъ. — Идѣтъ и переконаетеся.
> 
> Мае онъ тоже **велику галу** съ сценою для театральныхъ представленій, а тоже на весѣля, балѣ и мітинги. Такъ красныхъ галь якъ ВАРХОЛИКОВА, мало и въ Нью Іорку знайдеся.

289. Joseph Warcholic, 1908

> **Іосифъ Вархоликъ,**
> всѣмъ добре знаный Русскій человѣкъ
> Имѣетъ въ Ансоніи первокла́ссно заряженый Салонъ.
> **КРАСНА ГАЛЯ СО СЦЕНОЮ** для театральныхъ представленій и братскихъ митинговъ.
> 158-160-162 JERSEY ST.      ANSONIA, CONN.
> А-ну, Русины: Свой до свого!

290. Joseph Warcholic, 1910

> **JOSEPH WARCHOLIK,**
> **RUSSIAN LIQUOR DEALER**
> Imported Hungarian Wines and Slivovicz.
> WARCHOLIK HALL TO LET FOR DANCING AND MEETINGS.
> 43 JERSEY ST., ANSONIA, CONN.

291. Joseph Warcholic, 1904

---

**Andrew Warholak** was born on December 15, 1895, in the Lemko village of Świątkowa Wielka, Jasło County, Austro-Hungarian Empire [present-day Poland] and immigrated in 1913. He settled in Cleveland, Ohio, where in 1916 he was listed as a butcher and by 1917 had a grocery/meat store at 2568 St. Olga St. He still had this store in 1930 but by 1940 he was listed as a truck driver engaged in commercial trucking. He was married to Esther (née Walko, 1897–1964) with whom he had: Mary, Dorothy, and William. Warholak died on July 19, 1968, and was buried in St. Theodosius Orthodox Cemetery, Brooklyn, Ohio.

292. Andrew Warholak, 1922

**Nicholas Wartella** was born on December 18, 1869, in the Lemko village of Płonna, Sanok County, Austro-Hungarian Empire [present-day Poland] to Ivan Vorotyla and Mary (née Krzyzanowski / Kryzhanovskii). He immigrated around 1894, settled in Kingston, Pa., and by 1900 had moved to Edwardsville, Pa., working as a miner. By 1900 he had a home with nine boarders. In 1904 a fellow Lemko businessman, John *Repa, loaned Wartella money to buy the property at 73 Armstrong St. in Edwardsville. The house had pigs and chickens and a barn for two cows. In 1910 Wartella was still listed as a miner who owned six homes that were free of mortgages. In 1919 he bought a home at 217 Jackson St. and opened a grocery store there, employing his sons, Stephen and Michael. They competed with the mining company's store. Also, he purchased a vacant lot at 215 Jackson St. In 1920, despite all these investments, he was employed as a car oiler and was a coal mine foreman. In 1924 a house was built at 215 Jackson St. The store

293. Nicholas Wartella

294. The Wartella family, 1927

was moved there and began to expand. In addition to groceries, meat, and produce, on offer there was fresh baked bread from the bakery behind the store, dry goods (primarily clothing and shoes), and freshly killed chickens from the chicken coop out back. The store prospered. Wartella died on March 4, 1926, and was buried in Fern Knoll Burial Park, Dallas, Pa. He was married to Mary (née Senko, 1878–1956) with whom he had: Stephen, Michael, Metro, Nicholas, John, Anne, and Julia. After his death Stephen became the head of the household but Mary became the matriarch of the Wartella family, remembered as a "strong and proud woman" who felt she was successfully established in the community. It was said she could not speak English but had a chauffeur who had been hired to drive her in her expensive car, emphasizing her status. In 1930 sons Nick and Jack, were salesmen in the grocery store while Metro and Stephen were salesmen in the meat market. Metro also drove the Wartella truck, delivering meat and groceries to those who could not travel to the store.

НИКОЛАЙ ВОРОТИЛА
И СЫНОВЕ

Мае первоклассный Шторъ мѣшанныхъ товаровъ, Гросерню и Бучерню. У него можете достати найлучшій товаръ по дуже умѣренным цѣнамъ. — Попробуйте и не пожалѣсте. — Услуга совѣстная- щиро-русская.

ОРДЕРЫ ВСЕГДА ДОСТАВЛЯЮТСЯ
НА ДОМЪ.

УДАВАЙТЕСЬ ВСЕГДА ДО СВОЕГО
РУССКОГО ЧЕЛОВѢКА.

NICHOLAS VOROTILA
215 Jackson St., Edwardsville, Pa.
Bell Phone 2361-J.

295. Nicholas Wartella

**Nicholas M. Washienko** was born on March 31, 1876, in the Lemko village of Banica, Gorlice County, Austro-Hungarian Empire [present-day Poland] and immigrated in 1895. Until at least 1920 he worked as a railway conductor in Yonkers, N.Y., but later, in the 1920s, he had a grocery store. In 1930 he established an insurance and real estate business, which was located at 403 Nepperhan Ave. and later at 1750 Central Park Ave. He retired in 1960 and the business was taken over by his son Nicholas. He was one of the founders of the Carpatho-Russian American Center in Yonkers, N.Y.. and of the Lemko Association. He was married to Julia (née Hylwa, 1874–1967) with whom he had: Nicholas, Michael, Theodore, Alexander, William, Helen Buckley, Olga Crawford, and Mary Cyrulik. In 1966 Yonkers Mayor John E. Flynn proclaimed Sept. 5 to be "Mr. and Mrs. Washienko Sr. Day" to commemorate their 70th wedding anniversary. Washienko died on August 18, 1972, and was buried in Oakland Cemetery, Yonkers, N.Y.

**NICHOLAS M. WASHIENKO**

REAL ESTATE AND INSURANCE

403 Nepperhan Avenue

**YONKERS, NEW YORK**

TELEPHONE: YO 5-2424    5-5551

—:—

Удавайтесь до свого краяна, коли купуете або продаете домъ чи бизнесъ. Онъ дорадитъ и поможе при ассекураціи и при оплатѣ доходового податку.

296. Nicholas M. Washienko, 1956

```
             Tel. YOnkers 5-2424

              N. M. Washienko

             Real Estate & General
                  Insurance

           Notary Public — Income Tax
                    Service
           Appraiser & Licensed Real Estate
                    Broker.

           REAL ESTATE & GENERAL INSURANCE

      Удавайтеся до свого краяна, коли купуєте або продаєте дом
      ци бизнес. Он порадит и поможе при ассекурации и при
                уплаті доходового податку.

           403 NEPPERHAN AVENUE
              YONKERS, NEW YORK
```

297. Nicholas M. Washienko, 1957

---

**Andrew Warycha / Warycka** was born on December 5, 1895, in the Lemko village of Zdynia, Gorlice County, Austro-Hungarian Empire [present-day Poland]. He immigrated in 1913 and settled in Yonkers, N.Y., where he worked at Alexander Smith and Sons Carpet Company. In 1928 he opened a hotel/saloon with Andrew Guzy at 446 Saw Mill Rd. From 1929 to 1936 he was listed as a manager. He later lived in New York City and in the early 1940s he was employed by I.R.T. Power Station as an Assistant Stoker Operator. He was married to Anna (née Doshna, 1905–19??) with whom he had Michael and Samuel. Warycha died in March of 1977.

---

**John Worhach** was born on October 5, 1871, in the Lemko village of Florynka, Grybów County, Austro-Hungarian Empire [present-day Poland]. He immigrated in 1888 and settled in Shamokin, Pa. He moved to Mt. Carmel, Pa., in 1900 and by 1903 he owned and operated Liberty Hotel at 422 N. Maple St. in Diamondtown and did so until 1925. His building was destroyed in a fire in 1905. When it was replaced the next year with a three-story structure, it was noted that "the completion of this handsome building is indicative of the progressive spirit of our people." In 1930 he was listed as a merchant operating a cigar store. In 1937 he was described as a "prominent hotelman of Diamondtown" and in 1946 as a "well-known businessman." In the 1940s he had houses for rent. At the time of his death he operated a café at 422 N. Maple St. He was among the founders of Saints Peter and Paul Greek Catholic parish and was a charter member of the Ruthenian Greek Catholic Saint Demetri Benevolent Society of Mt. Carmel (1917). He was first married to Julia (née Homiak, 1879–1915) with whom he had: Stephen, Beatrice,

```
              Иванъ Воргачь,
      Всѣмъ знаный готельникъ. Шклянки у него якъ
                  старокраєвїі коновки.
      422 N. Maple Str.,                  Mt. Carmel, Pa.
```

298. John Worhach, 1903

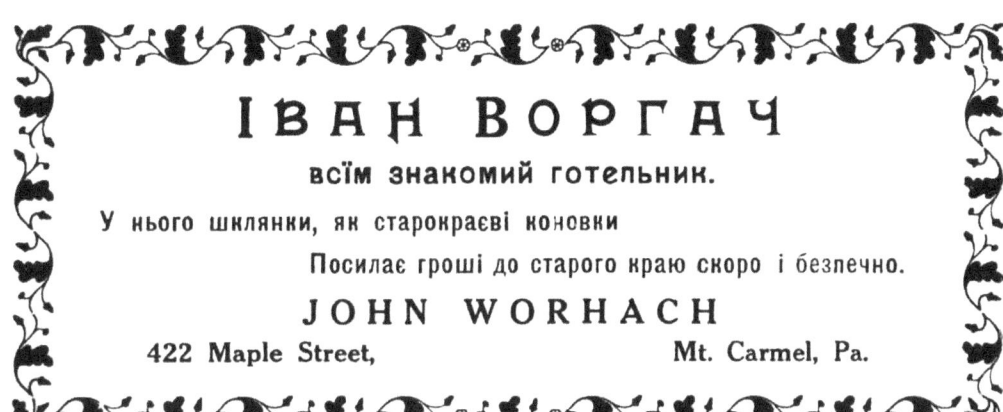

299. John Worhach, 1910

John, Anna, Barbara, and Julia. He was later married to Pauline (née Wilchacky, 1896–1985) with whom he had: Mary, Olga, Pearl, and Alex. Worhach died on April 29, 1950, and was buried in Saints Peter and Paul Greek Catholic Cemetery, Mt. Carmel, Pa.

300. John Worhach, 1925

301. John Worhach, 1925

**For Rent**

FOR RENT—Four-room house. Also a two-room house. Apply to John Worhach, 422 North Maple Street, Diamondtown.   26 3t*

302. John Worhach, 1942

**Theodore Worhacz** was born on June 26, 1869, in the Lemko village of Florynka, Austro-Hungarian Empire [present-day Poland] into the family of Filip. After serving in the army for three years, he arrived in the US in 1890. He made his home in Excelsior, Pa., and later moved to Brady, Pa., for a short time before moving to Shamokin, Pa. Until 1920 he worked as a miner and later became a cattle dealer. By 1921 he was involved in the beverage industry, including beer

Всїм знаменито відомий готельник:

## ІВАН ВОРГАЧ

має свій дім. Шклянки у нього як старо-краєві коновки.
Посилає гроші до старого краю скоро і безпечно.

JOHN WORHACH,
422 N. Maple Str.,            MT. CARMEL, PA.

303. John Worhach

distribution and a wholesale business, which was first listed at 326 Franklin St. at the corner of Spurzheim Street and later at 634 W. Pine St. He continued this business until the 1940s. He was one of the founders and organizers of the Greek Catholic parish of the Transfiguration and served on the church board for many years. Worhacz was also known as a teacher of the Ukrainian language and for many years conducted night classes in Shamokin, Brady and Excelsior. He was first married to Pearl/Paraska (née Ceklinski, 1875–1910) and later to Pearl (née Makuch, 1892–1954) and had the following surviving children: Michael, Mary Nicholis, Theodore, Lovie, Russell, Ophelia Kulonda, Daniel, Walter, Olga, Sylvester, and Mildred. Worhacz died on April 7, 1955, and was buried in Transfiguration Ukrainian Catholic Cemetery, Coal Township, Pa.

304. Theodore Worhach

**THEODORE F. WORHACZ**

ГУРТОВИЙ СКЛАД

ВСЯКОГО РОДА ПИВА.

FRANKLIN & SPURZHEIM STREETS,

**SHAMOKIN, PA.**

305. Theodore Worhach, 1925

**John Worona** was born on June 12, 1885, in the Lemko village of Krynica, Nowy Sącz County, Austro-Hungarian Empire [present-day Poland] and immigrated in 1905. He settled in Clifton N.J., where by 1917 he had a butcher shop at 87 Knapp Ave. and later at 319 Lakeview Ave. He was still in business in the late 1940s. In the early 1950s he worked as a meat cutter in Passaic, N.J. He was first married to Mary (née Jasenczak) who died by 1917. He was later married to Susanna (née Sedlak / Chabra, 1897–1973) and at the time of his death he was survived by two sons: Nestor and Nicholas. Worona died on April 6, 1967, and was buried in Saints Peter and Paul Orthodox Cemetery, Saddle Brook, N.J.

306. Nicholas Yackanicz

**Nicholas Yackanicz** was born on December 16, 1865, in the Lemko village of Muszynka, Nowy Sącz County, Austrian Empire [present-day Poland]. He immigrated in 1885 and settled in Beaver Meadows, Pa. Ten years later he set up the N. and W. Yackanicz Grocery Store with his brother Wasil. In 1910 he was listed as a hotel keeper and in 1913 as a restaurant owner, and a year later he left the grocery business. He ran his hotel for many years. In 1927, after retiring from the hotel business which he turned over to his son, Peter, he became president of the American Bank and Trust Co. of Hazleton, Pa., and later was a director of its successor, the Traders Bank and Trust Company. In 1929 he was named a director of the First National Bank of Weatherly. He also held directorship in Pilsner Brewing and Hazleton Syrup Co. He was active in civic and fraternal affairs, serving as councilman for the Borough of Beaver Meadow, including as the president. He was among the founders and the original trustees of the Saints Peter and Paul Greek Catholic parish. He was married to Olga (née Andrasz, 1876–1955) and had: Peter, (Msgr.) Joseph, Theresa, and Mary Mihalik. Yackanicz died on May 1, 1947, and was buried in Saints Peter and Paul Byzantine Catholic Cemetery, Beaver Meadows, Pa.

# Yackanicz Bros. Food Market

This page is dedicated to Nicholas and Wasil Yackanicz, the founders of Yackanicz Bros. Food Market — also two of the organizers of SS. Peter & Paul's Greek Rite Catholic Church of Beaver Meadows, Pa.

Wasil Yackanicz

Nikolaj Yackanicz, Sr.

307. Yackanicz brothers, Beaver Meadows, 1895

## American Bank & Trust Company of Hazleton, Pa.

| | |
|---|---:|
| CAPITAL | $ 400,000.00 |
| SURPLUS and UNDIVIDED PROFITS | 575,654.00 |
| DEPOSITS | 5,253,000.00 |

### OFFICERS

| | |
|---|---|
| Dr. J. C. Kochczynski | President |
| Nicholas Yackanicz | Vice President |
| John Yourishin | Vice President |
| Andrew J. Shigo | Treasurer |
| Sydney A. Alden | Asst. Treasurer |
| Walter H. Scheffley | Asst. Treasurer |
| Louis T. Gentillini | Asst. Treasurer |

### DIRECTORS

| | |
|---|---|
| Andrew Hourigan | Wilkes-Barre, Pa. |
| Dr. J. C. Kochczynski | Hazleton, Pa. |
| Andrew J. Kotch | Hazleton, Pa. |
| Dr. James A. Longo | Sheppton, iPa. |
| Louis Roman | Hazleton, Pa. |
| Pasco Schiavo | Hazleton, Pa. |
| Edmund Uffalussy | Wilkes-Barre, Pa. |
| M. G. Waschko | Hazleton, Pa. |
| Nicholas Yackanicz | Beaver Meadows, Pa. |
| John Yourishin | Hazleton, Pa. |

UNDER THE SUPERVISION OF THE STATE AND FEDERAL GOVERNMENTS

308. Yackanicz brothers, 1931

# ELEVENTH BIRTHDAY

On the Eleventh Birthday of the American Bank and Trust Company we are especially pleased to express appreciation of the good will and patronage of our customers.

Established April 2nd, 1917, this bank's chief aim has constantly been to render service that would be helpful to the miner, the worker in factory, office, store or shop, to the business house—to everybody who lives, works or transacts business in this community.

Here, where officers are always glad to serve customers personally—following at all times conservative banking practice under Federal and State Governments Supervision—we want you to regard this institution not only as an ideal place for your funds, but also a bank that you can count on as your business friend.

Looking to the steady growth of the Hazleton district, this bank pledges a continuance of the service that has kept it growing ever since it opened for business.

## OFFICERS:

| | |
|---|---|
| N. YACKANICZ | President |
| M. YURKANIN | Vice-President |
| EDWARD A. BYORICK | Treasurer |
| GEORGE A. SHIGO | Assistant Treasurer |
| SIDNEY A. ALDEN | Assistant Treasurer |

## DIRECTORS:

| | |
|---|---|
| J. C. KOCHCZYNSKI, M.D. | EDMUND UFFALUSSY |
| ANDREW HOURIGAN | M. G. WASCHKO |
| ANDREW J. KOTCH | NICHOLAS YACKANICZ |
| LOUIS ROMAN | M. YURKANIN |
| PASCO SCHIAVO | JOHN YOURISHIN |

# AMERICAN BANK AND TRUST COMPANY

HAZLETON, PA.

RESOURCES OVER - - - $6,000,000.00

"BUILT ON SERVICE"

309. Nicholas Yackanicz, 1928

REPORT OF THE CONDITION OF

# Traders Bank And Trust Company

Located at 2-8 East Broad Street, Hazleton, Pa., as of the Sixth day of November, 1936.

## RESOURCES.

RESERVE FUND:
| | | |
|---|---:|---:|
| *Cash, specie and notes | $ 59,789.84 | |
| Cash, due from approved reserve agents | 207,697.65 | |
| *TOTAL RESERVE FUND | | $ 267,487.49 |
| Cash Items | | 61.20 |
| Exchanges for Clearing House | | 4,029.05 |
| Due from banking institutions, excluding reserve | | 39,514.28 |
| Loans and discounts | | 1,228,587.15 |
| Bonds and stocks | | 1,125,252.13 |
| Office building and lot | | 291,200.00 |
| Furniture and fixtures | | 34,000.00 |
| Overdrafts | | 3.66 |
| Other resources not included in above | | 15,285.21 |
| Total | | $3,005,420.17 |

## LIABILITIES

| | | |
|---|---:|---:|
| Demand deposits | | $ 600,970.46 |
| Time deposits | | 1,735,739.75 |
| Certified and Cashier's or Treasurer's Checks | | 5,874.11 |
| Dividends unpaid | | 315.25 |
| Other liabilities not included in above | | 538.05 |
| CAPITAL PAID IN: | | |
| Common | $350,000.00 | |
| TOTAL CAPITAL PAID IN | | 350,000.00 |
| Surplus fund | | 190,000.00 |
| Undivided profits and reserves | | 121,982.55 |
| Total | | $3,005,420.17 |

Commonwealth of Pennsylvania, County of Luzerne, ss:

I, Walter H. Scheffley, Treasurer of the above named institution, do solemnly swear that the above statement is true to the best of my knowledge and belief.

(Signed) WALTER H. SCHEFFLEY,
Treasurer.

Sworn and subscribed to before me this sixteenth day of November, 1936.
(Signed) HENRY K. MARKMAN,
Notary Public.

[NOTARIAL SEAL]
My commission expires April 1, 1939.
Correct—Attest:
Signed—
**JOHN YOURISHIN,
NICHOLAS YACKANICZ,
GEORGE I. PUHAK,**
Directors.

310. Nicholas Yackanicz, 1936

**Wasil / Wasco Yackanicz** was born in February of 1866, in the Lemko village of Muszynka, Nowy Sącz County, Austrian Empire [present-day Poland]. He immigrated in 1887 (1889?). In 1895 he set up the N and W Yackanicz Grocery Store with his brother Nicholas, in Beaver Meadows, Pa. After his brother left the business in 1914 Wasil continued it under his own name until his death. At that time his wife, Tekla, formed a partnership with their sons, Paul and Nicholas, and the business continued as Yackanich Bros. until at least 1945, despite the death of Tekla and Paul. He was married to Tekla (née Lyga, 1873-1943) with whom he had: Paul, Nicholas, Demetrius, Mary Watro, Anna Bacon, Theresa, Olga and William. Yackanicz died on June 20, 1927, and was buried in Saints Peter and Paul Byzantine Catholic Cemetery, Beaver Meadows, Pa.

---

**Onufry Yonak** was born on August 15, 1892, in a Lemko village in Grybów County, Austro-Hungarian Empire [present-day Poland] a into a Iunak / Junak family. He immigrated in 1910 and settled in New York City. By 1917 he was working as a butcher and by 1925 he had his own butcher shop at 312 E. 71st St. in Manhattan. He was still in business in 1953 and had retired by 1957. He later lived on a farm in West Lebanon, N.Y., which he put up for sale in 1963 and moved to Monroe, N.Y. He was married to Mary (née Maksimchak, 1893–1987) with whom he had Paul J. Young and William. Yonak died on December 26, 1975, and was buried in Saint Vladimir's Russian Orthodox Cemetery, Jackson, N.J.

```
TEL. REgent 4—9518
ONUFRY YONAK
POULTRY, PROVISIONS & RESTAURANT
SUPPLIES—SPECIAL KOLBASY

КРАЯНЕ! Ордеруйте у нас на Хрестины, Весіля,
  Свята и предприятия. Завсе свіжы мяса.
Чужы люде задоволены, а и Вы будете як у свого
  спробуете. Ордеруйте сами, телефонуйте, або
      пиште, а радо Вам услужиме.

             O. YONAK
312 E. 71st ST.
Bet. First & Second Aves., NEW YORK,N.Y.
```

311. Onufry Yonak, 1942

---

**Thos / Thomas A. Youshock** was born on February 12, 1885, in the Lemko village of Łosie, Gorlice County, Austro-Hungarian Empire [present-day Poland] as Seman Jewusiak / Ievusiak and immigrated in 1889. His parents were Andryi and Anna. He settled in Olyphant, Pa., where by 1911 he had a plumbing / electric / heating business at 124 River Ave. In 1914 he was also listed as a hardware merchant in Peckville, Pa. By 1917 he had a car and in 1920 owned a house that was worth $10,000. By 1930 his brother Andrew and son Theofan had joined him in the business, which was now called Thos A. Youschock and Son or Youshocks Plumbers. In 1938 they were awarded plumbing contracts for $2,108 to work on the addition to the Wyoming County Court House. They were still in business in 1940. He was married to Rose (née Russen, 1890–1969) with whom he had: Theofan, Olga, Eugenia Poplavsky, Victor, Rose Butwick, and Vladimir. Youshock died on December 21, 1971, and was buried in All Saints Russian Orthodox Cemetery, Peckville, Pa.

312. Thos/Thomas Youschock, 1920

**Harry Zuraw** was born on December 23, 1871, in the Lemko village of Bartne, Gorlice County, Austro-Hungarian Empire [present-day Poland] into a Zhurav family. He immigrated in 1894 and via Philadelphia, Pa. came to Hazleton, Pa. (or possibly Olyphant, Pa.). He abandoned work in mines due to health reasons and in 1896 moved to Derby, Conn. where by 1899 he was engaged in business with Gabriel *Dziadik, running a store at 152 Main St. In 1902 this partnership was dissolved after Zuraw sold his share to his partner. He later engaged in business with Alexis *Horbal, with whom he had a saloon/hotel at 94 Main St. and also wired money. By 1902 they also offered help when it came to purchasing land in the Lemko Region. By 1903 Zuraw had a grocery store at 19 High St., which he eventually sold to Dimitro *Sydoriak. In 1904 Zuraw moved his family to Podolia, Russian Empire (present-day Ukraine), where he purchased land and engaged in farming, but returned to America a year later. He purchased a liquor store at 128 Main St., which he turned into a saloon under the name New York Café. He eventually became a real-estate agent, notary public, and insurance salesman. He also returned to providing private banking and later wired money as an American Express agent and sold steamship tickets out of his two offices at 128 Main St., Derby, Conn., and 20 High St., Ansonia, Conn. In the mid-1920s he ran a grocery store with his wife at 42 Factory St., Derby, Conn. but they retired by 1930.

313. Harry Zuraw, 1915

Zuraw served as a treasurer of the First Russian National Organization of the New England States, which was established in 1912 with the goal of "promoting the spiritual, moral and material welfare of its members." This organization consisted of five branches (Ansonia, New Britain, Waterbury, Bridgeport, and Seymour) and in 1913, under Zuraw's leadership, was transformed into a corporation. This move was challenged in court by the branches but Zuraw prevailed. He also served as a treasurer of the local Ruthenian

Greek Catholic St. Peter and St. Paul Church and was active on a national level in the Russian/Little Russian National Union (later Ukrainian National Association). In 1920 he joined a committee to organize a Ukrainian bank in America. He was married to Ksenia (née Horbal, 1876–by 1940) with whom he had: Anna, Maria, Katherine, and Marian Maissurow. Zuraw died on July 25, 1950, and was buried in St. Peter and St. Paul Ukrainian Greek Catholic Cemetery, Derby, Conn.

314. Harry Zuraw, 1919

Staro Dawnyj Bisnesista W Tej Okolicy Establish B 1889

## HARRY ZURAW

### STEAMSHIP TICKET AGENCY

NOTARY PUBLIC : INSURANCE : REAL ESTATE

128 MAIN STREET, DERBY
20 HIGH STREET, ANSONIA

315. Harry Zuraw

# ILLUSTRATION CREDITS

*Ameryka*, Toledo, Ohio: 190.

ancestry.com: 13, 29-30, 32-33, 35-36, 56, 58, 61, 69-70, 77, 94-95, 104, 128, 135-136, 157-160, 195, 201, 205, 230, 234-238, 246-247, 251, 272-273, 292, 304.

*Ansonia, Derby, Shelton, and Seymour, Connecticut City Directory*: 115, 211, 250, 291, 313.

Bavolack, Daniel: 21, 23, 244.

Basalyga, Piotr: A photo of a thatched-roof house before the Introduction.

Bell, George E., *The Pancios from Galicia: Centennial Reprint*, Ontario, N.Y.: Wayne & Ridge Publishing, 2017: 197-198.

*Boyd's Yonkers City Directory*: 240.

*Bridgeport, Fairfield, Southport, Stratford, Easton and Trumbull Directory*: 67.

Custer, Richard: 14, 84, 120, 146, 164, 183, 212, 217, 220, 295, 303, 306-307.

Decerbo, Michael: 6-8.

Google Patents: 98, 253.

Gordon, Kate and Wayne T. McCabe, Newton, Charleston SC: Arcadia, 1998: 34.

Hotz Café, https://hotzcafe.com/ : 119.

*Illiustrovannyi russko-amerikanski kalendar'* (later: *Russko-amerikanskii kalendar Obshchestva Russkikh Bratstv*): 3, 9-10, 26, 37, 49, 53, 73-74, 79, 90, 102, 106, 111, 116, 118, 121-123, 131, 139, 148-149, 151, 154, 174, 186, 192-193, 196, 203-204, 208, 214, 216, 233-234, 242, 258, 261-262, 278-279, 283-284, 287-289, 308, 312.

*Kalendar' dlia amerykanskykh Rusynov* (later *Kalendar' Rus'koho Narodnoho Soiuza v Amerytsi*, and *Kalendar Ukraïns'koho Narodnoho Soiuza*): 4, 12, 31, 51, 54, 63, 81, 85, 86, 89, 92, 99, 105, 107, 117, 124, 126-127, 156, 161-163, 167, 169-173, 209, 224-228, 232, 248, 259, 268, 270, 281-282, 298-301, 305, 314.

Klancko, Robert: 129-130.

*Karpatorusskii kalendar' Lemko-Soiuza*: 11, 17-19, 25, 27-28, 38, 50, 55, 57, 59, 64-66, 75, 80, 93, 97, 108-110, 112-114, 132-134, 137-138, 140-141, 147, 152-153, 155, 175-176, 179-182, 184-185, 187-188, 194, 210, 215, 218-219, 221-223, 229, 243, 245, 252, 255-256, 263, 271, 274-275, 280, 296-297, 311.

Madzik, John: 52.

*Mauch Chunk Times News*, Mauch Chunk, Pa.: 40.

*Moody's Manual of Corporation Securities*: 2.

*Moody' Manual of Investments*: 42.

*Mount Carmel Item*, Mt. Carmel, Pa.: 87, 91, 302.

*New Britain City Directory*: 202.

NYPL Digital Collections: 1.

*The New York Times*: 241.

*Pershii rusko-amerykanskii kalendar'*: 44, 83, 88, 101, 143, 168, 189, 191, 231, 266, 286.

*The Plain Speaker*, Hazleton, Pa.: 24, 206, 309-310.

*Postup*, New York: 103, 289.
*Pravda*, Philadelphia, Pa.: 48, 150.
*Pravoslavnyi russko-amerikanskiiкalendar*: 12, 71-72, 76, 78, 100, 285, 290.
*Republican Herald*, Pottsville, Pa.: 39, 41, 254, 257.
*Scranton Republican*, Scranton, Pa.: 16.
*The Scranton Truth*, Scranton, Pa.: 46.
*Shamokin News Dispatch*, Shamokin, Pa.: 249.
*Standard Sentinel*, Hazleton, Pa.: 22, 207.
Success Postal Card Co., Hazleton, Pa.: A photo of Ellis Island before the Introduction
*Svoboda*, Jersey City, N.J.: 5, 43-47, 60, 62, 82, 125, 142, 144, 177-178, 199-200, 213, 239, 264, 267, 269.
*The Wilkes Barre Record*, Wilkes Barre, Pa.: 165-166, 260.
*Wall Street Journal*, New York, N.Y.: 15.
Wartella Genealogy, http://wartella.com/ 293-294.

# INDEX

**A**

Adamiak, Constantine  28
Adamiak, Efrozima/Iefroska  28
Adamiak, Isidore  28
Adamiak, John  28
Adamiak, Melania Fedorczak  28
Adamiak, Olga  28
Adamiak, Peter  28
Adamiak, Rose  28
Adamiak, Stefania  28
Adamiak, Vladimir  28
Adamo, Natalie  173
Alberts, Helen  106
Alex Rusynyk and Son Funeral Home  138
Alexander Smith and Sons Carpet Co.  3, 35, 63, 94, 133, 159, 178
All Saints Cemetery, Peckville, Pa.  125, 130, 186
Allentown, Pa.  12, 89, 97, 135
American Bank and Trust Co., Hazleton, Pa.  181
American/Anaconda/Ansonia Brass Co.  3, 95, 132, 173
American Building Club, Detroit, Mich.  11, 154
Andruchowicz, Constantine  13
Ansonia, Conn.  3, 18, 19, 36, 45, 46, 47, 81, 95, 103, 116, 131, 132, 133, 134, 157, 173, 186
Antonik, Mary  45
Apster, Judith  152
Arlington Cemetery, Drexel Hill, Pa.  91
Arsenych, Ella  113
Assumption of Virgin Mary Cemetery, Northampton, Pa.  111, 125
Atlas, Pa.  64, 71, 84
Auburn, N.Y.  10, 106, 128

**B**

Bachyns'kyi, Iulian  6
Bacon, Anna  185
Balch, Emily Greene  13, 15, 16, 23
Balint, Olga  28
Balnica, Lisko County  81
Balut, Anna  113
Banica, Gorlice County  39, 59, 60, 152, 177
Banica, Grybów County  28, 35
Barna, Alexander C.  28
Barna, Eva  28
Barna, Ksenia/Sadie Fylak  28
Barna, Mary  55
Barna, Mary Fesh  29
Barna, Mike  28
Barna, Paul  28
Barna, Peter  28
Barna, Piza/Paiza Vatrolick  28
Barna, Stephen  28
Barna, Theodore  29
Barna, William  28
Barrett, M. J.  9
Bartne, Gorlice County  36, 45, 46, 86, 131, 132, 133, 186
Basalyga, Eva Stachura  29
Basalyga, John  31
Basalyga, Mary Warasicka  30
Basalyga, Onufrii  29
Basalyga, Pearl/Paraska Chomiak  31
Basalyga, Peter  9, 11, 29, 31
Basalyga, Simeon  31
Bavolack Jr., Daniel  32
Bavolack, Adam  32
Bavolack, Anastasia Cirkot  32
Bavolack, Anna Daniliak  31
Bavolack, Daniel  11647
Bavolack, Dmitro  32
Bavolack, Julia  32
Bavolack, Vasil  32
Bavolack, Vasyl'  31
Bayonne, N.J.  11, 91, 103
Beacon Falls, Conn.  95
Beaver Meadows, Pa.  102, 181, 185

Belle Vernon Cemetery, North Belle Vernon, Pa.   50
Bendinsky, Anna   156
Benson, Andrew   34
Berezynski, Sally/Salomea   113
Betula, Pa.   126, 128
Bielanka, Gorlice County   55
Bihuniak, Fatima Oseniak   34
Bihuniak, Tessie Parahus   34
Bihuniak, Theodore   34
Bihuniak, Vasyl   34
Bincarowsky, Helen   34
Bincarowsky, John   34
Bincarowsky, Joseph   34
Bincarowsky, Peter   34
Bincarowsky, Suzanna Sheer   34
Bincarowsky, William "Wasil"   34
Binczarowa, Grybów County   43, 69, 72, 162, 169
Bischak, Alexander   35
Bischak, Julius   35
Bischak, Olga Osterjohn   35
Bischak, Richard   35
Bischak, Robert   35
Bischak, Theodore   35
Bischak, William   35
Blackwood, Pa.   42
Blechnarka, Gorlice County   159, 160
Bochnak, Dolores   135
Bochnewich, Eva Paranich   35
Bochnewich, Fotii   35
Bochnewich, John   35
Bochnewich, Kirill   35
Bochnewich, Mary Wojtowicz   35
Bochnewich, Michael   35
Bochnewich, Paul   35
Bochnewich, Therese   35
Boght Corners, N.Y.   67
Bogusza, Grybów County   48, 63, 64, 71, 73, 88, 89, 111
Bohaczyk, Andrew   36
Bohaczyk, Anna Pecushak   36
Bohaczyk, Daniel   36
Bohaczyk, Mary Worobel   36
Bohaczyk, Peter   20, 36
Boroshovich, John   36
Boroshovich, Leshko   36
Boroshovich, Mary   36
Boroshovich, Maryia Smarz   36
Boroshovich, Nicholas   36
Boroshovich, Paiza/Pelagia Gbur   36
Boroshovich, Pauline   36
Boroshovich, Walter   36
Borowits, John   105
Borowski, Olga   82
Bosak, Michael   45147
Bosak Private Bank   9
Bosak State Bank, Scanton, Pa.   9
Brady, Mary   103
Brady, Pa.   179
Brenia, Peter   16
Bridgeport, Conn.   12, 18, 48, 50, 57, 74, 91, 100, 152, 163
Bristow, Mary   93
Broad Mountain Building and Loan Association   70
Broda, Damian "Demko"   11, 38
Broda, Sarah Ann Howell   38
Broderick, Mary   154
Brooklyn, N.Y.   34, 40, 91, 96, 142, 172
Brunary Niżne, Grybów County   52
Brunary, Grybów County   154
Buchanan, Helen   98
Buck Run, Pa.   139
Buckley, Helen   177
Buckley, Olga   162
Buffalo, N.Y.   154
Bunga, Anna   128
Bungo, Rose   126
Burnard, John H.   9
Bush, Anna   126
Butwick, Rose   186
Bybel, Alexander   39
Bybel, Andrew   39
Bybel, Anna   39
Bybel, Anna Pac   39
Bybel, Anna Szkymba   39
Bybel, Eva   39
Bybel, Eva Kycej   39
Bybel, Harry   39
Bybel, Ivan   39
Bybel, John   39
Bybel, Mary Florence Matika   39
Bybel, Paul   39
Bybel, Peter   39

Bybel, Petro  39
Bybel, Stephen  39
Bybel, Theodore / Frank D.  39
Bybel, William  39

## C

Calkins, Mildred  98
Calvary Cemetery, Maspeth/Woodside, N.Y.  128
Campana, Tessie  68
Capitan, Olga  55
Carbondale, Pa.  78
Carlstadt, N.J.  120
Carnegie, Pa.  48
Carpatho-Russian American Center  115, 177
Carpatho-Russian Literary Association  76
Carr, Charles M.  9
Carroll, John  104
Catawissa, Pa.  84
Cedar Lawn Cemetery, Paterson, N.J.  35, 55, 112, 117
Chamberlain, Anastasia/Nancy  119
Chandler, Justina  34
Charleroi Cemetery, Charleroi, Pa.  136
Charleroi, Pa.  48, 136
Charles Baber Cemetery, Pottsville, Pa.  42
Chicago, Ill.  6, 169
Chomiak, Anna  29
Chowanes, Eva Haluschak  41
Chowanes, George  41
Chowanes, Jean  41
Chowanes, John P.  10, 40
Chowanes, Michael  41
Chowanes, Nancy  41
Chowanes, Peter  41
Chylack, Akelena  42
Chylack, Alex C.  11, 42
Chylack, Anastasia Polansky  42
Chylack, Andrew  42
Chylack, Anna Bice/Bajas  42
Chylack, Harry  42
Chylack, Jerome  42
Chylack, John  20, 42
Chylack, Michael  42
Chylack, Nestor  42
Chylack, Peter  42
Chylack, Tekla Polefka  42
Chylack, Theodore  42
Chylack, Theodore P.  20, 42
Chylak Jr., George  45
Chylak, Anna Warcholak  42
Chylak, Annie  43
Chylak, George  8, 9, 20, 43
Chylak, Geraldine  42
Chylak, Helen  42
Chylak, Julia Czar  45
Chylak, Kundrad  43
Chylak, Leo  42
Chylak, Mary  42, 45
Chylak, Nestor  45
Chylak, Rosalie  42
Chylak, Tillie  45
Cidylo, John  40
Cidylo, Kalistrat  40
Cidylo, Nicholas  40
Cidylo, Olga  40
Cidylo, Paraska Zabowska  40
Cidylo, Peter  40
Cihi, Martha  148
Cikot, Anastasia Pirog/Wandzilak  45
Cikot, Annie  45
Cikot, Helen  45
Cikot, Hnat  45
Cikot, Iakov  45
Cikot, John  45
Cikot, Julia  45
Cikot, Mary  45
Cikot, Matrona  45
Cikot, Simon  45
Cikot, Steve  45
Cikoth, Theodore  19
Cirko Jr., Peter  45
Cirko, Anna Chomiak  45
Cirko, Michael  45
Cirko, Pearl Barna  45
Cirko, Peter  45
Cirkot, Alex  46
Cirkot, Elena  46
Cirkot, Joanna Stasienko  45
Cirkot, Olena Hodio  45
Cirkot, Olga  46
Cirkot, Osyf  45

Cirkot, Ruth  46
Cirkot, Sidor  19, 45
Cirkoth, Irene Dokla  46
Cirkoth, John  46
Cirkoth, Maryia Gbur  46
Cirkoth, Stella  46
Cirkoth, Theodore  46
Cirkoth, William  46
Citizens' Club of McAdoo  150
Citizens National Bank of Shenandoah, Pa.  40
Ciuryk, Alexander  47
Ciuryk, Anna Sarich  47
Ciuryk, Anthony  47
Ciuryk, Julia  47
Ciuryk, Larry  47
Ciuryk, Oscar  17, 47
Clark, Helen  116
Clemens, Annie  162
Cleveland, Eva  63
Cleveland, George  63
Cleveland, Maria Horbal  63
Cleveland, Michael  63
Cleveland, Ohio  7, 54, 63, 83, 89, 97, 138, 154, 174
Cleveland, Raymond  63
Cleveland, Rosa  63
Cleveland, Steven  63
Clifton, N.J.  18, 29, 31, 55, 112, 115, 117, 120, 123, 167, 181
Coaldale, Pa.  39, 135, 162
Cohoes, N.Y.  12, 20, 67, 68, 116, 117
Colgan, Vera  35
Colinton Cemetery  161
Colinton Hotel  160
Comcowich, Dorothy  47
Comcowich, Edward  47
Comcowich, Harry  47
Comcowich, Helen  47
Comcowich, John  47
Comcowich, Joseph  19, 47
Comcowich, Lillian  47
Comcowich, Mary Zanowiak  47
Comcowich, Michael  47
Comcowich, Paul  19, 47
Comcowich, Tekla  18
Comcowich, Tekla Tezbir  47
Comcowich, Theodore  47
Comcowich, Thomas  47
Comcowich, William  47
Comcowich, Joseph  174
Community Funeral Home  106
Cook, Margaret  103
Corba, Annie Fechosko  48
Corba, Harvey  48
Corba, Helen  48
Corba, Joseph  48
Corba, Mary Bock  48
Corba, Nick  48
Corba, Peter  48
Corba, Steve  48
Corba, Vladimir  48
Coriell, Mabel  38
Cosmarchike, John  92
Costeinek, John D.  171
Crawford, Olga  177
Crest Haven Memorial Park, Clifton, N.J.  120
Cross Fork, Pa.  126
Crush, Olga  162
Curth, Mildred  47
Cushon, Marry  46
Cusick, P. F.  9
Cyrulik, Mary  177
Czajkowski, Michael  112
Czaszyn, Sanok County  109
Czeremcha, Sanok County  112
Czertyżne, Grybów County  102, 114
Czyrna, Grybów County  40

**D**

Dailey, Edward J.  9
Daliowa, Sanok County  104, 134, 157
Danbury, Conn.  60
Danville, Pa.  65
Daytona Beach, Fla.  36
Deackon, Peter  57
Derby, Conn.  8, 45, 52, 86, 152, 186
Detroit, Mich.  11, 154
Detroit, Pa.  157
DiFate, Tekla/Tillie  154
Diamondtown, Pa.  71, 84
Diehl, Helen  48
Dime Trust and Safe Deposit Company, Shamokin, Pa.  141
Dragan, Andrew  16, 17, 48, 100, 163

Dragan, Anna  48
Dragan, Elsie  48
Dragan, Eva  48
Dragan, Eva Luciszyn  48
Dragan, Fannie/Euphemia Koltko  48
Dragan, John  48
Dragan, Mary  48
Dragan, Mykhal  48
Dragan, Olga  48
Dragan, Stefania  48
Dragan, Stella  48
Dragan, Vladimir  48
Dragon, William  100
Driscoll, Martha  119
Drosdak, Alex  48
Drosdak, George  48
Drosdak, Isaack  48
Drosdak, John  48
Drosdak, Joseph  48
Drosdak, Leo  48
Drosdak, Marianna Drozdiak  48
Drosdak, Mary  42, 48
Drosdak, Mary Warcholak  48
Drosdak, Metro  48
Drosdak, Michael  48
Drosdak, Simon  48
Drosdak, Walter  42, 48
Dudra, Anastazyia Szlanta  48
Dudra, Andryi  48
Dudra, Eva Trembacz  50
Dudra, John  48, 50
Dudra, Peter  50
Dudycz, George  50, 163
Dudycz, Helen  50
Dudycz, Lillian  50
Dudycz, Peter  50
Dudycz, Theodora/Dora  50
Dupay, Mary  81
Durka, Johanna  171
Durkot, Anthony  50
Durkot, Eva Sterzyn/Sturgeon  50
Durkot's Bar and Grill, Yonkers, N.Y.  50
Durkot, Michael  50
Durkot, Mixhael  50
Dutchess, N.Y.  120
Dutko, Betty  123
Dziadik, Catherine Wójcik  53
Dziadik, Edward  53
Dziadik, Gabriel  8, 16, 52, 53, 132, 186
Dziadik, Jaroslawa  53
Dziadik, Michael  53
Dziadik, Peter  53
Dziadik, Stephen  53
Dziama, Anastazyia  54
Dziama, Dan'ko  54
Dziama, Freida/Efroska Sudyk  54
Dziama, Peter  54
Dziama, Raymond  54
Dziama, Samuel  54
Dziama, Steven  54
Dziobko, George  14
Dzwinchik, Alex  55
Dzwinchik, Anna Cekleniak  55
Dzwinchik, Chester  55
Dzwinchik, John  55
Dzwinchik, Mary  55
Dzwinchik, Nicholas  55
Dzwonczyk, Anastazyia Wojtowicz  55
Dzwonczyk, Anthony  55
Dzwonczyk, Domka Maksimiak  55
Dzwonczyk, Eve  55
Dzwonczyk, Michael  55
Dzwonczyk, Mykolai  55
Dzwonczyk, Ozim  55
Dzwonczyk, Vasyl  55
Dzwonczyk, Victor  55
Długie, Gorlice County  68

**E**

East Ridgelawn Cemetery, Clifton, N.J.  31, 115, 123, 134
Edwardsville, Pa.  9, 28, 81, 113, 176
Elmira Heights, N.Y.  86
Elysburg, Pa.  36
Evergreen Cemetery, Hillside, N.J.  28
Excelsior, Pa.  14, 65, 68, 84, 85, 117, 179
Exchange, Pa.  84
Exchange Hotel and Restaurant  136

**F**

Fairfield, Conn.  50
Farmers Flour and Grain Co., Stratford, Conn.  12, 57

Fecko, Samuel   15
Fedorchak, Helen   55
Fedorchak, Jerry   55
Fedorchak, John   55
Fedorchak, Pelahia Bodin/Bodon   55
Fedorchak, Stephen   55
Fedorchak, Theodore   55
Fedorko, Cyril   57
Fedorko, Cyril W.   12, 56
Fedorko, Helen   57
Fedorko, Julia Preslovska/Pryslopska   57
Fedorko, Nicholas   57
Fedorko, Nicholas W.   21174
Fedorko, Peter   57
Fedorko, Tekla Dziubina   56, 57
Fedorko, Vasyl'   56, 57
Fedorko, William   57
Fekula, Anna Herbut   59
Fekula, Eva Yewusiak   57
Fekula, Hryhoryi/Harry   57
Fekula, Joseph Harry   11, 57
Fell Township, Pa.   55, 77
Ferants, Anna   103
Fern Knoll Burial Park, Dallas, Pa.   59, 81, 136, 176
Fesch, Adeline   60
Fesch, Eva   60
Fesch, Julia.   60
Fesch, Mary   60
Fesch, Mitro   17, 59
Fesch, Rose   60
Filak, Andryi   60
Filak, Justina   61
Filak, Mary   60
Filak, Mary Wysowski   62
Filak, Maryia Fesh   60
Filak, Michael   62
Filak, Paul   61, 62
Filak, Peter   11, 17, 60, 62
Filak, Stella   62
Filak, Thomas P.   61
Fill, Andrew   63
First National Bank, Olyphant, Pa.   9
First National Bank, Jessup, Pa.   9-10, 30
First National Bank, McAdoo, Pa.   9, 93
First National Bank, Weatherly, Pa.   181
Florynka, Grybów County   68, 76, 116, 117, 178-179
Follansbee, WV   136
Formas, Joyce   35
Forty Fort, Pa.   59
Frackville, Pa.   18, 70, 112, 139, 156, 162
Francik, Helen   152
Franklin, N.J.   38
Franko, Ivan   1
Freedom, Pa.   147
Freeland, Pa.   13, 157
Fregman, Helen   64
Furtak, Helen   63
Furtak, Kost   63
Furtak, Mary   63
Furtak, Paraska Dzubak/Holowiak   63
Furtak, Paraska Lazor   63

# G

G and G Potato Chip Co.   68
Galician-Russian American Club/ Russian American Club, Seymour, Conn.   95
Gambal, Alice   64
Gambal, Annie   64
Gambal, Barbara Malyjczak   64
Gambal, Catherine Swallow   64
Gambal, Daniel   64
Gambal, Dominka Felenchak   64
Gambal, Jacob   22, 63
Gambal, John   64
Gambal, Julius   64
Gambal, Lena   64
Gambal, Lottie   64
Gambal, Marie   64
Gambal, Mary   64
Gambal, Mary Duffalo   64
Gambal, Matei   64
Gambal, Melka Homiak   64
Gambal, Michael   64
Gambal, Mitrofan   20, 64
Gambal, Nicholas   64
Gambal, Olga   64
Gambal, Sophie   64
Gambal, Stephen   64

Gambal, Tatiana   64
Gambal, Vera   64
Gambal, Walter   64
Gambal, Wasco   64
Gamble, Anna   65
Gamble, Isadore   65
Gamble, Mary Schipchik   65
Gamble, Thomas M.   10, 64
Garfield, N.J.   22, 35, 73, 77, 133
Garland, Julia   42
Garofalo, Olga   50
Gary, Ind.   74
George Washington Memorial Park, Paramus, N.J.   120
Giffin, Anne C.   46
Gilberton, Pa.   109, 112
Glen Carbon, Pa.   139
Glinsky, Nellie   64
Glowa, Antoinette   66
Glowa, Catherine Chlebowsky   66
Glowa, Ella/Helen Emck   66
Glowa, John   9, 14, 20, 22, 65
Glowa, Matthew   66
Glowa, Michael   66
Glowa, Walter   66
Gogotz, Natalie   42
Gola, Julia   28
Goldsmith, Frances   38
Golowitz, Julia   39
Golubowski, Vera   133
Gould, Olga   151
Grab, Jasło County   112, 132, 136
Grandview Cemetery, Monessen, Pa.   104, 109
Grapeville, Pa.   157
Greenback, Pa.   141
Greek Catholic Union   9, 126
Greek Catholic Fraternal and Beneficial Society of Winton   30
Grega, Alexander P.   12, 67, 68
Grega, Anna Lazor   67
Grega, Peter   67
Greve, Rosalie   128
Grucelak, Anna Koznoski   67
Grucelak, Charles D.   11, 67
Grucelak, Ivan   67
Grucelak, Tessie "Teckla" Lawrick   68
Guba, Anna Kopcza   68
Guba, Harry   68
Guba, John H.   12, 67, 68
Guba, Walter   68
Gurin, Mary   157
Guzy, Andrew   178
Gładyszów, Gorlice County   56, 57, 105, 106, 119, 134, 148

## H
Habura, Andryi   68
Habura, Anna   69
Habura, Eva   69
Habura, Helen   69
Habura, Jeannie   69
Habura, Mary   69
Habura, Mary Dubec   68
Habura, Nicefor   14, 20, 21, 68
Habura, Paraska Maksymchak   68
Habura, Phoebe Murdza   69
Habura, Stella   69
Habura, Walter   69
Hackensack, N.J.   117
Halaburda, Alex   69
Halaburda, Dominika Homiak   69
Halenda, Anna Uhrin   70
Halenda, John   70
Halenda, Melvin   70
Halenda, Michael   70
Halenda, Olga   70
Halkovich, Anna   73
Halkovich, Eva.   73
Halkovich, Hilar   73
Halkovich, Julia Hatala   73
Halkovich, Peter   73
Halkovich, Sam   73
Halkowicz, Alexander   71
Halkowicz, Annie   71, 73
Halkowicz, Catherine   73
Halkowicz, Ella   73
Halkowicz, Elsie   71
Halkowicz, George   73
Halkowicz, Johanna   73
Halkowicz, John   71, 73
Halkowicz, Lora/Lucy Shiposh   71
Halkowicz, Mary   73
Halkowicz, Michael   73
Halkowicz, Michael N.   20, 71
Halkowicz, Nicholas   72

Halkowicz, Pearl   71
Halkowicz, Pearl/Paraska Wronik   73
Halkowicz, Thomas   71
Halkowicz, Victorola   73
Halkowicz, Walter   71, 73
Hall, Anna   148
Hannover, Pa.   91
Hardy, Anastasia   76
Hardy, Myron   12, 76
Hardy, Nadine   74, 76
Hardy, Peter S.   12, 20, 74-76
Harems, Dennis   15
Harrilchak, Anna   63
Harrington, Mary   41
Hassick, Dora Tatus'ko   76
Hassick, George   76
Hastings-on-the-Hudson, N.Y.   172
Hatala, Anna   77
Hatala, Joseph   77
Hatala, Julia   77
Hatala, Katrena Petryshyn   77
Hatala, Mary   77
Hatala, Mykhal   77
Hatala, Olga   77
Hatala, Paraska Demczko   77
Hatala, Stephen   77
Hatala, Thomas   22, 77
Havrilak, Anastasia   77
Havrilak, Annie   77
Havrilak, Ina   77
Havrilak, John   77
Havrilak, Joseph   77
Havrilak, Maria   77
Havrilak, Michael   77
Havrilak, Stephen   77
Hawran, Akim   22, 77
Hawran, Alex   78
Hawran, Anna Dudra   78
Hawran, Annie   78
Hawran, Christine   78
Hawran, Eva   78
Hawran, Evdokia   78
Hawran, Harry   78
Hawran, John   78
Hawran, Julia   78
Hawran, Maria   78
Hawran, Metro   78
Hawran, Michael   78

Hawran, Simeon   78
Hawran, Thomas   22, 78
Haze, Barbara   169
Hazleton Junction, Pa.   11, 31
Hazleton, Pa.   13, 132, 146, 150, 186
Hazleton Syrup Co.   181
Hańczowa, Gorlice County   1, 50, 85, 103, 123, 125
Health Developing Apparatus Co.   74
Heidelberg, Pa.   90
Heights Deposit Bank, Wilkes-Barre, Pa.   136
Heller, Anna   156
Hemlock Farm Dairy   130
Herkimer, N.Y.   116
Hess, Olga A.   53
Hladick, Johanna H. Wyslocky   79
Hladick, Victor P.   11, 78
Hoblak, Anna   81
Hoblak, Anna Vrabel   81
Hoblak, Ashton   81
Hoblak, Catherine   81
Hoblak, Elizabeth   81
Hoblak, George   81
Hoblak, Helen   81
Hoblak, Joseph   81
Hoblak, Michael   81
Hoblak, Olga   81
Hodio, Alexander   81
Hodio, Dorothy   81
Hodio, Faust   81
Hodio, Olga   81
Hodio, Stephen   17, 81
Hodio, Timothy   81
Holda, Anna   82
Holda, Barbara   82
Holda, John   20, 82
Holda, Myron   82
Holda, Olga   82
Holda, Paul   82
Holda, Walter   82
Hollywood, Fl.   57
Holod, Dionizi   82
Holod, Ivan   82
Holod, Matrona Pavlikovska   82
Holod, Olena Spiak   82
Holowczak, Anna Pelechaty   18, 83

Holowczak, Joseph  83
Holowczak, Paul  10, 83
Holowczak, Peter  83
Holowczak Funeral Home  83
Holy Ascension Cemetery, Frackville, Pa.  70, 112, 156, 162
Holy Cross Cemetery, Detroit, Mich.  155
Holy Cross Cemetery, North Arlington, N.J.  91, 103
Holy Ghost Cemetery, Jessup, Pa.  30
Holy Resurrection Cemetery, Plains, Pa.  131
Holy Sepulcher Cemetery, Cheltenham, Pa.  64
Holy Transfiguration Cemetery, Nanticoke, Pa.  158
Holy Trinity, East Taylor Township, Pa.  169
Homiak, Anna  84
Homiak, Anna Gardysh  85
Homiak, Celia  84
Homiak, Eddie  84
Homiak, Eugenia  84
Homiak, Eva Worhach  84
Homiak, George  85
Homiak, Isadore  84
Homiak, Jennie  84
Homiak, John  84, 85
Homiak, Justin  84
Homiak, Kate  84
Homiak, Mary Bencroski  84
Homiak, Olga  84
Homiak, Paul  21, 84
Homiak, Peter  85
Homiak, Sophie  84
Homiak, Steve  85
Homiak, Teodozii  21
Homiak, Thecla/Tillie Nowak  84
Homiak, Theodore  22, 85
Homiak, Walter  84
Homick, Anna  85
Homick, Anthony W.  85
Homick, Frank  85
Homick, John  85
Homick, Julia Sym  85
Homick, Mary  85
Homick, Stephen  85
Homick, William  85
Honcharik, Esther Mikuliak  86
Honcharik, Mary  86
Honcharik, Olga  86
Honcharik, Walter  16, 85
Honeybrook, Pa.  13
Hoover, Anna  42
Horbal, Alex  132
Horbal, Alexis  86, 186
Horbal, Andrew  87
Horbal, Dorothy  87
Horbal, Ivan  86
Horbal, Louise  87
Horbal, Maryia Dutkanych  86
Horbal, Myron  87
Horbal, Olena  87
Horbal, Peter  87
Horbal, Theodosia/Tevdozka Felenchak  18, 87
Horoschak, Mary  88
Horoschak, Paul  88
Horoschak, Peter  22, 88
Horoschak, Sophia Shuptar  88
Horoschak, Stella  88
Horoschak, Theodore  88
Horoshchak, Anna  18, 89
Horoshchak, August  89
Horoshchak, Fenna Chermanski  89
Horoshchak, Jacob  89
Horoshchak, Osyf  89
Horoshchak, Simon  14, 21, 22, 89
Horoshchak, Theodore  89
Horoshchak, Walter  89
Hotel Vanderbilt  161
Hotz Café, Cleveland, Ohio  7, 89, 188
Hotz, Andrew  89
Hotz, Anna Paryllo  89
Hotz, Barbara Zaporach  89
Hotz, Freida Rusin  89
Hotz, John  7, 89
Hotz, Mike  89
Hotz, Peter  89
Hotz, Steve  89
Hotz, William  89
Howard, Mary  89
Hoxie, Mary Theodora  128
Hrishko, Anastazyia Guzy  89
Hrishko, Antonii  89

Hrishko, Basil 89
Hrishko, Daniel 90
Hrishko, Gregory 90
Hrishko, Myron 90
Hrishko, Olga 90
Hrishko, Rose Homik 90
Hrobuchak, Olga 104
Hudson, Pa. 131, 136
Humecki, Daniel 90
Humecki, Dolores 91
Humecki, Dorothy 91
Humecki, Frances E. Mahaven 91
Humecki, Francis 91
Humecki, Irene 91
Hungarian Russian Slavonic State Bank, Johnstown, Pa. 169
Hylwa, Andrew 81
Hylwa, Ann 81
Hylwa, Antinette 81
Hylwa, Elias 81, 128
Hylwa, Esther 81
Hylwa, Helen 81
Hylwa, John 81
Hylwa, Mary 81
Hylwa, Stephanie 81
Hylwa, Theckla Ciok 81
Hyra, Anna Durniak 91
Hyra, Hryts 91
Hyra, Katrena Fylak 91
Hyra, Orest 12, 91

## J

Jadick, Pearl 76
Jastrzębik, Nowy Sącz County 167
Jaszkowa, Gorlice County 64
Jeannette, Pa. 122
Jeansville, Pa. 149
Jeddo, Pa. 136
Jermyn, Pa. 13, 166
Jersey City, N.J. 10, 12, 29, 47, 61, 77, 78, 82, 86, 91, 106, 128, 159
Jessup, Pa. 47371
Jewusiak, Anna Mashonski 91
Jewusiak, Harry 91
Jewusiak, Helen 91
Jewusiak, Ivan 91
Jewusiak, Joseph 91
Jewusiak, Mary 91
Jewusiak, Maryia Voitovych 91
Jewusiak, Michael 91
Jewusiak, Stephen J. 10, 91
Jewusiak, Walter 91
John W. Turko Funeral Home 171
Johnstown, Pa. 4, 20, 169
Joseph, John 68
Jowyk, Helen 90
Jurowce, Sanok County 74

## K

Kaczmarczyk, Anna 92
Kaczmarczyk, Basil 92
Kaczmarczyk, Ethel/Natalka Korin 92
Kaczmarczyk, Iefroska Borik 92
Kaczmarczyk, Isabela 92
Kaczmarczyk, John 92
Kaczmarczyk, Joseph 92
Kaczmarczyk, Julia 92
Kaczmarczyk, Mary 92
Kaczmarczyk, Michael 92
Kaczmarczyk, Mikhal 92
Kaczmarczyk, Mykhal 92
Kaczmarczyk, Olga 92
Kaczmarczyk, Stephen 92
Kaczmarczyk, Theodore 92
Kaczmarczyk, Vladimir 92
Kaczmarczyk, William 92
Kalinyak, Anna 169
Kamianna, Grybów County 42, 113, 120
Kamionka, Sanok County 28, 29, 45
Kandel, Sylvia 11
Kapitula, Gmitro 7, 9, 20, 92
Kapitula, Julia 93
Kapitula, Mary Koban 92
Kapitula, Matrona Segletsky/Hladym 93
Kapitula, Teodor 92
Kaprowski, Michael 13
Karandisevski, Frank J. 12, 74
Karell, Alexander 94
Karell, Eva Wojtovich 94
Karell, John 94
Karell, Michael 17, 94
Karell, Walter 94
Karlak, Annie 96
Karlak, Dimitry/Michael W. 95

Karlak, Helen/Olena   95
Karlak, Ignatius /Hnat Selvestroff   96
Karlak, Ignaty/Otto   95
Karlak, John   95
Karlak, Joseph   96
Karlak, Julia   96
Karlak, Mary   96
Karlak, Mary Michniak   95
Karlak, Michael   95
Karlak, Mildred/Melania Mikulak   96
Karlak, Nicholas   96
Karlak, Paul   96
Karlak, Peter   95
Karlak, Stephen   96
Karlak, Ustina/Eunice   95
Karlak, Victoria Michniak   95
Karlak, Wasil   95, 96
Karlak, William   95
Kashytskii, Iurko   1
Kasych Jr., Charles   98
Kasych, Andrew   97
Kasych, Anna   98
Kasych, Charles   12, 97
Kasych, Daniel   97
Kasych, Eva Popowchak   97
Kasych, Mary Nestor   97
Kasych, Raymond   97
Kasych, Vera   98
Kasych Service Station   97
Katrinics, Anna   81
Kearny Point, N.J.   29
Keetsock, Metreo   156
Kelley, Julia   106
Kemmerer, Emily   90
Kinanrd, Anne   154
Kingston, Pa.   81, 136, 176
Klein, Louise D.   46
Klimkosky, Susan   102
Klimkówka, Gorlice County   28
Klymash, Peter   100
Klymash, Tillie/Tekla Pupchyk   100
Koban, Anastasia Kieselowska   100
Koban, Cost   100
Koban, Fotina   18
Koban, Fotina Czar   100
Koban, Ivan   100
Koban, John   100
Koban, Lena   100

Koban, Nellie   100
Koban, Peter   100
Koban, Vera   100
Koban, William   100
Koblosh, Aftanazy   100
Koblosh, Anna Durkot   100
Koblosh, Eva Hatala   100
Koblosh, Helen   100
Koblosh, Michael   100
Koblosh, Mytro   100
Kochansky, John   102
Kochansky, Joseph   102
Kochansky, Lewis   102
Kochansky, Louis   102
Kochansky, Susanna Larzo   102
Kochansky, William   102
Kolody, Catherine   111
Kolynack, Michael   14
Kopp, Mildred   152
Kopyscianski, Anna Chlebowsky   102
Kopyscianski, Anthony   102
Kopyscianski, Helen   102
Kopyscianski, Henry   102
Kopyscianski, Ioanna   102
Kopyscianski, Ivan   102
Kopyscianski, Jeannine   102
Kopyscianski, John   102
Kopyscianski, Julian   21, 102
Kopyscianski, Michael   102
Kopyscianski, Theodore   102
Kopystianski, Julian   114
Koralko, Alexander   104
Koralko, Annie Wencl/Wenzel   104
Koralko, Eva Stehnach   104
Koralko, Fetsko Kurylko   104
Koralko, Maryia Syjczak   104
Koralko, Metro   104
Korbelak, Alexander   103
Korbelak, Anna Janiga   103
Korbelak, Annie   103
Korbelak, George   103
Korbelak, Helen   103
Korbelak, John   11, 103
Korbelak, Juli Rotko   103
Korbelak, Lida   103
Korbelak, Louise   103
Korbelak, Michael   103
Korbelak, Stephen   103

Korbelak, William   103
Korbicz, Anthony   103
Korbicz, Helen Fedko   103
Korbicz, John   103
Korbicz, Joseph   103
Korbicz, Levi   103
Korbicz, Michael   103
Korbicz, Paul   103
Korbicz, Roman   103
Korbicz, Stephen   103
Korin, Philip   165
Kotań, Jasło County   97
Kotys, Alex   104
Kotys, Eva   104
Kotys, Mary   104
Kotys, Mary Gabla   104
Kotys, Miroslav   104
Kotys, Nick   104
Kotys, Olga   104
Kotys, Rose   104
Kotów, Nowy Sącz County   131, 151
Kowalchik, Alexander   11, 18, 20, 104
Kowalchik, Amelia   104
Kowalchik, John   104
Kowalchik, Kathryn   18
Kowalchik, Kathryn Chowanski   104
Kowalchik, Olga   104
Kowalchik, Stephen   104
Kowalchik, Theofan   104
Kowalczyk, Alexander   106
Kowalczyk, Emelia/Mildred Kurylak   106
Kowalczyk, Harry   10, 106
Kowalczyk, Jacob   17, 105, 106
Kowalczyk, Johanna Skripak   106
Kowalczyk, John   10, 106, 107
Kowalczyk, Kyrylo "Kerey"   106
Kowalczyk, Lavonia   107
Kowalczyk, Leon   10, 16, 17, 106
Kowalczyk, Lillian   106
Kowalczyk, Marion   107
Kowalczyk, Matthew   107
Kowalczyk, Michael   106
Kowalczyk, Paul   107
Kowalczyk, Rose   105
Kowalczyk, Stella Spewak   107
Kowalczyk, Stephen   105, 106
Kowalczyk, Theodore   105
Kowalczyk, Theresa Doshna   105
Kowalczyk, Walter   10, 106
Kowalczyk, William   10, 106
Kowalczyk Funeral Home   106
Kowtko, Julia   107
Kowtko, Onufer   20, 107
Kowtko, Stephanie   107
Koziel, Nellie   146
Krashkevich, Mary   136
Krempna, Jasło County   89, 149
Krenicki, Olga   120
Krenitsky, Al   108
Krenitsky, Anna   108
Krenitsky, Harry   108
Krenitsky, Hilary   108
Krenitsky, Mary Kuzmich   108
Krenitsky, Olga   108
Krenitsky, Peter   108
Krenitsky, Rose   108
Krenitsky, Secelia   108
Krill, Anna   162
Krynica, Nowy Sącz County   181
Krzywa, Gorlice County   39
Kudlik, Ilko   109
Kudlik, John   109
Kudlik, Justyna   109
Kudlik, Olga   109
Kudlik, Walter   109
Kufrovich, Helen   41
Kulanda Jr., Phillip   111
Kulanda, Afton   109, 110
Kulanda, Alfred   110
Kulanda, Amelia   111
Kulanda, Anna   110
Kulanda, Anna Krupa   110
Kulanda, Catherine Moskaluk   111
Kulanda, Dennis   14, 110
Kulanda, Dennis A.   21, 109
Kulanda, Eva Murdza   109, 110
Kulanda, Joseph   111
Kulanda, Julia   110
Kulanda, Nicholas   21, 110
Kulanda, Phillip   21, 109, 110
Kulaszne, Sanok County   139, 156
Kulmatycki, Julia   71
Kulonda, Ophelia   180
Kulpmont, Pa.   36
Kunkowa, Gorlice County   55, 78, 136

Kurey, Ahafia Salei/Peiko Fedko 111
Kurey, Daniel 111
Kurey, John 111
Kurey, Joseph 111
Kurey, Julia 111
Kurey, Mary 111
Kurey, Waldemar 111
Kushvara, Mykhal 13
Kuziw, Mary 66
Kuzmicz, Katie Anderson 111
Kuzmicz, Peter C. 21, 22, 111
Kuzmicz, Rosie 111
Kuzmicz, Stephen 111
Kwiatkowski, Rose 126
Kłopotnica, Jasło County 48, 100

**L**

Labowsky, Anna Sladechak Pelak/ Pellack 112
Labowsky, George 112
Labowsky, John 112
Labowsky, Mildred 112
Labowsky, Samuel Paul 112
Lackawanna County Funeral Directors' Association 171
Ladika, Anna 122
Lahutsky, John 112
Lahutsky, Paraska / Margare Baran 112
Lahutsky, Peter 112
Lahutsky, Russell 112
Lahutsky, Thomas 112
Lakeview Cemetery, Bridgeport, Conn. 81
Lakewood, Ohio 11, 64
Lalka, Paulina 130
Lansford, Pa. 39, 40, 42, 162
Larksville, Pa. 55
Legosh, Helen 113
Legosh, Mary Kanik/Konic 113
Legosh, Mathew 113
Legosh, Olga. 113
Legosh, Peter 9, 22, 0112
Leluchów, Nowy Sącz County 67
Lemko Association 18, 23, 25, 73, 86, 146, 177
Lemko Hall see Carpatho-Russian American Center

Lemko Relief Committee 76
Lemkos' Committee 78
Lesko, Helen 50
Leszczyny, Gorlice County 35, 48
Liberty Hotel 178
Lipscius, Catherine 139
Liptak, Olga 133
Little Falls, N.J. 122
Little Russian Cooperative Association/ Little Russian Corporation, Yonkers, N.Y. 15, 48, 86, 106, 116, 135, 148, 154, 163, 172
Little Russian National Union see Russian National Union
Little, Anna 151
Lower Askam, Pa. 45
Luczkowec, Efrem 21, 113
Luczkowec, Maria Steranka 113
Luczkowec, Michael 113
Lukasik, Stanley 40
Lynn, Jacob M. 9
Lysiak, Mary 82

**Ł**

Łabowa, Nowy Sącz County 109, 110, 120, 121, 122, 160-161
Łosie, Gorlice County 48, 57, 63, 91, 94, 106, 107, 143, 168, 185
Łosie, Nowy Sącz County 171
Ług, Gorlice County 61, 82, 154

**M**

Madigosky, Ella 46
Madzelan, Anna Dutko 114
Madzelan, Evheniia 114
Madzelan, Iefrozka 114
Madzelan, Ivan 114
Madzelan, Tymko 114
Magnitzky, Anastasia 148
Mahanoy City, Pa. 8, 70, 92, 112, 125
Maissurow, Marian 187
Majchrowicz, Anna 146
Maksymik, Mary 126
Maliniak, Anna Moskaluk 114
Maliniak, Eugene 114
Maliniak, Gabriel 21, 102, 114
Maliniak, Henry 114
Maliniak, Michael 114

Maliniak, Walter   114
Malinowki, Bolesław   1
Malutich, Barbara Mikuliak   115
Malutich, Havryl   115
Malutich, Iuliia Dankovska   115
Malutich, John   17, 115
Malutich, Simon   115
Manhattan, N.Y.   151
Manitoba Historical Society   172
Manko, Anna   137
Mantone, Rose   132
Maplewood, N.J.   28
Market Street National Bank, Shamokin, Pa.   9-10, 65
Marko's Bar and Grill Restaurant   159
Marko's Wine and Liquor Package Store   159
Markowicz, Mary   98
Masley, Antoinette Wujcicka   115
Masley, Jerry   115
Masley, Michael A.   115
Masley, Peter   115
Masley, William   115
Mauch Chunk, Pa.   34, 48
Maurer, Mary   36
Mayfield, Pa.   28, 55, 108, 140, 143, 168, 171, 172
McCurdy, Antoinette   119
McAdoo, Pa.   9, 31, 92, 150
McAdoo Property Owners' Association   93
McGivney, Mary   53
McKees Rocks, Pa.   134
Medenek, Anna   47
Meder, Mary   104
Melia, Stella   36
Merancy, Mary   132
Merena, Aleksander   117
Merena, Anna   116
Merena, Anna Dubetz   117
Merena, Basil   117
Merena, Damian   17, 20, 116
Merena, Denni   116
Merena, Dennis   16, 17, 19
Merena, Elsie   116
Merena, Eva   116, 117
Merena, Eva Haszczyc   116
Merena, Fannie   116

Merena, Gregory   117
Merena, Helen   117
Merena, Jean   117
Merena, John   117
Merena, John L.   20, 117
Merena, Mary   116, 117
Merena, Maryna Murawski   117
Merena, Metro   116
Merena, Michael   116, 117
Merena, Moxy   116
Merena, Olga   117
Merena, Pauline   116
Merena, Pearl   117
Merena, Peter   116
Merena, Stella   117
Merena, Stephen   116
Merena, Walter   117
Merena, Zachary   117
Merva, Justina   140
Meschan, Elizabeth   39
Metrinko, Seman   20
Miami, Fl.   73
Miczejewski, John   57
Mihalak, Anastasia Woytowik   119
Mihalak, Harold   119
Mihalak, Lucas   119
Mihalak, Peter   119
Mihalak, Rose/Eufrozina Schmyda   119
Mihalak, Simeon   119
Mihalik, Mary   181
Mikailek, Frank E.   92
Mildred, Amelia   148
Miller, Justine   146
Minersville, Pa.   115, 135
Miners' Bank of McAdoo, Pa.   31
Miner's National Bank, Wilkes-Barre, Pa   113
Miner's Savings Bank, Olyphant, Pa.   44, 104
Mitrenko, Anastazyia Swiatko   117
Mitrenko, Anna   118
Mitrenko, Eva   118
Mitrenko, Harry   118
Mitrenko, John   118
Mitrenko, Lubor   118
Mitrenko, Michael   118
Mitrenko, Mykhal Mytrenko   117

Kurey, Ahafia Salei/Peiko Fedko    111
Kurey, Daniel    111
Kurey, John    111
Kurey, Joseph    111
Kurey, Julia    111
Kurey, Mary    111
Kurey, Waldemar    111
Kushvara, Mykhal    13
Kuziw, Mary    66
Kuzmicz, Katie Anderson    111
Kuzmicz, Peter C.    21, 22, 111
Kuzmicz, Rosie    111
Kuzmicz, Stephen    111
Kwiatkowski, Rose    126
Kłopotnica, Jasło County    48, 100

**L**
Labowsky, Anna Sladechak Pelak/ Pellack    112
Labowsky, George    112
Labowsky, John    112
Labowsky, Mildred    112
Labowsky, Samuel Paul    112
Lackawanna County Funeral Directors' Association    171
Ladika, Anna    122
Lahutsky, John    112
Lahutsky, Paraska / Margare Baran    112
Lahutsky, Peter    112
Lahutsky, Russell    112
Lahutsky, Thomas    112
Lakeview Cemetery, Bridgeport, Conn.    81
Lakewood, Ohio    11, 64
Lalka, Paulina    130
Lansford, Pa.    39, 40, 42, 162
Larksville, Pa.    55
Legosh, Helen    113
Legosh, Mary Kanik/Konic    113
Legosh, Mathew    113
Legosh, Olga.    113
Legosh, Peter    9, 22, 0112
Leluchów, Nowy Sącz County    67
Lemko Association    18, 23, 25, 73, 86, 146, 177
Lemko Hall see Carpatho-Russian American Center

Lemko Relief Committee    76
Lemkos' Committee    78
Lesko, Helen    50
Leszczyny, Gorlice County    35, 48
Liberty Hotel    178
Lipscius, Catherine    139
Liptak, Olga    133
Little Falls, N.J.    122
Little Russian Cooperative Association/ Little Russian Corporation, Yonkers, N.Y.    15, 48, 86, 106, 116, 135, 148, 154, 163, 172
Little Russian National Union see Russian National Union
Little, Anna    151
Lower Askam, Pa.    45
Luczkowec, Efrem    21, 113
Luczkowec, Maria Steranka    113
Luczkowec, Michael    113
Lukasik, Stanley    40
Lynn, Jacob M.    9
Lysiak, Mary    82

**Ł**
Łabowa, Nowy Sącz County    109, 110, 120, 121, 122, 160-161
Łosie, Gorlice County    48, 57, 63, 91, 94, 106, 107, 143, 168, 185
Łosie, Nowy Sącz County    171
Ług, Gorlice County    61, 82, 154

**M**
Madigosky, Ella    46
Madzelan, Anna Dutko    114
Madzelan, Evheniia    114
Madzelan, Iefrozka    114
Madzelan, Ivan    114
Madzelan, Tymko    114
Magnitzky, Anastasia    148
Mahanoy City, Pa.    8, 70, 92, 112, 125
Maissurow, Marian    187
Majchrowicz, Anna    146
Maksymik, Mary    126
Maliniak, Anna Moskaluk    114
Maliniak, Eugene    114
Maliniak, Gabriel    21, 102, 114
Maliniak, Henry    114
Maliniak, Michael    114

Maliniak, Walter   114
Malinowki, Bolesław   1
Malutich, Barbara Mikuliak   115
Malutich, Havryl   115
Malutich, Iuliia Dankovska   115
Malutich, John   17, 115
Malutich, Simon   115
Manhattan, N.Y.   151
Manitoba Historical Society   172
Manko, Anna   137
Mantone, Rose   132
Maplewood, N.J.   28
Market Street National Bank, Shamokin, Pa.   9-10, 65
Marko's Bar and Grill Restaurant   159
Marko's Wine and Liquor Package Store   159
Markowicz, Mary   98
Masley, Antoinette Wujcicka   115
Masley, Jerry   115
Masley, Michael A.   115
Masley, Peter   115
Masley, William   115
Mauch Chunk, Pa.   34, 48
Maurer, Mary   36
Mayfield, Pa.   28, 55, 108, 140, 143, 168, 171, 172
McCurdy, Antoinette   119
McAdoo, Pa.   9, 31, 92, 150
McAdoo Property Owners' Association   93
McGivney, Mary   53
McKees Rocks, Pa.   134
Medenek, Anna   47
Meder, Mary   104
Melia, Stella   36
Merancy, Mary   132
Merena, Aleksander   117
Merena, Anna   116
Merena, Anna Dubetz   117
Merena, Basil   117
Merena, Damian   17, 20, 116
Merena, Denni   116
Merena, Dennis   16, 17, 19
Merena, Elsie   116
Merena, Eva   116, 117
Merena, Eva Haszczyc   116
Merena, Fannie   116

Merena, Gregory   117
Merena, Helen   117
Merena, Jean   117
Merena, John   117
Merena, John L.   20, 117
Merena, Mary   116, 117
Merena, Maryna Murawski   117
Merena, Metro   116
Merena, Michael   116, 117
Merena, Moxy   116
Merena, Olga   117
Merena, Pauline   116
Merena, Pearl   117
Merena, Peter   116
Merena, Stella   117
Merena, Stephen   116
Merena, Walter   117
Merena, Zachary   117
Merva, Justina   140
Meschan, Elizabeth   39
Metrinko, Seman   20
Miami, Fl.   73
Miczejewski, John   57
Mihalak, Anastasia Woytowik   119
Mihalak, Harold   119
Mihalak, Lucas   119
Mihalak, Peter   119
Mihalak, Rose/Eufrozina Schmyda   119
Mihalak, Simeon   119
Mihalik, Mary   181
Mikailek, Frank E.   92
Mildred, Amelia   148
Miller, Justine   146
Minersville, Pa.   115, 135
Miners' Bank of McAdoo, Pa.   31
Miner's National Bank, Wilkes-Barre, Pa   113
Miner's Savings Bank, Olyphant, Pa.   44, 104
Mitrenko, Anastazyia Swiatko   117
Mitrenko, Anna   118
Mitrenko, Eva   118
Mitrenko, Harry   118
Mitrenko, John   118
Mitrenko, Lubor   118
Mitrenko, Michael   118
Mitrenko, Mykhal Mytrenko   117

Mitrenko, Olga   118
Mitrenko, Pelagia Mudryk   118
Mitrenko, Peter   118
Mitrenko, Sam   118
Mitrenko, Seman / Simon Metrinko / 117
Mochnaczka Niżna, Nowy Sącz County 77, 78
Mochnaczka, Nowy Sącz County   146
Monchak, Helen Grusha   120
Monchak, Joseph   120
Monchak, Peter   120
Monchak, Samuel   120
Monessen, Pa.   104, 109
Monroe, N.Y.   115, 185
Morawska, Eva   20
Moritz, Joseph   112
Moszak, Teresa   126
Mszana, Krosno County   128
Mt. Carmel, Pa.   20, 22, 36, 69, 71, 72, 73, 82, 85, 88, 121, 122, 160, 169, 178
Mt. Hope Cemetery, Hastings-on-Hudson, N.Y.   86, 106, 107, 146, 159, 160, 173
Mt. Olivet Cemetery, Maspeth, N.Y. 40, 96, 104, 148
Muchnacky, John   120
Muranko, Stephen   107
Murdza, Anna   122
Murdza, Benedict (Benjamin)   122
Murdza, Catherine Fetko   122
Murdza, Lena   122
Murdza, Magdalena   122
Murdza, Maria Halaburda   122
Murdza, Mary   122
Murdza, Maryia Bobak   121, 122
Murdza, Natalie   122
Murdza, Nicholas   122
Murdza, Olga   122
Murdza, Onufry Joseph   22, 121
Murdza, Osyf   121, 122
Murdza, Phillip   121, 122
Murdza, Stephen   121, 122
Murdza, Theodora Moszczar   122
Murdza, Vladimir   122
Mustorick, Lovie   64
Muszynka, Nowy Sącz County   102, 141, 163, 181, 185
Myscowa, Krosno County   139
Męcina Wielka, Gorlice County   92

**N**

N and W Yackanicz Grocery Store   185
Nanticoke, Pa.   29, 45, 55, 157
Nayduch, Olga   170
Nepperhan Valley Realty Company, Yonkers, N.Y.   148
Nescott, Aksenty   122
Nescott, Catherine   122
Nescott, Ellen   122
Nescott, George   122
Nescott, Maria Stashchak   122
Nescott, Mary Elizabeth Zawada   122
Nescott, Nicholas   122
Nescott, Paul   122
Nescott, Pearl   122
Nescott, William   122
Nesquehoning, Pa.   42
Nevick, Rose   146
New Britain, Conn.   81, 128, 139
New Haven, Conn.   139
New York City, N.Y.   1, 12, 41, 91, 96, 104, 128, 136, 140, 149, 150, 178, 185
Newark, N.J.   28, 115, 161
Newtown Cemetery, Newtown, N.J. 38
Newtown, N.J.   11, 38
Nicholis, Mary   180
North Catasauqua, Pa.   123
Northampton, Pa.   22, 111, 125
Nowa Wieś, Nowy Sącz County   172
Nowak, Annie   113
Nowica, Gorlice County   34, 95, 96

**O**

Oak Lawn Cemetery, Hanover Township, Pa.   45
Oakland Cemetery, Yonkers, N.Y.   39, 50, 63, 100, 107, 115, 119, 133, 135, 151, 154, 170, 177
Olaynick, Julia   98
Old Forge, Pa.   20, 64
Olean, N.Y.   126, 128

Olenich, Helen Smarsh   123
Olenich, Justyna Jankoski   122
Olenich, Paul W.   122
Olenich, Walter   123
Olenich, Wasil   122
Olesnewicz, Anna   24
Olesnewicz, Helen   24
Olesnewicz, Jeannie   24
Olesnewicz, Joseph   24
Olesnewicz, Julian   24
Olesnewicz, Mary   24
Olesnewicz, Pearl   24
Olesnewicz, Sally   24
Olson, Pauline   119
Olyphant, Pa.   8, 9, 11, 13, 18, 20, 22, 25, 36, 44, 59, 63, 91, 100, 104, 107, 117, 125, 130, 171, 185
Olyphant Business and Professional Men's Club   171
Olyphant Dairy   130
Onuschak, Aleksander   123, 125
Onuschak, Anna Hadik   125
Onuschak, Anna Warren/Wawryn   123
Onuschak, Aquilina Pyrcz   123
Onuschak, Elizabeth   125
Onuschak, Harry   123
Onuschak, Helen   125
Onuschak, Jacob   22, 92, 125
Onuschak, Jerome   125
Onuschak, John   125
Onuschak, Maria Durniak   125
Onuschak, Michael   125
Orange, N.Y.   82
Oseniak, Genevieve   125
Oseniak, Joseph   125
Oseniak, Martha   125
Oseniak, Mary   125
Oseniak, Olga   125
Oseniak, Theodosia Hopiak   125
Ożenna, Jasło County   173
O'Malley, James J.   9

**P**
Pabis, Julia   103
Padlo, Anna   126
Pagkos, Olga   35
Palko, John P.   171
Pancio, Anastasia (Nellie)   128
Pancio, Anastasia Lega   126
Pancio, Anastasia/Nellie Pushkar   126
Pancio, Andrew   126
Pancio, Catherine   126
Pancio, Daniel   126, 128
Pancio, Frank   126
Pancio, George   126
Pancio, John   126
Pancio, Michael   126
Pancio, Panko   128
Pancio, Paul   126
Pancio, Pelagia Shwahla   128
Pancio, Peter   126, 128
Pancio, Petro   126, 128
Pancio, Platt   128
Pancio, Rozalyia Pushkar   126, 128
Pancio, Stephen   126
Pancio, Theodore   126
Pancio, Theodore /Frank   128
Pancio, Wasyl (Charles)   128
Park Hotel   41
Parma, Ohio   138
Parcit Manufacturing Co.,   74
Parylak, Alex   128
Parylak, Annie   128
Parylak, Eva Hasko   128
Parylak, Il'ko   128
Parylak, John   81, 128
Parylak, Justina Broda   128
Parylak, Michael   128
Parylak, Nicholas   128
Parylak, Olga   128
Parylak, Tekla   128
Parylak, William   128
Passaic, N.J.   67, 73, 115, 148, 168, 181
Pastorak, Josephine   154
Patrycia, Sylvester   15
Paukztis, Sylvester   9
Paulishak, Anna   130
Paulishak, Emil J.   130
Paulishak, Eugene   130
Paulishak, Joseph   130
Paulishak, Julia Lashenik   130
Paulishak, Olga   130
Paulishak, Stephen   130
Paulishak, Theofan   130
Paulishak, Vera   130
Paulishak, William   130

Pawlik, Mary  78
Pearce, Martha  133
Peckville, Pa.  185
Pedbereznak, Andrew  19, 131
Pedbereznak, Helena  131
Pedbereznak, John  131
Pedbereznak, Joseph  131
Pedbereznak, Mary  131
Pedbereznak, Michael  131
Pedbereznak, Theresa  131
Peerless Aluminum Foundry Co.  12, 74
Peiko, Vasyl'  14
Pelak, Anastasia  131
Pelak, Andryi  131
Pelak, Anna  131
Pelak, Anna Ference  131
Pelak, John  131
Pelak, Joseph  131
Pelak, Mary  131
Pelak, Maryia Olenich  131
Pelak, Max  14, 21, 22, 131
Pelak, Michael  131
Pelak, Nathalie  131
Pelak, Peter  131
Pelak, Stephen  131
Pelak, Tekla Kopysczianski  131
Pelak, Theodore  131
Pelak, Tillie  36
Pelak, Timothy  131
Pelak Café  131
Pelak's Tavern.  131
Pelechacz, Andrew  132
Pelechacz, Anna  132
Pelechacz, Helen  132
Pelechacz, Klimkosky  132
Pelechacz, Mary  132
Pelechacz, Michael  132
Pelechacz, Peter  132
Pelechacz, Solowich  132
Pelechacz, Susan Gutter/Goodard  132
Pelesh, Annie  133
Pelesh, Dimitro  19, 132
Pelesh, Eva Koval  132
Pelesh, Harry  133
Pelesh, Helen Felenchak  133
Pelesh, John  132
Pelesh, Julian  133
Pelesh, Lillian  133
Pelesh, Louis  132
Pelesh, Peter T.  19, 132
Pelesh, Sophia  133
Pelesh, Teofil  132
Pelesh, William/Basil  132
Peoples Banking Company, Shamokin, Pa.  141
People's National Bank of Edwardsville, Pa.  9, 112-113
Peoples Trust Co./People's Trust Bank, Shamokin, Pa.  68, 70, 117, 141
Perich, Andrew  133
Perich, John  133
Perich, Katherine Taciga  133
Perich, Maryia Cimbalak  133
Perich, Petro  133
Perich, Theodore  133
Perich, Theodozy /Teodozii P.  133
Perog, Olga  39
Perun, Anna Tezbir  133
Perun, John  133
Perun, Stephen  133
Perun, Teresa Chomik  133
Perun, Toma  133
Peters, Sonia  151
Petersburg, VA  3
Petsock, Anna  76
Philadelphia, Pa.  13, 36, 59, 91, 169, 186
Piechota, Mary  126
Pielgrzymka, Jasło County  55, 122, 140, 146, 166
Pietruszewski, Anna  28
Pilsner Brewing  181
Pine Grove Cemetery, Ansonia, Conn.  95, 103, 132, 139, 173, 174
Pittsburgh, Pa.  90, 126
Plano, Eva  126
Ploxa, Mary  156
Plymouth, Pa.  45090
Polanchyck, Mary  71
Polany, Grybów County  116
Polany, Krosno County  133
Polany, Nowy Sącz County  34
Pompano Beach, Fl  159
Popiwchak, Anastasia/Nellie Glaskow  133

Popiwchak, Anna   134
Popiwchak, Helen   134
Popiwchak, John   133
Popiwchak, Mary   134
Popiwchak, Nicholas   133
Popiwchak, Olga   134
Poplavsky, Eugenia   186
Porada, Cecilia Redmerska   134
Porada, John   134
Porada, Mary   134
Porada, Michael / Mytro /Metro   134
Port Jervis, N.Y.   82
Potato Chip Manufacturing Co.   68
Powanda, Anna Kowtko   134
Powanda, Charles   16, 19, 134
Powanda, Daniel   134
Powanda, Elsie   134
Powanda, Emma   134
Powanda, Helen   134
Powanda, John   134
Powanda, Joseph   134
Powanda, Milia   134
Powanda, Rose   155
Powanda, William   134
Powoloskie, John   40
Providence, RI   63
Providence Association of Ukrainian Catholics in America   18, 36, 172
Przegonina, Gorlice County   47, 107, 173
Przysłup, Gorlice County   96
Pupchyk, Aftan   16, 17, 135
Pupchyk, Anna   135
Pupchyk, Paraska/Tessie Yacewycz   135
Pupchyk, Peter   135
Pursel, Anna   36
Puschak, Anna   135
Puschak, John   20, 135
Puschak, Mary   135
Puschak, Mary Hernaga   135
Puschak, Mary Hudock   135
Puschak, Nicholas   135
Puschak, Theodore   135
Pyle, Olga Vander   123
Pyvovarchyk, Il'ko   1
Pętna, Gorlice County   81, 122
Płonna, Sanok County   176

## Q
Queens, N.Y.   128

## R
Rad, Nicholas   135
Radio, Catherine Evanik   135
Radio, John   135
Radio, Michael   135
Radio, Peter   135
Radio, William   135
Radko, Stefan   15
Radocyna, Gorlice County   104
Ralpho, Pa.   103
Ramsay, Lydia   148
Ranshaw, Pa.   117
Regietów Nyżni, Gorlice County   50
Regietów Wyżny, Gorlice County   147
Regietów, Gorlice County   47
Regula, Olga   131
Reid, Julia   151
Renchkovsky, John   50, 136
Renchkovsky, Mary Trembach   136
Renchkovsky, Maryia Andrash   136
Renchkovsky, Michael   136
Renchkovsky, Mykhal   136
Renchkovsky, Nicholas   136
Renchkovsky, Olga   136
Repa, George   136
Repa, John   22, 136, 176
Repa, Joseph   136
Repa, Julia   136
Repa, Julianna Vanat   136
Repa, Maryia Hoshko   136
Repa, Michael   136
Repa, Osyf   136
Retick, Alfred   137
Retick, Ella   137
Retick, George   137
Retick, Helene   137
Retick, Joseph   137
Retick, Mary Fecica Dudek   137
Ritzko, Metro   18
Ritzko/Hrytsko, Metro   156
Ropki, Gorlice County   45, 115
Ross, Elisabeth   47
Rossi, Helen   146
Rothbart, Ron   7
Rozstajne, Jasło County   54

Roztoka Wielka, Nowy Sącz County 112
Rudin, Olga 173
Ruschak, Mary 68
Russian Brotherhood Organization (RBO) 9, 18, 23, 25, 45, 73, 78, 85, 91, 95, 104, 108, 128, 131-132, 134 142, 144, 157, 170, 174
Russian/Little Russian National Union (later Ruthenian/Ukrainian National Association) 20, 44-45, 53, 66-67, 86, 93, 100, 121, 141, 144, 162, 187
Russian National Brotherhood of St. Cyril and Methodius, Yonkers, N.Y. 60
Russian Mercantile Association Limited/ Russian Mercantile
Company 13-14, 65, 68, 122, 141, 151
Russian Orthodox Catholic Mutual Aid Society of the United
States of America 25, 64, 136
Russian Orthodox Fraternity "Lubov" 64, 144, 166
Rusyn, Anna 48
Rusynyk, Alex 138
Rusynyk, Alex Anthony 10, 138
Rusynyk, Anna 138
Rusynyk, Antoni 138
Rusynyk, Antonii 138
Rusynyk, Eva Kieleczawa Kovalczyk 138
Rusynyk, Funeral 138
Rusynyk, George 138
Rusynyk, Helen 138
Rusynyk, John 138
Rusynyk, Julia 138
Rusynyk, Julia Bagan 138
Rusynyk, Julia Greshko 138
Rusynyk, Olga 138
Rusynyk, Prokop /Perry 138
Rusynyk, Stephan 138
Rusynyk, Teresa 138
Rusynyk-Yurch Funeral Home 138
Ruthenian Building and Real Estate Company, Shamokin, Pa. 141
Ruthenian Greek Catholic Saint Demetri Benevolent Society, Mt. Carmel, Pa. 82, 122

Ruthenian National Association see Russian National Union
Ruthenian (today Ukrainian) National Home, McKees Rocks, Pa. 134
Ruthenian National Society, McKees Rocks, Pa. 134
Ruthenian Store Company, Shamokin, Pa. 14, 68, 89, 109
Rutherford, N.J. 120
Rychwałd, Gorlice County 67
Rzepedź, Sanok County 135

S
Sabat, Ivan 15
Sacred Heart Cemetery, Jeannette, Pa. 122
Saginaw, Mich. 154
Savitsky, Jennie 162
Scheiner, Philip 11
Schenectady, N.Y. 12
Schnell, Mae 107
School Directors' Association of Lackawanna County 143
Scott, Helen 126
Scott, Helena 126
Scranton, Pa. 7, 9, 11, 29, 67, 89, 136, 154, 171
Seedor, Anabelle 139
Seedor, Anna Hanczar 139
Seedor, Anna Socker 139
Seedor, John 139
Seedor, Marie 139
Seedor, Vera 139
Seedor, Wasyl 139
Sekelsky, Mary 100
Senkowicz, Daniel 139
Serafin, Anastazyia Myscovski 140
Serafin, Hnat 140
Serafin, Mary Fedak 140
Serafin, Michael 140
Serafin, Steve 140
Serafin, William 140
Serniak, John 140
Serniak, Julia 140
Serniak, Justina Gunia 140
Serniak, Mary Roman / Gunia 140
Serniak, Nicholas 140
Serniak, Paul 140

Serniak, Peter   140
Serniak, Stephen   140
Seventh Ward of Shamokin, Pa.   85
Seymour, Conn.   16, 81, 95, 132, 134, 152
Seymour Russian Company   16, 95
Shamoki, Pa.   76
Shamokin, Pa.   9, 13, 14, 18, 21, 22, 24, 42, 43, 55, 65, 68, 84, 89, 102, 103, 109, 110, 111, 113, 114, 116, 117, 121, 122, 131, 141, 160, 161, 163, 178, 179
Sharshon, Alexis   21, 141
Sharshon, Anna Dzhumbeliak   141
Sharshon, Anna Koval'chŷk   141
Sharshon, Anna Leszczynska   141
Sharshon, George   141
Sharshon, Ivan   141
Sharshon, Peter   141
Sharshon, Walter   141
Shenandoah, Pa.   5, 8, 13, 40, 45, 77, 115, 137, 141
Shkimba, Joseph   143
Shkimba, Julia Obuch   143
Shkimba, Julia Wolovich   143
Shkimba, Michael H.   142
Shkimba, Olga   143
Shlanta, Alex   20, 143
Shlanta, Barbara   144
Shlanta, Bohdan   144
Shlanta, Martha Kossman   144
Shlanta, Myra   144
Shlanta, Nestor   144
Shlanta, Olga   144
Shlanta, Walter/Vladimir   144
Shost, Daniel   11, 146
Shost, Mary Duda   146
Shost, Olga   47
Shost, Paul   146
Shost, Peter   146
Shost, Thomas   146
Shostak, Andrew   146
Shostak, Eva   146
Shostak, John   146
Shostak, Michael   20, 146
Shostak, Pauline/Pajza Valko   146
Shostak, Terrence   146
Shostak, Tomkiewicz   146
Shutowich, Barbara Chuchta   148
Shutowich, Nicholas   147
Simchok, Mary   82
Simpson (Fell Township), Pa.   153
Simpson, Pa.   22, 77, 78, 108
Sirotiak, Alexander   148
Sirotiak, George   148
Sirotiak, Hendricks   148
Sirotiak, Iefroska Skripak   148
Sirotiak, Iustin   148
Sirotiak, Konrad   148
Sirotiak, Lazor   11, 16, 0148
Sirotiak, Marina (Mary) Cecewa   148
Sirotiak, Marion   148
Sirotiak, Peter   148
Sirotiak, Simeon   148
Skimba, Hnat   149
Skimba, Maria Wyslocki   149
Skimba, Maryia Shkymba   149
Skimba, Stephen   149
Skrulsky, Alice   100
Skweir, Anna   141
Skwier, Andrew   20, 149
Skwier, Anna   150
Skwier, Anna Doliniak   149
Skwier, Anthony   150
Skwier, Eva Yonkovig/Jankowicz   150
Skwier, Helen   150
Skwier, John   150
Skwier, Julia   150
Skwier, Mary   150
Skwier, Michael   150
Skwier, Skvir   149
Slavonic Deposit Bank, Wilkes-Barre, Pa.   9
Slivka, Martha   115
Slota, Olga   119
Slovik, Helen   93
Smakula, Mary   107
Smakula, Samuel   107
Small, Irene   169
Smerechniak, Jerry   151
Smerechniak, John   150
Smerechniak, Mary Haytko   150
Smerechniak, Walter   151
Smerek, Anna   18
Smerek, Anna Kurylo   151
Smerek, Elias   151

Smerekowiec, Gorlice County   47, 135, 150
Smetana, Alexander   151
Smetana, Alice Yadlowsky   151
Smetana, Helen   151
Smetana, Marko   14, 21, 151
Smey, Anna   152
Smey, John   152
Smey, Kuzma   152
Smey, Mary   152
Smey, Nikolay   16, 152, 163
Smey, Peter   152
Smey, Sophia Telep   152
Smey, William   152
Smolnycki, Eva   126
Snyder, Mary   103
Sopchak, Aleksander   153
Sopchak, Alex   153
Sopchak, Anna   153
Sopchak, Daniel   153
Sopchak, George   153
Sopchak, Helen Patsey/Pecuch   153
Sopchak, Jaqueline Adamiak   153
Sopchak, Martha   153
Sopchak, Michael   153
Sopchak, Peter   153
Sopchak, Wasil   153
Soroka, Mildred   171
Spadaro, Susan   156
Spak, Helen   85
Spiak, Andrew   154
Spiak, John   16, 154, 172
Spiak, Justina Waszczyszak   154
Spiak, Peter   154
Spiak, Stephen   154
St. Alphonsus Cemetery, Windsor, ON   172
St. Andrew's Insurance Association, Shamokin, Pa.   111
St. Basil's Cemetery, Simpson, Pa.   77, 108, 153
St. Bonaventure Cemetery, Allegany, N.Y.   126
St. Boniface Cemetery, Elmont, N.Y.   162
St. Clair, Pa.   11, 20, 41-43
St. Demeter Russian Society of Mt. Carmel   71
St. John Russian Cemetery, Mayfield, Pa.   169
St. John the Baptist Beneficial Society, Olpyphant, Pa.   44, 107
St. John the Baptist Cemetery, Mayfield, Pa.   167, 171
St. John the Baptist Cemetery, Stratford, Conn.   48, 57, 76, 100, 153, 163
St. John the Baptist Society, Yonkers, N.Y.   170
St. John's Cemetery, Mayfield, Pa.   28, 55, 140, 144
St. John's Cemetery, Pringle, Pa.   28
St. John's Russian Cemetery, Nesquehoning, Pa.   34
St. Joseph Cemetery, Yonkers, N.Y.   35
St. Louis, Mo.   154
St. Mary's Cemetery, Fox Chase, Pa.   37
St. Mary's Cemetery, Fullerton, Pa.   90, 98, 135
St. Mary's Cemetery, Herkimer, N.Y.   116
St. Mary's Cemetery, Kennedy Township, Pa.   134
St. Mary's Cemetery, McAdoo, Pa.   32, 93, 150
St. Mary's Cemetery, Port Jervis, N.Y.   82
St. Mary's Cemetery, St. Clair, Pa.   42
St. Mary's Cemetery, Summit Hill, Pa.   39, 48, 135
St. Mary's Cemetery, Waterbury, N.Y.   149
St. Mary's Church, St. Clair, Pa.   42
St. Mary's (Old) Cemetery, Mahanoy City, Pa.   92
St. Michael's Cemetery, Old Forge, Pa.   64, 91
St. Michael's Cemetery, Frackville, Pa.   139
St. Michael's Cemetery, Hazleton, Pa.   132, 146
St. Michael's Cemetery, Mt. Carmel, Pa.   36, 71
St. Michael's Cemetery, Old Forge, Pa.   64
St. Michael's Cemetery, Shenandoah, Pa.

41, 45, 137
St. Michael's Church, Mt. Carmel, Pa. 84
St. Nicholas Cemetery, Boght Corners, N.Y. 68
St. Nicholas Cemetery, Mahanoy City, Pa. 92
St. Nicholas Cemetery, Nanticoke, Pa. 55
St. Nicholas Cemetery, Pringle, Pa. 113
St. Nicholas Church, St. Clair, Pa. 42
St. Nicholas Half Acre Cemetery, Half Acre, N.Y. 128
St. Peter's Cemetery, Garfield, N.J. 77
St. Theodosius Cemetery, Brooklyn, Ohio 63, 89, 97, 138, 175
St. Vladimir Cemetery, Jackson, N.J. 79, 140, 185
Stamford, Conn. 165
State Banking Co. in McKees Rocks, Pa. 134
State Russian American Political Club, Conn. 95
Stawisza, Grybów County 29, 31, 38, 100
Steele, Pauline 152
Stefanisko, Stella 93
Stefansky, George 155
Stefansky, John 155
Stefansky, Mary Onuschak 155
Stefansky, Michael 11, 154
Stefansky, Peter 155
Sternowsky, Julie 68
Stewart, Delores 36
Stone, Evelyn 47
Stoppi, Fannie 18, 156
Stoppi, Frank 156
Stoppi, John 156
Stoppi, Joseph 18, 156
Stoppi, Michael 156
Stoppi, Peter 156
Stratford [Avenue] Cemetery, Scranton, Pa. 68
Stratford, Conn. 12, 57
Sts. Cyril & Methodius Cemetery, North Catasauqua, Pa. 123
Sts. Cyril & Methodius Cemetery, Peckville, Pa. 100, 104, 107, 118, 171
Sts. Peter & Paul Cemetery, Beaver Meadows, Pa. 102, 181, 185
Sts. Peter & Paul Cemetery, Derby, Conn. 46, 47, 52-53, 81, 131, 133, 134, 187
Sts. Peter & Paul Cemetery, Mt. Carmel, Pa. 69, 73, 82, 85, 88, 122, 179
Sts. Peter & Paul Cemetery, Parma, Ohio 83
Sts. Peter & Paul Cemetery, Saddle Brook, N.J. 34, 168, 181
Sts. Peter & Paul Cemetery, Scott Township, Pa. 48
Sts. Peter & Paul Cemetery, Simpson, Pa. 78
Sudia, Anna Barna 157
Sudia, Annie 157
Sudia, Ivan 157
Sudia, James 157
Sudia, John 157
Sudia, Maria Hudak 157
Sudia, Michael 157
Sudia, Walter 157
Sudia, Wasily 157
Sura, Mary 39
Super Crisp Potato Chip Co. 68
Surowica, Sanok County 135
Sussex County 11
Swantko, Andrew 158
Swantko, Anna Hromchak 158
Swantko, John 157, 158
Swantko, Mary 158
Swantko, Michael 158
Swantko, Peter 157, 158
Swantko, Russell 157, 158
Swantko, Steven 157, 158
Swantko, Teodore 157
Swantko, Theodore 158
Sweeney Hotel 40
Sweeney, William L. 40
Sydoriak, Anna 157
Sydoriak, Antoinette 157
Sydoriak, Dimitro 19, 157, 186
Sydoriak, Esther 157
Sydoriak, Lena 157
Sydoriak, Mary Tanich 157

Sydoriak, Mike   157
Sydoriak, Nasta   157
Sydoriak, Wasil   157
Syminovitch, Volodymyr   13
Symochko, Anna Fedorko   160
Symochko, Eva Dzula   159
Symochko, Hilar   159, 160
Symochko, Marko   159
Symochko, Nicholas   17, 159, 160
Symochko, Stephanie Durkot   160
Symochko, Tekla Hatala   159, 160
Szczawne, Sanok County   89
Słotwiny, Nowy Sącz County   77

Ś

Śnietnica, Grybów County   103, 108, 111, 114, 153
Świerżowa Ruska, Jasło County   31, 82, 97
Świątkowa Wielka, Jasło County   85, 92, 138, 174

T

Talpash, Alice   161
Talpash, Anastasia Maliniak   162
Talpash, Anna   161
Talpash, Barbara Molodchak   160
Talpash, Ben   161
Talpash, Eugene   162
Talpash, Helen   162
Talpash, John   121, 160, 162
Talpash, Julia   161
Talpash, Kate   161
Talpash, Katrena Polianska   161
Talpash, Luka   161
Talpash, Mary   161
Talpash, Michael   161
Talpash, Millie   161
Talpash, Sadie   161
Talpash, Sally   161
Talpash, Samuel   161
Talpash, Teodozii   21, 22
Talpash, Theodore   161
Talpash, Twins A and B   161
Tatusko, Genevieve   162
Tatusko, John   162
Tatusko, Mary Dubec   162
Tatusko, Michael   162
Tatusko, Nicholas   162
Tatusko, Russel   162
Tatusko, Steven   162
Tayblyn, Anne   106
Tehansky, Andrew   163
Tehansky, Anna Galak   163
Tehansky, Anthony   163
Tehansky, Emily   163
Tehansky, John   163
Tehansky, Joseph   163
Tehansky, Julia   163
Tehansky, Mary   163
Tehansky, Michael   21, 163
Tehansky, Nellie   163
Tehansky, Pearl   163
Tehansky, Peter   163
Tehansky, Stephen   163
Tehansky, Tehan   163
Telep, Andrew   166
Telep, Awksenty   16, 48, 50, 100, 163
Telep, Catherine   163
Telep, Clement   163
Telep, Eufrosine/Rose Gibey   163
Telep, Eugene   163
Telep, Fetsko   166
Telep, George   163
Telep, Helen   166
Telep, Joseph   163
Telep, Justina   166
Telep, Katherine   165
Telep, Maria   165
Telep, Mary Senio   166
Telep, Maryia Paiko   166
Telep, Olga   165
Telep, Samuel   48, 50, 152
Telep, Samuel Andrew   163
Telep, Stephen F.   166
Telep, Walter   166
Telischak, Alexander   168
Telischak, Anna   168
Telischak, Fotia Markovich   168
Telischak, John   168
Telischak, Nazar   167
Terryville, Conn.   128
Thissell, Mary   118
Thomson, John Malcolm   74
Thorpe, Olga   112
Thos A. Youschock and Son   185

Three Saints Cemetery, Derby, Conn.
  133
Three Saints Church, Garfield, N.J.   73
Tiscar, Fortunato   9
Transfiguration Cemetery, Coal
  Township, Pa.   66, 69, 76, 84, 89,
  102-103, 110-111, 114, 117, 122,
  131, 141, 151, 163, 180
Trembach, Aleksander   15
Trembach, Anastasia Pawlak   168
Trembach, Arkhip/Archie   168
Trembach, Dorothy   169
Trembach, Evhenia   169
Trembach, Jerome   169
Trembach, John   169
Trembach, Julia   169
Trembach, Ludmila   169
Trembach, Nikolay   169
Trembach, Solomia Telech   169
Trembach, Stefka   169
Trembach, Theodore   168
Trembach, Virginia   169
Trembath, W. J.   9
Trochanowski, Bertha Skindzier   169
Trochanowski, Enoch /Hnat   169
Trochanowski, Leon/Lee   169
Trochanowski, Walter   169
Trohanowsky, Barbara Talabovich   169
Trohanowsky, John   169
Trohanowsky, Julia   169
Trohanowsky, Mary   169
Trohanowsky, Olga   169
Trohanowsky, Samuel A.   169
Trumbull, Conn.   20, 76
Turchick, Boris   170
Turchick, Margaret   170
Turchick, Simon T.   17, 170
Turko, Eugen   171
Turko, John   171
Turko, John W.   10, 25, 0171
Turko, Mary   171
Turko, Mary Pitenko   171
Turko, Tekla / Tillie Sanko   171
Turko, Wasyl   171
Turula, Stephena   53
Tylawa, Krosno County   126, 128
Tylicz, Nowy Sącz County   40, 83, 130
Tymkevych, Fr. Pavlo   15

**U**
Uhryń, Nowy Sącz County   1, 115
Ukrainian Brotherhood, Shamokin, Pa.
  111
Ukrainian National Association see
  Russian National Union
Ukrainian Republican Division of
  Lackawanna County   171
Uranko, Margaret   156
Uście Ruskie, Gorlice County   90, 104,
  125, 137

**V**
Vassalo, Anna   41
Verbicky, Mary   125

**W**
Wachna, Ann Prygrocky   172
Wachna, Antonia   172
Wachna, Claudia   172
Wachna, Elijah   172
Wachna, Johan   172
Wachna, Katherine   172
Wachna, Kozma   172
Wachna, Maria   172
Wachna, Olena   172
Wachna, Olga   172
Wachna, Theodor   20, 171
Wachna, Theodora Mieiska   171
Wachna, Theodosy   20, 172
Wachna, Wolodimyr B   172
Wachna, Wyronia   172
Wachna, Zofia   172
Wagiel, Anna   125
Wan, Wasil   16
Wandzilak, Jacob   16, 17, 154, 172
Wandzilak, Melania Honcharik   173
Wandzilak, Paraska   172
Wandzilak, Rosalie   173
Wandzilak, Teodor   172
Wandzilak, Theodore   173
Wandzilak, William   173
Waniga, Fred   173
Waniga, Howard   173
Waniga, Joseph   19, 173
Waniga, Julia   173
Waniga, Nicholas   173
Waniga, Peter   173

Waniga, Ross   173
Waniga, Tillie/Tekla Zawada   173
Warcholic, Anastasia Zhelem   173
Warcholic, Anna   174
Warcholic, Anton   174
Warcholic, Daniel   173
Warcholic, Joseph   173
Warcholic, Julia Bilcznianski   174
Warcholic, Mary   174
Wargo, Anna   68
Warholak, Andrew   174
Warholak, Dorothy   175
Warholak, Esther Walko   175
Warholak, Mary   175
Warholak, William   175
Warne, Frank Julian   4, 5
Wartella, Anne   176
Wartella, Ivan Vorotyla   176
Wartella, Jack   177
Wartella, John   176
Wartella, Julia   176
Wartella, Mary   18
Wartella, Mary Krzyzanowski   176
Wartella, Mary Senko   176
Wartella, Metro   176
Wartella, Michael   176
Wartella, Nicholas   18, 176
Wartella, Nick   177
Wartella, Stephen   18, 176
Warycha, Andrew   178
Warycha, Anna Doshna   178
Warycha, Michael   178
Warycha, Samuel   178
Washburn, W. O.   9
Washienko, Alexander   177
Washienko, Julia Hylwa   177
Washienko, Michael   177
Washienko, Nicholas   177
Washienko, Nicholas M.   17, 177
Washienko, Theodore   177
Washienko, William   177
Wasicko, Rose   154
Waterbury, Conn.   85, 140, 142, 149
Watro, Mary   185
Wawrzka, Grybów County   36, 84, 85
Way, Melanie   36
Weight Scales, Pa.   84
West Hazleton, Pa.   20, 146
West Lebanon, N.Y.   185
West Troy, N.Y.   91
Whitehall, Pa.   97, 125
Wilchek, Elizabeth   170
Wilkes-Barre, Pa.   9, 22, 84, 113, 131, 136
Williams, Anna   136
Williams, Fred   9
Windish, Victoria   117
Winters, Helen   148
Winton, Pa.   11, 29-30
Wirchne, Gorlice County   132, 163
Wislosky, Anthony   13
Wislowskie, Susan   103
Wisłok Górny, Sanok County   70
Wola Cieklińska, Jasło County   131
Wolanski, Ivan   13
Wolf, Olga   36
Wood, Anna   116
Woodland Cemetery, Stamford, Conn.   165
Worhach, Alex   179
Worhach, Anna   179
Worhach, Barbara   179
Worhach, Beatrice   178
Worhach, John   178, 179
Worhach, Julia   179
Worhach, Julia Homiak   178
Worhach, Mary   179
Worhach, Olga   179
Worhach, Pauline Wilchacky   179
Worhach, Pearl   179
Worhach, Stephen   178
Worhacz, Daniel   180
Worhacz, Lovie   180
Worhacz, Michael   180
Worhacz, Mildred   180
Worhacz, Olga   180
Worhacz, Pearl Makuch   180
Worhacz, Pearl/Paraska Ceklinski   180
Worhacz, Russell   180
Worhacz, Sylvester   180
Worhacz, Theodore   21, 179, 180
Worhacz, Walter   180
Worona, John   181
Worona, Mary Jasenczak   181
Worona, Nestor   181
Worona, Nicholas   181

Worona, Susanna Sedlak / Chabra   181
Woytowich, Mary   64
Woytowick, Mary   47
Wołowiec, Gorlice County   63, 142, 149, 157
Wyshowsky, Theodore   14
Wysowa, Gorlice County   77, 100, 133, 151

## Y
Yackanicz, Demetrius   185
Yackanicz, Joseph   181
Yackanicz, Nicholas   20, 181, 185
Yackanicz, Olga   185
Yackanicz, Olga Andrasz   181
Yackanicz, Paul   185
Yackanicz, Peter   181
Yackanicz, Tekla Lyga   185
Yackanicz, Theresa   181, 185
Yackanicz, Wasil / Wasco   185
Yackanicz, William   185
Yackanich Bros.   185
Yakobchak, Anna   64
Yandrofski, Mary   146
Yanovich, Stephen   13
Yarosh, Amros   16
Yaskowsky, Olga   31
Yeager, Eva   50
Yonak, Grybów County   185
Yonak, Mary Maksimchak   185
Yonak, Onufry   185
Yonak, William   185
Yonkers, N.Y.   3, 11, 12, 15, 17, 18, 34, 35, 39, 47, 48, 50, 56, 57, 59, 60, 63, 77, 81, 85, 91, 94, 100, 105-107, 115, 116, 119, 133, 135, 146-148, 150, 151, 154, 159, 160, 162, 163, 170, 172, 177, 178
Young, Paul J.   185
Youshock, Andryi   185
Youshock, Anna   185
Youshock, Olga   186
Youshock, Rose Russen   185
Youshock, Theofan   186
Youshock, Thos / Thomas A.   185
Youshock, Victor   186
Youshock, Vladimir   186
Youshocks Plumbers   185

Yurch Funeral Home   138

## Z
Zadosko, Anna   155
Zajacz, Nikolaj   3
Zarayko, Margaret   125
Zarutskie, Nita   162
Zawadka Rymanowska, Sanok County   65, 117, 157, 171
Zdynia, Gorlice County   91, 178
Zieniewicz, Stephanie   114
Zimmer, Henry   11
Zoliak, Mykhal   1
Zuk, Sophia   85
Zuraw, Anna   187
Zuraw, Harry   52, 86, 157, 186
Zuraw, Katherine   187
Zuraw, Ksenia Horbal   187
Zuraw, Margaret   107
Zuraw, Maria   187

## Ż
Żydowskie, Jasło County   170

www.ingramcontent.com/pod-product-compliance
Lightning Source LLC
Chambersburg PA
CBHW081916180426
43199CB00036B/2733